2-16-79

D1088031

Roman Historical Portraits

ASPECTS OF GREEK AND ROMAN LIFE

General Editor: H. H. Scullard

ROMAN HISTORICAL PORTRAITS

J. M. C. TOYNBEE

Cornell University Press

ITHACA, NEW YORK

First published 1978 by Cornell University Press.

Library of Congress Cataloging in Publication Data
(For library cataloging purposes only)

Toynbee, Jocelyn M. C.
    Roman historical portraits.

    (Aspects of Greek and Roman life)
    Includes index.
    1. Portrait sculpture, Roman. 2. Rome—Biography—Portraits. 3. History, Ancient—Portraits. I. Title. II. Series.
NB1296.3.T69   731'.8'2   75-38428
ISBN 0-8014-1011-8

Printed in Great Britain

Contents

Abbreviations of Bibliographical Sources

AA	*Archäologischer Anzeiger*
AJA	*American Journal of Archaeology*
Alföldi 1959	A. Alföldi, 'Das wahre Gesicht Cäsars' in *Antike Kunst*, ii, 1959, pp. 27–31, pl. 16
Bernareggi 1973	E. Bernareggi, 'La monetazione in argento di Marco Antonio', in *Numismatica e Antichità Classiche*, 1973, pp. 61–105
BCH	*Bulletin de Correspondance Hellénique*
BMCCRE	*British Museum Catalogue of Coins of the Roman Empire*
BMCGC	*British Museum Catalogue of Greek Coins*
CAH	*Cambridge Ancient History*
Carson and Sutherland 1956	R. A. G. Carson and C. H. V. Sutherland (ed.), *Essays in Roman Coinage Presented to Harold Mattingly*, 1956
CIG	*Corpus Inscriptionum Graecarum*
CIL	*Corpus Inscriptionum Latinarum*
Crawford 1974	M. Crawford, *Roman Republican Coinage*, 1974
Davis and Kraay 1973	N. Davis and C. M. Kraay, *The Hellenistic Kingdoms: Portrait Coins and History*, 1973
DC	Dio Cassius
Evans 1935	E. C. Evans, 'Descriptions of Personal Appearance in Roman History and Biography', in *Harvard Studies in Classical Philology*, xlvi, 1935, pp. 43–84
Furtwängler 1900	A. Furtwängler, *Antike Gemmen*, 1900
Ghirshman 1962	R. Ghirshman, *Iran: Parthians and Sassanians*, 1962
Göbl 1971	R. Göbl, *Sasanian Numismatics*, 1971
Grant 1946	M. Grant, *From Imperium to Auctoritas*, 1946
Grueber 1910	H. A. Grueber, *Coins of the Roman Republic in the British Museum*, 1910
Head 1911	B. V. Head, *Historia Numorum*, 2nd ed., 1911
Herbig 1959	R. Herbig, 'Neue Studien zur Ikonographie des Gaius Julius Caesar', in *Kölner Jahrbuch*, iv, 1959, pp. 7–14
Herrmann 1969	G. Herrmann, 'The Darabgird Relief – Ardeshir or Shahpur? A Discussion in the Context of Early Sasanian Sculpture', in *Iran*, vii, 1969, pp. 63–88
Herzfeld 1938	E. Herzfeld, 'Khusraus II Krone: Al-Tadj Al-Kabir: die Kronen der sasanidischen Könige', in *Archäologische Mitteilungen aus Iran*, ix, 1938, pp. 101–58
Iran	*Iran* (published by the British Institute of Persian Studies)
Jahreshefte	*Jahreshefte des Österreichischen Archäologischen Institutes in Wien*
JDAI	*Jahrbuch des Deutschen Archäologischen Instituts*
Johansen 1967	F. S. Johansen, 'Antichi ritratti di Caio Giulio Cesare nella scultura', in *Analecta Romana Instituti Danici*, iv, 1967, pp. 7–68
JRS	*Journal of Roman Studies*
Krämer 1973	K. Krämer, 'Zum Freundschaftsvertrag zwischen Rom und Parthien unter Augustus', in *Klio*, lv, 1973, pp. 247–8
MacDermot 1954	B. C. MacDermot, 'Roman Emperors in Sassanian Reliefs', in *JRS*, xliv, 1954, pp. 76–80
Mazard 1955	J. Mazard, *Corpus Nummorum Numidiae Mauretaniaeque*, 1955
Michel 1967	D. Michel, *Älexander als Vorbild für Pompeius, Caesar und Marcus Antonius*, 1967
NC	*Numismatic Chronicle*
Newell 1937	E. T. Newell, *Royal Greek Portrait Coins*, 1937
NH	Pliny, *Naturalis Historia*

NZ   *Numismatische Zeitschrift*

Paruck 1924   F. D. J. Paruck, *Sassanian Coins*, 1924

RA   *Revue Archéologique*

RIC   *The Roman Imperial Coinage*

Richter 1965   G. M. A. Richter, *The Portraits of the Greeks*, iii, 1965

RM   *Mitteilungen des Deutschen Archäologischen Instituts: Römische Abteilung*

RN   *Revue Numismatique*

Sands 1908   P. C. Sands, *The Client Princes of the Roman Empire under the Republic*, 1908

Schweitzer 1948   B. Schweitzer, *Die Bildniskunst der römischen Republik*, 1948

Scullard 1970   H. H. Scullard, *Scipio Africanus: Soldier and Politician*, 1970

SHA   Scriptores Historiae Augustae

Sydenham 1952   E. A. Sydenham, *The Coinage of the Roman Republic*, 1952

Toynbee 1957   J. M. C. Toynbee, 'Portraits of Julius Caesar', in *Greece and Rome*, ser. 2, iv, 1957, pp. 2–9

Vessberg 1941   O. Vessberg, *Studien zur Kunstgeschichte der römischen Republik*, 1941

Vollenweider 1960   M.-L. Vollenweider, 'Die Gemmenbildnisse Cäsars', in *Antike Kunst*, iii, 1960, pp. 81–8

Vollenweider 1964   M.-L. Vollenweider, 'Die Gemmenbildnisse Cäsars', in *Gymnasium*, lxxi, 1964, pp. 505–18, pls. 13–18

Vollenweider 1966   M.-L. Vollenweider, *Die Steinschneidekunst und ihre Künstler in spätrepublikanischer und augusteischer Zeit*, 1966

ZfN   *Zeitschrift für Numismatik*

Ziegler 1964   K. H. Ziegler, *Die Beziehungen zwischen Rom und dem Partherreich*, 1964

Introduction

For the purposes of this book a Roman historical portrait is defined as the true, individual, realistic likeness of an identifiable, specific personage who played a part in Roman history – a Roman 'notable', that is, one who figured in public life in republican or early Augustan times, or a foreign potentate or leader, whether of republican or of imperial times, who had significant contacts with Rome. It must be a portrait that was made either during the subject's lifetime or soon after his or her death, while his or her features were still familiar; or it must be a later portrait that can establish its claim to be based on a contemporary likeness. Obviously the most authentic of the portraits that concern us here are those on coins, on which the names and titles of the individuals represented are normally inscribed beside them. And it is generally from their numismatic likenesses that the sculptural portraits of public characters can be identified.

When did true portraits as we have just defined them apropos of Rome first make their appearance in the ancient world? In the late fifth century BC local dynasts in Lycia had the right of issuing coins under the Persian Empire; one of them, Khäräi, struck silver staters, obviously the work of Greek artists, on the reverses of which are distinctively oriental male heads, either wearing an elaborate 'Phrygian' cap or wreathed and with the hair curled up behind after the eastern fashion. These heads were probably intended to portray the dynast himself, or perhaps a satrap, and they have a definitely individual look. But we have no evidence that they were portraits made from life: they could merely represent the Greek engravers' conception of an ethnic type.[1]

At first sight, references in imperial-age literature to the early fourth-century Athenian sculptor Demetrius of Alopeke suggest that he could be reckoned as a portraitist in the strict sense. Lucian describes his rendering of the Corinthian general Pelichos as αὐτοανθρώπῳ ὅμοιον, with a hanging paunch, bald head, wind-swept beard, and carelessly worn cloak;[2] and Quintilian says that Demetrius was 'keener on likeness than on beauty' ('similitudinis quam pulchritudinis amantior').[3] But Lucian's phrase precisely means 'just like a human being', that is, a highly naturalistic representation of what a man is like in old age: it does not necessarily mean like the specific, individual man Pelichos; and Quintilian's *similitudo* could mean likeness to nature, not likeness to an individual.

A true portrait has sometimes been recognized in the statue of Demosthenes that was made by the sculptor Polyeuktos in *c.* 280 BC and set up in the Athenian Agora,[4] and which may have been the one with folded hands mentioned by Plutarch.[5] The features of the orator have been identified from a bronze head from Herculaneum inscribed with his name;[6] and it is noteworthy that in all the copies that have come down to us, whether of the head alone or of the whole statue,[7] these features never vary. We do not, in fact, have various types of Demosthenes as we have, for instance, of Socrates. All the same, Polyeuktos' statue was made some forty to fifty years after the orator's death in 322 BC and we have no record of any likeness of him having been taken during his lifetime. The statue could simply represent the sculptor's idea of what he must have looked like. The same would apply to all the naturalistic 'portraits' made in Hellenistic times of famous Greek statesmen, poets, philosophers, and so forth, of earlier generations. These are often extremely life-like and suggestive of the characters and achievements of the personalities that they purport to represent. But naturalism, however vivid it may be, is not enough to constitute a true portrait. The same applies again to Roman imaginary 'portraits' of the kings and early republican heroes.

The first ancient personage who is known for certain to have had his likeness taken in his lifetime and who presumably sat for portraitists is, of course, Alexander the Great (356–323 BC); and it was with him that portraiture in the strict sense was born. Pliny states that the sculptor Lysippus made many portraits of Alexander, beginning with one of him as a boy – the latter reputed to be extant in Nero's time nearly three centuries later (whether in the original or in a copy is not known). According to Plutarch, Lysippus was the only portraitist by whom Alexander liked to be portrayed, since he rendered with great exactness two of the king's personal traits – the inclination of his head a little on one side towards the left and the melting glance of his eyes.[9] This turn of the head, together with the upward glance of the eyes and the leonine mane of hair, is particularly clearly shown in the well-known head in the British Museum.[10] Probably the earliest extant portraits of Alexander that can be dated with some precision are the heads on the obverses of coins struck by Lysimachus in Thrace[11] and by Ptolemy I in Egypt[12] about 300 BC. But Alexander was a god as well as a man; and here the individual features are combined with the ram's horns of Zeus Ammon who had recognized the king as his son (Lysimachus and Ptolemy I) and with the elephant's scalp of Dionysus (Ptolemy I). In Part II of this book we shall meet this fusion of realistic likeness and idealism again, in the portraits of some foreign rulers known to Roman history. And it is often to be found in material that is not included in this book, namely in the portraits of some emperors and, above all, in those of some empresses, who are not infrequently represented as being many years younger than they actually were at the time when their likenesses were made.

Despite this idealizing element the portraits of Alexander are portraits in the full meaning of the term; and they set the pattern for the portraits of the Hellenistic kings who succeeded to his empire in Egypt, Syria, Asia Minor, Greece, Sicily, Bactria and India – including those kings who entered Roman history and whose likenesses qualify in that sense as Roman historical portraits. Moreover, not a few of the Hellenistic ruler portraits, so far from idealizing their subjects, show a ruthless, almost brutally realistic, individualization, in which a man's facial peculiarities and blemishes are starkly chronicled. To this trend in portraiture the term 'veristic' has been applied; and it can also be traced in 'non-historical' Hellenistic portraits of unknown private persons from the late third century BC onwards. This was just the time when the influence of Greek art and Greek artists, first from Magna Graecia and then from the East, was beginning to penetrate to Rome in a steady stream; and when Hellenistic 'verism' in particular was soon to set its stamp upon two Roman social practices that were not indeed confined to historical characters, but naturally included them and had their repercussions on their portraits.

One of these practices concerns the Roman funerals which Polybius witnessed when he was in Rome about the middle of the second century BC and describes in a famous passage:[13] 'Next after the burial they place the image [τὴν εἰκόνα] of the departed in the most conspicuous place in the house, enclosed in a wooden shrine. This image is a mask reproducing the deceased with remarkable fidelity as regards both modelling and drawing [ἡ δὲ εἰκών ἐστι πρώσωπον, εἰς ὁμοιότητα διαφερόντως ἐξειγασμένον καὶ κατὰ τὴν πλάσιν καὶ κατὰ τὴν ὑπογραφήν]. On the occasion of public sacrifices they display these images and decorate them with much care; and when any distinguished member of the family dies, they take them to the funeral, putting them on men who seem to bear the closest resemblance to the originals in stature and general appearance.' Polybius' words imply that these masks were of light material, of terracotta or of wax; and Pliny, writing in the first century AD, says that 'apud maiores' (i.e. under the Republic) faces modelled in wax ('expressi cera vultus') were kept each in a cupboard in the atrium of the house to serve as portraits attending family funerals ('ut essent imagines quae comitarentur gentilicia funera').[14] What the Roman ancestral masks were like in earlier times we do not know, since none have survived. They may have been of a quite generalized and conventional character. But from Polybius' description it is clear that by the middle of the second century BC they had become a highly realistic and individualistic type of portrait, which, he goes on to say, served as a means of edification for the young and of the maintenance of what had come to be regarded as the Roman national virtues.

Originally and officially the right to keep and display these ancestral *imagines* was a privilege of the patrician *gentes* (although there are some passages in Latin literature which indicate that plebeian families occasionally possessed themselves of *imagines* unofficially). *Novi homines* did not have this right – 'quia imagines non habeo et quia nova mihi nobilitas est', as Marius is recorded by Sallust as saying;[15] and Cicero in the *De lege agraria*, delivered in 63 BC, the year of his consulship, declared to the Quirites 'si quid deliquero nullae sunt imagines quae me a vobis deprecentur'.[16] What, then, did Cicero mean by saying in the *Verrines* that his curule aedileship had secured for him the 'ius imaginis ad memoriam posteritatemque prodendae'?[17] He must have meant by this the right granted to curule magistrates, of plebeian as well as of patrician stock, to set up, with State permission, statues of themselves in public places during their lifetimes. And it must be to this second Roman social practice, which was affected by the veristic trend in Hellenistic portraiture, that Pliny refers when he states that in 158 BC the censors removed from the Forum all statues of magistrates that had not been 'populi aut senatus sententia statutae'.[18] Such statues in the collection as were erected round about the time of this clearance can hardly have been other than realistic likenesses.

Such, then, briefly sketched, is the iconographic background, in the East and in the West, against which Roman historical portraits were evolved during Hellenistic/republican times. The following studies of historical characters – taken in their chronological order, more or less, so far as the Roman notables are concerned, and geographically, in the case of foreign rulers – are centred on selections from their well, or reasonably well, authenticated likenesses; and the illustrations, which thus constitute the essence of this book, are accompanied by brief descriptions, short factual notes where these are necessary in order to explain a given personage's place in Roman history, ancient writers' comments, where such exist, on the characters' physique, and some bibliographical information.

As far as possible (subject to quality) the coin portraits illustrated have been enlarged to twice actual size. The great majority of the works of art that are here reproduced have often been published before and can be found in the standard works in English, French, German and Italian on Hellenistic and Roman portraiture, both sculptural and numismatic. But classical students and others who are interested in what some of the actors on the stage of Roman history actually looked like may, it is hoped, find it helpful to have their portraits assembled between the covers of a single volume.

The choice of portraits of republican and early Augustan Roman notables and of foreign rulers as the subject of this book has been governed by the fact that these are, with a few exceptions, relatively unfamiliar, their previous publications being widely scattered through a large number of different sources. An attempt is made here to bring together as complete as possible a portrait-gallery of these persons (all but a few being represented by at least one illustration showing a well-preserved likeness); and for our knowledge of the likenesses of one particular group of Roman worthies, provincial governors and local magistrates of the last century BC, we are especially indebted to the work of Michael Grant who, in his *From Imperium to Auctoritas* (1946), rescued their coin issues from virtual oblivion. Under the Empire, while honorific and sepulchral portraits of private persons, many of them named, abounded, those of a historical and public character were in the main confined to emperors, empresses, their relatives and close associates, and some usurpers of imperial power. Only members of the imperial house had the right of numismatic portraiture. The long and important series of official, historical Roman portraits of imperial times must, for our present purposes, be reckoned as a separate study, which can, in fact, already be quite satisfactorily pursued by students and non-specialists in the easily accessible volumes of the *British Museum Catalogue of Coins of the Roman Empire* and of the corpus known as *The Roman Imperial Coinage* (providing a complete sequence of authentic likenesses) without essential recourse to other works. Meanwhile, on the various fringes of the Roman Empire many numismatic and some sculptural portraits of foreign rulers who made their impact on that Empire or were at any rate recognized by it, continued to be produced, some of them as long as Roman history lasted.

In Part II, in the course of our study of the non-Roman rulers, we shall circle the Mediterranean world, beginning with Egypt and passing thence westward along the northern coast of Africa, then going north to Sicily, Spain, Britain, Gaul, and Dacia, southwards and eastwards to Illyricum, Macedonia, Achaia, the Aegean Islands, Thrace, the kingdoms of Asia Minor and the Black Sea regions, Armenia and Commagene, then south to Edessa, Syria, Palestine and Arabia, and lastly east again to Parthia and the empire of the Sassanian Persians. The royal portraits of a number of the Hellenistic kingdoms that had contacts with Rome are among the finest, if indeed they are not the finest, works of numismatic art that the Graeco-Roman world produced. They are obviously by the hands of the very best Greek die-engravers whose services the sovereigns could command. These outstanding masterpieces were issued in Ptolemaic Egypt, Sicily, Macedonia, Bithynia, Pontus, Pergamon, Cappadocia, Syria and Parthia. Other less distinguished groups of likenesses of kings, queens and leaders are no less clearly the productions of Greek artists or of men who had been trained in the traditions of Greek art. Finally, among the coin-types depicting the features of Roman notables struck in Rome, or at extra-Italian mints under Roman control, there are some superbly realistic portraits which can claim to rank with the most arresting late-Hellenistic veristic works that have come to light in east Mediterranean lands. It is therefore to be hoped that the present book may make some appeal to students of classical art as well as to those of Roman history.

Foreign rulers who were client kings – and they formed a large proportion of those in contact with Rome – had either to obtain Roman approval for some of their activities, notably in matters of foreign policy, or allow Rome to act in their behalf. They owed Rome certain services, receiving in return her protection, security for their thrones, and sometimes active aid; and in this way Rome gradually extended her protectorate and the recognition of her power throughout the Mediterranean world, particularly when she was called upon to arbitrate between rival claimants to the kingship. Rome formally accepted the claim to the personal title of 'king' – a claim that had to be renewed at each accession – of those absolute Hellenistic monarchs, in the first place, who gave her their allegiance and services and thus became *amici* or *socii et amici* of the Roman State. Rich gifts often accompanied the Senate's confirmation of a king's position. But the term 'ally' did not necessarily imply a definite treaty by which both parties bound themselves, on equal terms, to help one another in war. The title of 'ally of Rome' was a source of moral support to the client, whose relationship with Rome was actually no more than that of friend. Only occasionally and for fixed periods did Rome make true alliances with her client kings, when she herself was in real need of their help. In theory the aid rendered by the kings to Rome and the money payments made to her were voluntary, but difficult to refuse in the face of Rome's superior strength and prestige; and under the Principate the term 'ally' came to designate those kings who were reckoned as members of the Empire and bound to supply contingents to the Roman army.

As regards the details of the client kings' foreign policy, no king could enter into friendship with one who was not a friend of Rome; and no king could make war or peace without Rome's consent. But a king could suppress a revolt among his own dependencies, wage a defensive war, if the victim of an unprovoked attack, and extend his own conquests if Rome was not interested in preventing them. Aggression by one friend of Rome against another was, in theory, at any rate, immediately checked by Rome's intervention and arbitration, generally by means of a commission, between the contestants.

To turn to the internal affairs of the client kings – under the Republic their kingdoms were, unlike the provinces, outside the scope of Rome's *imperium*. They remained owners and masters of their own territories and could do with them what they pleased, enjoying undisputed sovereignty and jurisdiction within them. Not until the time of Augustus did Rome interfere in the interests of a king's subjects. It goes without saying that the kings possessed the full right of coinage, sometimes in gold, as well as in the other metals. They also had the right of personally leading the forces that served as auxiliaries for Rome. They could make bequests and nominate their successors for Rome to recognize, according to the traditional hereditary principle. They could and did leave their kingdoms temporarily in order to lodge complaints or make requests before the Roman Senate or emperor. When in Rome they were duly honoured; and their princes living as hostages in the capital were treated with every kindness and trained in Roman ways. There is no evidence of regular tribute being exacted from any client king under the Republic and under the Empire instances of it are few. But in the form of irregular contributions and bribes money often flowed into Roman pockets from the royal clients. In imperial times a number of kings received the Roman citizenship and adopted Roman names.

Such, in brief outline, was the role played in Roman history by those characters whose likenesses are the most aesthetically impressive of Roman historical portraits.

1   C. Seltman, *Greek Coins*, 1933, pl. 31, nos. 2, 3.
2   *Philopseudes* 18.
3   *Institutio oratoria* xii, 10, 9.
4   Pseudo-Plutarch, *Vitae oratorum* x, 847.
5   *Demosthenes* 31.
6   M. Bieber, *The Sculpture of the Hellenistic Age*, 1961, fig. 214.
7   E.g. the Ny Carlsberg, Copenhagen, copy, on which the missing hands have been correctly restored as clasped: G. M. A. Richter, *The Portraits of the Greeks*, 1965, ii, figs. 1397–1513 – in particular figs. 1398–1400 (Copenhagen).
8   *NH*, xxxiv, 63: 'fecit et Alexandrum Magnum multis operibus a puertia eius orsus, quam statuam inaurari iussit Nero princeps delectatus admodum illa.'

9   *Alexander* 4: τήν τε ἀνάτασιν τοῦ αὐχένος εἰς εὐώμενον ἡσυχῇ κεκλιμένου καὶ τὴν ὑγρότητα τῶν ὀμμάτων, διατετήρηκεν ἀκριβῶς ὁ τεχνίτης [sc. Lysippus].
10 G. M. A. Richter, *The Sculpture and Sculptors of the Greeks*, 4th ed., 1970, fig. 745.
11 Davis and Kraay 1973, figs. 4, 6.
12 Ibid., figs. 7, 8.
13 vi, 53.
14 *NH*, xxxv, 6.
15 *Jugurtha* lxxxv, 25.
16 ii, 36, 100.
17 v, 14, 36. Cf. *Pro Rabirio Postumo* 7, 16: 'imago ipsa ad posteritatis memoriam prodita'.
18 *NH*, xxxiv, 30.

PART I

Republican and Early Augustan Roman Notables

Footnotes are placed at the end of the text section to which they refer.

MARCUS CLAUDIUS MARCELLUS
(consul 222 BC)
Ills. 1, 2

Marcus Claudius Marcellus, hero of the Hannibalic War, who defeated the Carthaginians in Sicily in his campaign of 214–211 BC, died in 208 BC. The only portraits that definitely purport to represent him are the heads, facing towards the right and with a *triskele* (the symbol of Sicily) behind them, on the obverses of the denarii issued by his descendant, Publius Cornelius Lentulus Marcellinus, in 50 BC (*Ill. 1*).[1] These heads are very different in style from the coin portraits that can be safely attributed to the late third and early second centuries BC (cf. pp. 18–21). They are executed in the highly veristic manner of the first century BC; and they show the subject with a large, long nose, prominent cheek-bones, sunken cheeks, a scraggy neck and a pronounced 'Adam's apple'. This might well suggest an imaginary portrait invented in the moneyer's own time.[2] On the other hand, these heads have something in common with the portrait that may well be that of Scipio Africanus on a late third- or early second-century gem at Naples (see *Ill. 4*); and we know that one portrait at least of Marcellus was erected in Rome during the first half of the second century, when his grandson Marcus Claudius Marcellus set up statues of himself, his father and his grandfather in the temple of Honos and Virtus.[3] Moreover, Plutarch describes an inscribed statue of Marcellus at Lindos on the island of Rhodes;[4] and Cicero mentions statues of him in Sicily.[5]

The first-century coin portraits could, then, have been based on a second-century portrait tradition, which might, in its turn, have been formed at a time at which Marcellus' features were still remembered as they were shortly before his death, when he was about sixty years old. But there still remains the long gap between the erection of his portrait in Rome and the striking of Marcellinus' denarii. Meanwhile, all the details of these denarii allude to the great Marcellus – the *triskele* on the obverse to his capture of Syracuse in 211 BC; the reverse type of Marcellus carrying a trophy to a temple to his dedication to Jupiter Feretrius of the Gallic spoils that he had taken after defeating the Insubres in 222 BC; and the reverse legend MARCELLVS COS QVINQ to the fact that he was five times consul (222, 215, 214, 210 and 208 BC).

The subject of one sculptural portrait has been identified as Marcellus. This is a marble, smaller than life-size head in relief in Berlin, which has features very similar to those of the coin portraits, although the hair is somewhat differently treated (*Ill. 2*). It has been suggested that this was a

1 M. Claudius Marcellus: obverse of denarius, posthumously minted, 50 BC.

2 M. Claudius Marcellus: marble head, possibly contemporary.

'private' portrait, contemporary with Marcellus himself and possibly made in southern Italy.[6]

1   Vessberg 1941, pp. 127–8, pl. 3, nos. 2, 3; Sydenham 1952, p. 187, no. 1147, pl. 29; Crawford 1974, no. 439, pl. 52.
2   Cf. *RM*, lxxv, 1968, pp. 70–1, pl. 14, fig. 4, pl. 15, fig. 4.
3   Asconius, *In Pisonem* 11.
4   *Marcellus* 30, 5.
5   *Verrines* ii, 4, 40, 86.
6   *RM*, lxxv, 1968, pp. 71–3, pl. 15, figs. 1, 3.

PUBLIUS CORNELIUS SCIPIO AFRICANUS (236/5–184/3 BC)

Ills. 3, 4

In 209 BC Scipio captured New Carthage, together with its mint, so suddenly that the craftsmen and their workshops were taken intact and could at once be set to work for the conqueror. There then appeared in the city's coin series, on silver shekels and half-shekels and on bronze, an entirely new obverse portrait type, completely different from the portrait types hitherto minted of Carthaginian rulers (cf. § Spain, below), namely the head, facing left, of a clean-shaven Roman, with close-cropped hair cut in a fringe across the brow, but growing rather long on the nape of the neck, a prominent chin, and a long, pointed nose with a pronounced bridge. The reverses continue the old Carthaginian type of horse and palm-tree.[1] It is difficult to see who in this context the Roman can be if it is not Scipio himself.

The same applies to the leftward-facing head on the obverses of some rare bronze coins struck at Canusium in Apulia, which represent a unique irruption into the Canusine repertory. This head is very similar to the New Carthage portrait, with its close-cut hair combed forward onto the brow, but somewhat long behind, its prominent chin and long, pointed nose. On the reverse is a galloping horseman.[2] After the Roman debacle at Cannae the survivors, including Scipio, retreated to Canusium, where Scipio rallied the Roman troops – an event that the city could well have commemorated by putting a portrait of Scipio on its coinage, after he had become a celebrity.

The long locks on the nape of the neck in these two portrait heads recall literary descriptions of Scipio's appearance – Livy's *promissa caesaries*[3] and Silius Italicus' picture of his warlike expression, with long, flowing locks behind, blazing eyes, and a mien in which ferocity and kindliness were mingled.[4]

Very different from the New Carthage and Canusium heads are those on the obverses of denarii struck *c.* 112 BC by the moneyer Cnaeus Cornelius Blasio.[5] There can be little doubt that they are meant for Scipio, since the moneyer belonged to the *gens Cornelia* and the Capitoline triad on the reverses is obviously a reference to Scipio's special association with the temple of Jupiter Capitolinus. The only point in common which these rightward-facing heads have with the New Carthage and Canusium portraits is the long, pointed nose. The brow appears to be wholly bald and only a wisp of hair is occasionally visible below the Greek Corinthian helmet, which would seem to be a type of headgear completely irrelevant to Scipio. These heads could be imaginary 'portraits' of the moneyer's famous forbear, conceived of as he might have been in his concluding years, with prominent cheek-bones and long, thin, scraggy neck with 'Adam's apple'.

A far better claim to be a real likeness of Scipio can be made for the leftward-facing portrait on a gold signet-ring from Capua, signed by Herakleidas and now in the Naples Museum (*Ill. 4*).[6] It

3, 4   P. Cornelius Scipio Africanus: obverse of silver shekel, New Carthage, *c.* 209 BC; and portrait on gold signet-ring signed by Herakleidas, from Capua, late 3rd or early 2nd century.

shows the head of a clean-shaven Roman with neat, straight hair clinging to the head like a cap and combed forward onto the brow, while quite luxuriant locks cover the nape of the neck. The nose is long and pointed, the chin prominent, and there is a slight 'Adam's apple'. The somewhat sunken cheeks and scraggy neck proclaim a subject rather more advanced in years than the New Carthage and Canusium personage. The lettering of the inscription indicates a late third- or early second-century date for the ring. That Scipio's features were portrayed on a signet-ring is known from the fact that his son Lucius wore a ring 'in quo caput Africani sculptum erat'.[7]

Recently the identification as a portrait of Scipio has been suggested for a marble head in the castle of Erbach, west of Wiesbaden, on the right bank of the Rhine.[8] The subject wears a close-fitting cap of animal pelt, with a metal band worn diadem-wise across the brow. The nose is unfortunately restored. There are side-burns, which do not occur on any of the portraits that have so far been connected with Scipio. But the small mouth and large eyes recall those of the Canusium heads; and the locks escaping from below the cap down the nape of the neck are reminiscent of the *promissa caesaries* attributed to Scipio by Livy and Silius Italicus. The pelt cap is described by Polybius as characteristic of the lightly armed Roman *velites* – a simple headpiece sometimes covered with wolf-skin or something of the kind.[9] In his account of the Roman cavalrymen Polybius recounts how in his day the old-style equipment had been exchanged for the Greek type;[10] and although he does not mention their former helmets, it seems to be implied by the context that they were not of metal, lacking, that is to say, the peak above the brow, the neckguard, and the cheek-pieces that accompany the skin cap normally worn by Roman cavalrymen on funerary stelae of the first century A D.[11] Precisely when these metal items were added we do not know, but it is likely to have been some time before Polybius wrote; and since the cap of the Erbach head is without them, the most probable date of its original would be *c.* 200 B C or a decade later.

That Scipio should have been portrayed with the light cavalry headgear of his day is a reasonable supposition in view of his special interest in providing the Roman army with adequate cavalry units.[12] It was, in fact, the cavalry that contributed not a little to his victory at Zama.[13] We recall that a horseman is the reverse type of Canusium portrait coins (see above); and also the fact that Scipio in his youth commanded a cavalry squadron at the battle of the Ticinus and charged forward to rescue his wounded father. The original behind the Erbach head could, indeed, have been an equestrian statue, with the diadem signifying his superhuman

exploits and the close association with the gods that he claimed to enjoy. It would seem to be most improbable that after Zama no honorific statues of him were set up. According to Appian[14] and Valerius Maximus[15] a private statue of Scipio was erected in the Capitolium. That there was a good portrait tradition of him is implied by his grandson's statement that he knew his grandfather's features better from his likenesses than from his childhood recollections of him.[16]

1   Carson and Sutherland 1956, pp. 41–3, 52, pl. 3, nos. 7(h), 7(i), 7(l), 7(m), 7(p); Scullard 1970, pls. 3, 16; *Museum Helveticum*, xv, 1958, pl. 3, no. 11.
2   Carson and Sutherland 1956, pp. 41–2, fig. 4, C, D; Scullard 1970, pls. 4, 17; *Museum Helveticum*, xv, 1958, pl. 3, nos. 2–6, 8, 9.
3   xxviii, 35, 6.
4   viii, 559–61: 'martia frons facilisque comae nec pone retroque/caesaries brevior; flagrabant lumina miti/ aspectu gratusque inerat visentibus horror'.
5   Vessberg 1941, pp. 126–7, pl. 3, nos. 4–6; Sydenham 1952, p. 75, no. 561, pl. 19; Scullard 1970, pls. 2, 15; Crawford 1974, no. 296, pl. 40 (interprets as Mars).
6   *JRS*, xlv, 1955, p. 44, pl. 6, fig. 22; *Museum Helveticum*, xv, 1958, pp. 27–32, pl. 1; Scullard 1970, pl. 1.
7   Valerius Maximus, iii, 5, 1.
8   *AA*, 1972 (1973), pp. 474–89, figs. 1–7, 9, 13, 17.
9   vi, 22: προσεπικοσμεῖται δὲ καὶ λιτῷ περικεφαλαίῳ ποτὲ δὲ λυκείαν ἤ τι τῶν τοιούτων ἐπιτίθεται.
10 Ibid., 25.
11 *AA*, 1972 (1973), p. 488, fig. 19, pp. 490–92.
12 Scullard 1970, pp. 230, 232.
13 Polybius xv, 14; Livy xxx, 35.
14 *Roman History*, vi, 23.
15 viii, 15, 1.
16 Cicero, *Somnium Scipionis* 10: 'Africanus se ostendit ea forma, quae mihi ex imagine eius quam ex ipso erat notior'.

TITUS QUINCTIUS FLAMININUS
(consul 198 B C; died 174 B C)
Ill. 5

Unique in the Roman republican coinage are the gold staters issued in the name of Titus Quinctius Flamininus after his victory over Philip V of Macedon at Cynoscephalae in 197 B C. On the reverses is a figure of Victory with the legend T QVINCT; while the obverses, which carry no inscription, display Flamininus' likeness. Here the ardent philhellenist is portrayed in the guise of a Hellenistic ruler, if without a royal diadem, with far-away gaze, a square head, untidy, agitated hair growing low on the nape of the neck, projecting lower brow, a long, thin and hooked nose, a slightly pouting mouth, a prominent chin, an 'Adam's apple', a moustache and a short, scrubby beard.[1] The head faces to the right and nearly fills the flan. There can be little doubt that these types were designed and struck under Flamininus' own direction; and it is the first 'labelled', absolutely certain self-portrait of a Roman to feature on a coin. Five examples (in Athens, Berlin, Paris, the British Museum (*Ill. 5*), and a private collection) are now known.[2] All seem to be from different dies, which

5   T. Quinctius Flamininus: obverse of gold stater, 197 BC (British Museum).

suggests that the issue was quite a large one. The occasion for the issue could have been Flamininus' proclamation of the freedom of Greece in 196 BC; and their purpose may have been to serve as presentation pieces.

If the reverse legend is Roman, the style of the obverse portraits is indisputably Greek and must have emanated from a Greek mint. These portraits bear so close a resemblance to the coin portraits of Philip V and Perseus of Macedon (qq.v.) that they could well be the work of the same school of court die-engravers. Furthermore, a life-size portrait head at Delphi, carved in Parian marble, has recently been plausibly identified as Flamininus' likeness, its profile in particular being very close in its details to the coin portraits.[3] That a portrait of the Roman philhellenist should have been erected at Delphi is extremely probable. There is, in fact, an inscription there recording the setting up and dedication to Apollo of a bronze statue of him by the city in recognition of his valour (ἀρετή) and beneficence (εὐεργεσία).[4] Plutarch gives a list of the dedications that he made at the Delphic sanctuary;[5] and it is more than likely that he visited Delphi in person when in Greece, leaving the city under the control of the Aetolians, who were allied with Rome.

Plutarch also tells us that anyone wishing to know what Flamininus looked like could study the bronze statue of him that stood in Rome beside the great figure of Apollo from Carthage, opposite the Circus and carrying a Greek inscription.[6] Unfortunately Plutarch does not provide us with any description of Flamininus' features; nor does he tell us whether this portrait was contemporary or of later date.

1   Vessberg 1941, pp. 124–6, pl. 3, no. 1; Richter 1965, fig. 1761; Scullard 1970, p. 195, pl. 36.
2   A. A. Boyce, 'The Gold Staters of T. Quinctius Flamininus', in *Hommages à Albert Grenier*, 1962, i, pp. 342–50. Cf. R. A. G. Carson, *NC*, 1959, pp. 4–6, pl. 1, no. 4.
3   F. Chamoux, 'Un portrait de Flamininus à Delphes', in *BCH*, lxxxix, 1965, pp. 214–24, figs. 1, 4, 5, 9.
4   Ibid., pp. 218–19.
5   *Flamininus* 12.
6   Ibid., 1: ἰδέαν μὲν ὁποῖος ἦν πάρεστι θεάσασθαι τοῖς βουλομένοις ἀπὸ τῆς ἐν Ῥώμῃ χαλκῆς εἰκόνος, ἢ κεῖται παρὰ τὸν μέγαν Ἀπόλλωνα τὸν ἐκ Καρχηδόνος ἀντικρὺ τοῦ ἱπποδρόμου, γράμμασιν Ἑλληνικοῖς ἐπιγεγραμμένη.

LUCIUS AEMILIUS PAULLUS
(*c.* 230–160 BC)
Ill. 6

Of L. Aemilius Paullus no coin portraits have come down to us. But what is very likely to be a contemporary sculptural likeness of him exists in relief on the frieze of the monument erected by him at Delphi to commemorate his victory over Perseus of Macedon at Pydna in 168. It is, indeed, difficult to see whom else the prominent rider in this battle scene, with a distinctively portrait-like head facing towards the right, could be intended to represent.[1] Very close to this head in features are those of a terracotta relief found in the Kerameikos in Athens, obviously depicting a Roman and most probably a 'private', reduced copy of a monumental portrait of a Roman general who had served in Greece before 146 BC (*Ill. 6*).[2] These two heads

6   L. Aemilius Paullus: portrait on a terracotta relief, Athens.

portray an elderly man about sixty years of age, with fleshy, creased cheeks and a large thick nose; and with them again may be compared the head of a marble herm in the Palazzo dei Conservatori in Rome, the nose of which is unfortunately a restoration – apparently a late republican or early imperial copy of a second-century BC original.[3] That portrait statues of Paullus were erected soon after Pydna both in Greece and in Rome is a reasonable supposition. But the attribution to him of the Athens and Conservatori portraits, for all their resemblance to the Delphi head, is far from certain.

1 H. Kähler, *Der Fries vom Reiterdenkmal des Aemilius Paullus in Delphi*, 1965, pp. 14, 17, 18, pl. 22.
2 G. Hafner, 'Das Bildnis des L. Aemilius Paullus', in *Jahreshefte*, xlviii, 1966–7, pp. 5–15, figs. 2, 3.
3 Ibid., figs. 1, 4, 7.

AULUS POSTUMIUS ALBINUS
(consul 99 BC; died 89 BC)
Ill. 7

Two main types of coin portrait, both facing to the right, of A. Postumius Albinus occur on the denarii issued *c.* 49–48 BC by Decimus Postumius Albinus, son of Brutus.[1] One type portrays him as old, with a narrowish head, a powerfully built, long and creased face, a deeply furrowed brow, a large nose that bulges at the tip, thick lips, and a stocky neck with an 'Adam's apple'. In this case the treatment of the portrait is more graphic than plastic (*Ill. 7*). In the second type, which is more monu-

from two different sculptural originals. There can be little doubt that Albinus is the subject of a marble head in the Louvre, a copy attributable to the second half of the first century AD.[2]

1 Vessberg 1941, pp. 132–4, pls. 4, nos. 8–10, pl. 5, nos. 1, 2; Sydenham 1952, p. 158, no. 943, pl. 26; Crawford 1974, no. 450a–c, pl. 53.
2 Schweitzer 1948, figs. 53, 55, 57.

CAIUS COELIUS CALDUS (consul 94 BC)
Ill. 8

Denarii of the moneyer Caius Coelius Caldus issued in 51 BC carry on their obverses the rightward-facing portrait of his grandfather of the same name, who as tribune of the plebs in 107 or 106 BC had introduced a *lex tabellaria* providing that in trials for high treason the votes of the voting units should be secretly inscribed on tablets – hence the tablet that appears behind his head on some obverses, while the vexillum, boar standard, and *carnyx* (Celtic trumpet) found on other obverses allude to his conquests in Spain in 99 BC (*Ill. 8*).[1] These portraits show extremely life-like and individual features – tufty, woolly hair, a very large aquiline nose, pronounced 'crow's feet' at the corners of the eyes, thick, slightly parted lips striking a 'pathetic' note, a somewhat receding chin, hollow cheeks, slashed by vertical folds of skin on some dies, deep-set eyes that sometimes gaze upwards in the 'inspired' Hellenistic manner. These highly personal traits suggest that the coin portraits, although

7 A. Postumius Albinus: obverse of denarius, minted *c.*49–48 BC.

8 C. Coelius Caldus: obverse of denarius, posthumously minted, *c.*62 BC.

mental, the head is broader, the eyes are more deeply set, the folds of flesh are softened down, the mouth is more sloping, and the whole expression more benign.

Albinus was the moneyer's adoptive father and both variants of his coin portraits would appear to be too personal and realistic to be wholly posthumous. Possibly the two variants were derived

struck some forty years after the probable date of Caldus' death, were based on a lifetime original. No sculptural portraits, so far as the present writer is aware, have been attributed to Caldus.

1 Vessberg 1941, pp. 128–9, pl. 3, nos. 7, 8, pl. 14, no. 7; T. R. S. Broughton, *The Magistrates of the Roman Republic*, ii, 1952, p. 3, n. 2; Crawford 1974, no. 437, 1a–4b, pl. 52.

LUCIUS CORNELIUS SULLA FELIX
(138–78 BC; consul 88 BC)
Ills. 9–11

Portrait heads of Sulla, facing towards the right, appear on the obverses of denarii struck in 54 BC by the moneyer Quintus Pompeius Rufus, whose forbear, the Quintus Pompeius Rufus who was Sulla's colleague in the consulship in 88 BC, is portrayed on the reverses. Sulla's portraits reveal a number of dies that differ quite noticeably from one another in their details.[1] Among these dies there are three main variants, of which the most striking in its effect of elderliness, restlessness and 'pathos' has upward-gazing eyes, two vertical gashes or folds down the cheeks, and a furrowed brow (*Ill. 9*).

the gap of over twenty years between their issue and his death.

Various attempts have been made to identify sculptural portraits of Sulla. For instance, L. Curtius[2] and R. Herbig[3] have argued that a head in Venice represents him,[4] while others have firmly rejected this identification.[5] There is, indeed, some slight resemblance between its features and those of the coin portraits. But the hair of the Venice head is much neater and the face more veristically treated. This is also the case with the travertine head in Copenhagen (Ny Carlsberg Glyptotek) assigned to Sulla by Herbig,[6] where the features are even more starkly chronicled and the close-fitting cap of very sketchily worked hair wholly different from the

9 L. Cornelius Sulla Felix: obverse of denarius, posthumously minted, 54 BC.

10 L. Cornelius Sulla Felix: obverse of denarius, 54 BC, showing variant portrait.

11 L. Cornelius Sulla Felix (?): travertine head (Ny Carlsberg Glyptotek, Copenhagen).

The second variant is much calmer and more conventional in expression, with smoother cheeks and brow and an altogether younger look; while the third variant is closer to the first than to the second, but plumper in the face than the first. But all variants are alike in their untidy, tufty, woolly hair, large aquiline nose, slightly double chin, curving, full-lipped mouth, and 'Adam's apple' (*Ill. 10*). All these dies must be based on one or more portraits made during Sulla's lifetime, despite

long, lanky locks of the coins (*Ill. 11*). It would seem to be unlikely that the latter's sculptural counterpart has as yet been found.

That monumental portraits of Sulla did exist we know from literary sources. Suetonius tells us that Julius Caesar restored the statues of Sulla and Pompey in Rome that the Roman mob had overthrown.[7] Plutarch gives us a quite detailed description of Sulla's portrait statues,[8] but unfortunately tells us little of his actual features, concentrating on his colouring – on the sharp and powerful gleam of his grey eyes and on his blotchy red and white complexion, which gave him a terrifying look. He probably had painted statues of the dictator in mind.

1 Vessberg 1941, pp. 129–31, pl. 4, nos. 2–4, pl. 14, no. 6; Schweitzer 1948, pp. 67–8; R. Herbig, 'Zur Ikonographie des Lucius Cornelius Sulla Felix', in *Würzburger Jahrbücher für die Altertumswissenschaft*, i, 1946, pp. 108–10, pls. 3, fig. 6, and 4, figs. 7–10; B. Schweitzer, 'Monumentale Bildnisse des Diktators Sulla?', in ibid., pp. 258–67, pl. 6, fig. 3; Sydenham 1952, p. 150, no. 908, pl. 25; Crawford 1974, no. 434, 1, pl. 52.
2 *RM*, xlvii, 1932, pp. 202–12.
3 See note 1.
4 See note 2: figs. 1, 3. See note 1: pl. 1, fig. 2, pl. 3, fig. 5, pl. 5, fig. 1, pl. 6, fig. 4.
5 E.g. F. Poulsen, *Römische Privatporträts und Prinzen-bildnisse*, 1939, pp. 3, 4; Schweitzer (see note 1).
6 See note 1: pl. 1, fig. 1, pl. 2, figs. 3, 4.
7 *Julius* 75: 'statuas Luci Sullae atque Pompei a plebe disiectas reposuit'.
8 *Sulla* 2, 1.

QUINTUS POMPEIUS RUFUS
(consul 88 BC, with Sulla)
Ill. 12

Quintus Pompeius Rufus, Sulla's colleague in the consulship in 88 BC and associate in his march on Rome, was murdered when left in charge of Italy on Sulla's departure for the East. His rightward-facing portraits appear on the reverses of the denarii, struck in 54 BC by his grandson of the same name, with obverse portraits of Sulla (q.v.).[1] At least three different dies were used. One shows a middle-aged man with vertical folds of flesh down the cheeks (*Ill. 12*). Two other dies, more idealizing, portray him as somewhat younger and fuller in the face. But all show him with the tufty, woolly hair displayed by Sulla's portraits, a large, very aquiline nose, deep-set eyes, and an 'Adam's apple'. It is improbable that the moneyer used no

12 Q. Pompeius Rufus: reverse of denarius, post-humously minted, 54 BC (cf. *Ill. 9*).

contemporary portraits of his grandfather, who died not more than thirty years before these coins were issued. According to Cicero, Publius Cornelius Lentulus, a member of the Catiline faction, had a signet-ring carrying his grandfather's likeness.[2]

1 Vessberg 1941, pp. 131–2. pl. 4, nos. 5–7; Sydenham 1952, p. 150, no. 908, pl. 25; Crawford 1974, no. 434, pl. 52.
2 *Catilines* iii, 5, 10. For a similar case cf. Scipio Africanus above.

QUINTUS ARRIUS (praetor 72 BC?)
Ill. 13

What is probably the rightward-facing portrait of the Quintus Arrius, who, as praetor in c.72 BC, fought against Spartacus and Crixus, appears on the obverses of denarii issued c.41 BC by Marcus Arrius Secundus (*Ill. 13*).[1] The praetor was certainly the most distinguished member of the

13 Q. Arrius: obverse of denarius, c.41 BC.

moneyer's *gens*; and the portrait, *pace* Vessberg, who dismisses it as 'unpersönlich' (impersonal), shows distinctively individual features – long, lanky locks of hair, a long, narrow face, a long, thin nose, slightly smirking lips, a weak chin, lightly bearded, below which the long curving neck is thrust well forward.

1 Vessberg 1941, p. 165, pl. 14, no. 5; Sydenham 1952, p. 180, nos. 1084–5, pl. 28 (where the curious suggestion is made that the portrait is that of Octavian); Crawford 1974, no. 513, 2, 3, pl. 64.

CAIUS ANTIUS RESTIO
(tribune of the plebs c.72 BC)
Ill. 14

The coin portrait of Caius Antius Restio, tribune of the plebs in c.72 BC, which appears on the obverses of the denarii struck by the moneyer C. Antius Restio in 47 BC, represents the acme of the Roman veristic portrait style (*Ill. 14*).[1] The head, facing right, is round, the hair lank, the long, narrow face is almost grotesque, with its prominent

flesh gash the cheeks from nose to chin. The long nose bulges pronouncedly at the tip, the distance between the nostrils and the upper lip is unusually

14   C. Antius Restio: obverse of denarius, posthumously minted, 47 BC.

15   Cn. Pompeius Magnus: obverse of denarius struck in Spain, 46–45 BC.

cheek-bones, two deeply cut, vertical folds of flesh on the cheeks, long, pointed, thin nose thickening at the tip, thick lips, protruding chin, and a scraggy neck with 'Adam's apple'. The origin of this outstandingly striking likeness must have been a portrait made during Restio's lifetime.

1   Vessberg 1941, p. 134, pl. 4, no. 1; Schweitzer 1948, pp. 75–6, fig. 87; Sydenham 1952, p. 162, no. 970, pl. 26; Crawford 1974, no. 455, 1a, b, pl. 54.

CNAEUS POMPEIUS MAGNUS (106–48 BC)
Ills. 15–21

Of the coin portraits of Pompey the Great there are five different series:

(i) On the obverses of denarii struck in Spain in the names of Pompey's elder son Cnaeus and Marcus Minatius Sabinus in 46–45 BC Pompey's head faces to the right and is accompanied by the legends CN MAGN or MAGNVS IMP, CN MAGN or MAGNVS IMP F(*ilius*).[1] This may be described as the 'Hellenistic' type, distinguished by its markedly untidy hair, long on the nape of the neck and with Pompey's peculiarly characteristic long, waving, and upstanding 'crest' (ἀναστολή, *anastole*) above the brow, a feature noted by Plutarch, Lucan, and Silius Italicus as emphasizing the nobility of his forehead and as enhancing his generally handsome and commanding mien (*Ill. 15*).[2] This 'crest' could, indeed, have been a conscious imitation on Pompey's part of Alexander's leonine mane. No less characteristic are the 'whiskers' in the form of a thick lock of hair on each cheek in front of the ear. Here the glance of the large eyes is directed upwards, two strongly marked transverse lines furrow the brow, and two very deep, vertical folds of

long, the chin is double, and there is a small 'Adam's apple' on the thick neck.

(ii) On the obverses of denarii struck by Pompey's younger son, Sextus Pompeius Magnus Pius, in Spain in 45–44 BC there is a portrait of Pompey, facing either to the right or to the left, which is utterly different from any of his other likenesses – showing him as youthful, plump in the cheeks, with the head tilted forward on a relatively thin neck, woolly curls covering the head in an almost negroid manner, and a very summarily rendered 'crest'. The accompanying legends are SEX MAGN or MAGNVS IMP SAL(*utatis*) or SAL IMP; and the reverses carry the figure of PIETAS.[3] But of the same date and from the same mint are asses with a Janus head with both faces displaying Pompey's distinctively bulbous nose and full chin and surmounted by the legend MAGN or MAGNVS.[4]

(iii) On the obverses of denarii issued by Sextus in Sicily in 42–38 BC Pompey's head appears facing rightwards with the hair arranged in three neat, superimposed tiers on the crown, luxuriant locks on the nape of the neck, and a 'crest' above the brow less unruly than in (i) above (*Ill. 16*). The brow is

16   Cn. Pompeius Magnus: obverse of denarius struck in Sicily, 42–38 BC.

furrowed and the bull-like neck is double-creased in front, but the cheeks show only one short vertical fold of flesh. The eyes are smaller than in (i). Behind the portrait is a sacrificial jug and on some dies there is also a *lituus* (augural staff) in front of it. The accompanying obverse legend is MAG PIVS IMP ITER, while the reverse legends read PRAEF(*ectus*) CLAS(*sis*) ET ORAE MARIT(*imae*) EX SC or PRAEF ORAE MARIT ET CLAS EX SC.[5]

(iv) Aurei issued in the same years as (iii) and also in Sicily by Sextus carry on their reverses the heads of Pompey and his elder son Cnaeus Pompeius Iunior (q.v.) confronted. Pompey's portrait, which is on the left, facing right, shows the same hair-style, cheeks and neck as (iii) and has a *lituus* behind it, while the reverse legends are almost identical with those of (iii).[6] A portrait of Sextus Pompeius (q.v.) is on the obverse.

(v) Portraits of Pompey facing right or left on the obverses of denarii struck at an uncertain mint in 44–43 BC by Quintus Nasidius, who had held a naval command under Sextus, have the same 'crest', hair-style, cheeks and neck as (iii) and (iv); and there are a dolphin below the neck and a trident in front of the face (*Ill. 17*). The obverse legend is NEPTVNI – 'Neptune's own'. Sextus had styled himself 'son of Neptune'. But here, accompanying a likeness of Pompey the Great, the legend like the dolphin and trident, must refer to him and to his maritime exploits against the pirates as Neptune's protégé.[7]

Pompey died in 48 BC at the age of 58 and he is, with the exception of the series (ii) denarii, always shown as elderly on his coin portraits. There can be little doubt that these reflect his monumental lifetime likenesses.

Two gems also present certain portraits of Pompey that are close to the numismatic series. One, an aquamarine in the Devonshire Collection, shows his head facing to the left with hair, 'crest', and nose very close to those of the 46–45 BC series (i), while the cheeks and neck resemble those of series (iii); and the presence of the dolphin below

17 Cn. Pompeius Magnus: obverse of denarius (mint uncertain), 44–43 BC.

the neck and of the trident in front of the face would seem to indicate that the gem was not cut until after the Nasidius coin portraits of series (v) has been issued.[8] A jasper in the Berlin Antiquarium displays Pompey's head facing right, with features very similar to those of series (i), but with the tiered hair that characterizes series (iii). It has been suggested that the letters P P that flank the neck on this gem stand for 'Pompeius Patronus'.[9]

Of the sculptural portraits of Pompey in the round by far the best known is the marble bust in Copenhagen (Ny Carlsberg Glyptotek) (*Ills. 18, 19*).[10] The hair on the crown of the head resembles that of the Devonshire aquamarine, but the 'crest' is lower and neater and more like that of the Berlin jasper. The very much furrowed, worried-looking brow and double chin recall the coin portraits of series (i). But the cheeks are fuller and the mouth more set than on the gems and most of the coins. The eyes are small and rather mean. The thick, bulbous nose is very definitely Pompey's. The Copenhagen bust is obviously an imperial-age copy of a republican original; and on the score of its technique F. Poulsen and B. Schweitzer have assigned the copy to Hadrianic times. But the technical arguments are not conclusive; and since the bust is said to have been found in the family tomb of the Licinii near Rome, it may well date from the time of Marcus Licinius Crassus Frugi, consul in AD 27, who gave his son the name of Cnaeus Pompeius Magnus to mark his descent from Pompey the Great through his mother.[11] This dating, now accepted by F. Poulsen,[12] would account for the inclusion of Pompey's portrait in the Licinian tomb more reasonably than a Hadrianic dating.

Very close to the Copenhagen bust is a much more recently published marble head of Pompey now in the Frank Brown collection and acquired in Rome (*Ill. 20*).[13] It has, indeed, been claimed as the original head of the statue of Pompey at the feet of which Julius Caesar met his death or as being at least a contemporary copy of it. On this question both D. Michel and the present writer would suspend judgment, since neither has examined the head itself; and Michel suggests that the discrepancies between it and the Copenhagen portrait which F. Brown detects – the larger eyes, more curved and kindlier mouth, and slightly less wind-blown hair – may be partly, at least, illusory.[14]

From their close correspondence with his coin likenesses two terracotta heads have been most reasonably identified as portraits of Pompey. One is in the Museo Nazionale Romano (*Ill. 21*),[15] the other at Stuttgart.[16] Neither of these, however, has 'whiskers'.

Of the sculptural portraits attributed to Pompey

18, 19　Cn. Pompeius
Magnus: front and profile
views of marble bust,
posthumous (Ny Carlsberg
Glyptotek, Copenhagen).

20 Cn. Pompeius Magnus: marble head, possibly contemporary (Yale University Art Gallery; lent by Frank Brown).

21 Cn. Pompeius Magnus: terracotta head (Museo Nazionale, Rome).

the least close to the coins is the head at Venice, of which the nose, the chin and parts of the eyebrows and lips are restorations.[17] Characteristic of Pompey are its locks growing low on the neck, its thick 'whiskers', its furrowed brow and its creased neck. But the 'crest' is almost rudimentary.[18]

1   Vessberg 1941, pl. 5, no. 3; Sydenham 1952, pp. 173–4, nos. 1036–9, pl. 27; Michel 1967, pl. 13, no. 3; Crawford 1974, no. 470, pl. 55.

2   *Pompey* 2: τὴν ὄψιν ἔσχεν οὐ μετρίως συνδημαγωγοῦ-σαν . . . ἦν δέ τις καὶ ἀναστολὴ τῆς κόμης ἀτρέμα καὶ τῶν περὶ τὰ ὄμματα ῥυθμῶν ὑγρότης τοῦ προσώ-που, ποιοῦσα μᾶλλον λεγομένην ἢ φαινομένην ὁμοιότητα πρὸς τὰς Ἀλεξάνδρου τοῦ βασιλέως εἰκόνας. ('His [Pompey's] countenance contributed in no small degree to his winning the people's good-will . . . he had also a slightly upstanding "crest" of hair and a melting expression of the eyes that produced a resemblance to the portraits of Alexander the Great that was more talked of than apparent.') Lucan viii, 680–1: 'hirta coma et generosa fronte decora/caesaries' ('his shaggy hair and the long locks that graced his noble brow'). Silius Italicus xiii, 860–1: 'ille, hirta cui subrigitur coma fronte, decorum/et gratum terris Magnus caput' ('Magnus, with his shaggy locks rising above his brow, a handsome and gracious presence among men'). Velleius Paterculus (ii, 29) writes of Pompey's 'forma excellens', Pliny (*NH*, vii, 12 (53)) of his 'os probum' ('noble countenance') and 'honorem eximiae frontis' ('fine and majestic brow').

3   Sydenham 1952, p. 174, nos. 1041–3, pl. 27; Crawford 1974, no. 477, pl. 56.

4   Sydenham 1952, no. 1044; Michel 1967, pl. 13, no. 5; Crawford 1974, no. 479, pl. 56.

5   Vessberg 1941, pl. 5, nos. 4, 6; Sydenham 1952, p. 210, nos. 1344–5; Michel 1967, pl. 13, no. 1; Crawford 1974, no. 511, 3, pl. 62.

6   Vessberg 1941, pl. 5, nos. 8, 9; Sydenham 1952, p. 210, no. 1346, pl. 30; Crawford 1974, no. 511, 1, pl. 61.

7   Vessberg 1941, pl. 5, no. 5; Sydenham 1952, p. 211, nos. 1350–1, pl. 30; Michel 1967, pl. 13, no. 2; Crawford 1974, no. 483, pl. 57.

8   Furtwängler 1900, pl. 50, no. 43; Michel 1967, pl. 13, no. 6.

9   Furtwängler 1900, pl. 47, no. 38; Michel 1967, p. 61, pl. 13, no. 4.

10   Schweitzer 1948, figs. 117, 124, 125; Michel 1967, pl. 14.

11   V. H. Poulsen, *Journal of the Walters Art Gallery, Baltimore*, xi, 1948, p. 10.

12   *Ny Carlsberg Catalogue*, 1951, p. 414, no. 597.

13   Ed. G. E. Mylonas, *Studies Presented to David Moore Robinson*, i, 1951, pp. 761–4, pls. 95–7; Michel 1967, pls. 15–17.

14   Michel 1967, pp. 64–5.

15   Vessberg 1941, pl. 54.

16   Michel 1967, pl. 20.

17   Schweitzer 1948, figs. 121, 123; Michel 1967, pls. 18, 19.

18   For the so-called Pompey statue in the Palazzo Spada, Rome, see D. Faccenna in *Archeologia Classica*, viii, 1956, pp. 173–201, pls. 41–5. For a general survey of portraits of Pompey, including the head, very dubiously attributed to him, in the Uffizi Gallery, Florence, see F. Poulsen in *RA*, ser. 6, vii, 1936, pp. 16–52.

MARCUS TULLIUS CICERO (106–43 BC)
Ills. 22, 23

Several descriptions of Cicero's physique survive in the works of ancient writers. According to the orator himself, he was a very thin and weedy boy with a long and scraggy neck; but when he was in Greece in 79 BC – for the sake of his health and for study purposes – he grew strong in lungs and average in build.[1] Plutarch, too, records his early slenderness and leanness and his increase in strength as he advanced in vigour through the practice of gymnastic exercises.[2] Plutarch also comments on Cicero's genial and serene expression;[3] and Asinius Pollio informs us that he retained his good looks and good health even when ageing.[4]

No coins bear Cicero's portrait and none of his sculptural likenesses shows him in his fragile youth. All portray him in his solid middle age and all are copies executed in imperial times. The most important of them is a bust in Apsley House, London, much restored, but identified by an inscription, CICERO, at the base of the bust, that has been generally accepted by epigraphists as genuinely ancient.[5] Here we see a quite benevolent-looking individual with a high, furrowed brow, above which the hair grows sparsely, but thickens on the crown and at the sides of the head. The eyes are deep-set, two small creases spring diagonally from just above the bridge of the nose, and two much deeper creases starting from the nostrils line the full and rather flabby cheeks. The lips are slightly parted; there is a double chin and heavy creasing in the now stocky neck. Portraits in the Uffizi, Florence (*Ills. 22, 23*),[6] in the Vatican (Museo Chiaramonti),[7] and in the Capitoline Museum[8] obviously show the same person, but as slightly older, with 'crow's feet' at the corners of the eyes.

Finally, there are two portraits on gems that can be identified as Cicero with reasonable certainty.[9] These show the same hair, scanty above the brow, but with quite plentiful, lanky locks on the sides and back of the head; a high, furrowed brow; vertical folds of flesh on the cheeks, at the corners of the nose, and at the corners of the mouth; and a double chin. Here Cicero is definitely growing older and putting on more flesh.

1   *Brutus* 91: 'erat eo tempore in nobis summa gracilitas et infirmitas corporis, procerum et tenue collum . . . lateribus vires et corporis mediocris habitus accesserat.'

2   *Cicero* 3, 4: καὶ γὰρ ἦν ὄντως ἰσχνὸς καὶ ἄσαρκος . . . καὶ τὸ σῶμα τοῖς γυμνασίοις ἀναρρωνύμενον εἰς ἕξιν ἐβάδιζε νεανικήν.

3   *Comparison of Demosthenes and Cicero* 1, 6: τό τε πρόσωπον αὐτοῦ μειδίαμα καὶ γαλήνην παρεῖχε.

4   In Seneca *Suasoriae* vi, 74: 'facies decora ad senectutem prosperaque permansit valetudo.'

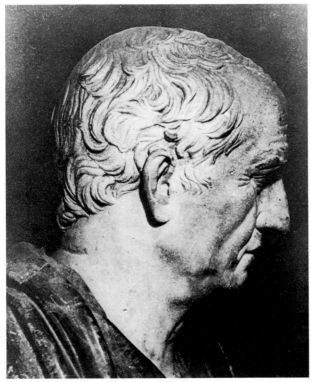

22, 23 M. Tullius Cicero: front and
profile views of portrait bust (Uffizi,
Florence).

5 Schweitzer 1948, figs. 135, 137, 156.
6 Ibid., figs. 143, 147.
7 Ibid., figs. 138, 139.
8 Ibid., figs. 142, 146.
9 Furtwängler 1900, pl. 47, no. 58 (Berlin), pl. 65, no.
   36 (Marlborough Collection). Cf. also ibid., pl. 50,
   no. 3 (Naples) and no. 5 (Paris), which probably
   depict Cicero.

CAIUS JULIUS CAESAR (c. 100–44 BC)
Ills. 24–37

Suetonius has bequeathed to us a vivid picture of Julius Caesar's physical characteristics.[1] 'He is said to have been tall of stature [excelsa statura], with a fair complexion [colore candido], shapely limbs [teretibus membris], a somewhat disproportionately large [or fleshy?] mouth [ore paulo pleniore – which some scholars translate as "with a somewhat full face", but the most authentic coin portraits do not, as we shall see, bear this out], and keen black eyes [nigris vegetisque oculis]. . . . His baldness was a disfigurement that worried him greatly [calvitii vero deformitatem iniquissime ferret]. . . . Because of it he used to comb his scanty locks forward from the crown of his head [ideoque et deficientem capillum revocare a vertice adsueverat; cf. Plutarch, *Caesar* 4, 4: τὴν κόμην οὕτω διακειμένην περιττῶς – "hair carefully arranged"] and of all the honours voted him by the Senate and people there was none that he accepted and made use of more gladly than the privilege of wearing a laurel-wreath on all occasions [ius laureae coronae perpetuo gestandae]'.[2] According to Plutarch, he was lean (ἰσχνός) and fair- and soft-skinned (τὴν σάρκα λευκὸς καὶ ἁπαλός).[3]

There are at least seven references in ancient writers to honorific portrait statues of Caesar erected during his lifetime. Caesar himself and Dio Cassius, apropos of 48 BC, mention a statue set up in the temple of Nike at Tralles in Asia Minor, perhaps as early as 74 BC, when Caesar was active in Asia.[4] Three more passages in Dio Cassius describe respectively a bronze statue on the Capitol, with an inscription entitling Caesar 'demi-god', decreed by the Senate after his return from Africa in 46 BC;[5] an ivory statue for display in the Circus; a statue inscribed 'to the invincible god' in the temple of Quirinus, and another statue on the Capitol, all voted by the Senate in 45 BC;[6] and statues in the cities (of Italy? or of the Roman world?), in every temple in Rome, and two on the Rostra, all in 44 BC.[7] From Pliny we hear of a cuirass-statue (*loricata*) in the Forum of Caesar,[8] from Appian of a statue of him as a god in the temple of Clementia.[9] Furthermore, A. E. Raubitschek has listed eighteen inscriptions from the bases of statues of Caesar that were set up during his lifetime, some as early as 48 BC, in east-Mediterranean lands – in Greece proper (including Athens), on some of the Greek islands, and in Asia Minor:[10] a nineteenth inscription, from Mytilene, probably relates to a posthumous statue of Augustan date;[11] and there is yet another reference in Dio to a posthumous bronze statue, with a star above the head, dedicated by Octavian in the temple of Venus in Rome in 44 BC, shortly after Caesar's murder and well before his consecration in 42 BC.[12] There was thus a good tradition of portraits of Caesar made either during his life or soon after his death; and there can be little doubt that these now vanished statues of the Dictator are at least reflected in some, at any rate, of the numerous coin portraits and portraits in the round that have come down to us. Among the portraitists who worked in Rome, there must have been some at least for whom he sat.

The earliest known coin portraits of Caesar are two that were issued in the Greek East. A bronze coin with the legend ΝΙΚΑΙΕΩΝ was struck at Nicaea by the moneyer Caius Vibius Pansa in 48–47 BC with Caesar's bare head facing to the right (*Ill. 24*).[13] Here we have the somewhat idealized profile and slightly upward-tilted glance that are reminiscent of the coin portraits of Alexander and the Hellenistic kings. The cheeks are smooth and the chin pointed; but the neck is long and thin and features an 'Adam's apple' below the chin – traits which recur on the coin portraits issued by the moneyers Lucius Certus Aeficius and Julius Caesar in Corinth in 46–44 BC, with the Latin legend LAVS IVL CORIN (*Ill. 25*).[14] But here the neck is even longer and thinner and the head, also facing right, is laurel-wreathed, with a few locks of hair appearing in front of the wreath, above the brow, which is wrinkled. The nose is very long, protruding, and pointed. The flabby cheeks hang in heavy, vertical folds. But it is to some of the Roman denarii, issued by the official moneyers in the capital, that we must turn for the most veristic renderings of Caesar's physiognomy. Caesar obtained from the Senate in 44 BC the right to have his title of 'Father of his Country' stamped upon the Roman coinage – presumably to accompany a portrait.[15]

In these metropolitan coin likenesses the head is always facing to the right. They reveal many different types – types that differ, not only as being the products of different groups of moneyers, but also sometimes within the same moneyer's issues. They have been divided by Vessberg into three main categories: A, veristic portraits; B, idealizing portraits; C, monumental portraits that form a link between A and B. We observe, on the whole, a gradual evolution from the starkness of the earliest portraits to the monumentalizing of the later ones; but there are a few examples of later portraits that revive the early realistic style.

Of the category A portraits there are three types, all showing thick and bushy laurel-wreaths, under which the baldness of the high, massive brow disappears. On the obverses of Marcus Mettius, struck in 44 BC the legends are CAESAR IMPER and CAESAR DICT QVART and on some there is a *lituus* (augural staff) behind the head (*Ill. 26*).[15] The heads on L. Mussidius Longus' obverses, struck in 42 BC, have no accompanying legends (*Ill. 27*),[16] while some of those of Publius Sepullius Macer, dated to *c.* 44, have the legends CAESAR IMP, CAESAR IMPER and CAESAR DICT PERPETVO and sometimes have a star behind (*Ill. 28*).[17] All of these Type I portraits are prosaic likenesses and some are veristic in the extreme, ruthless and uncompromising; those on Mettius coins with the legend CAESAR IMPER are frankly caricatures, although they can hardly have been intended as such. The abnor-

mally thin, giraffe-like, scraggy neck is diagonally scored across, with row upon row of sagging folds of skin; and on it the head is thrust forward awkwardly. The eyes are large, the nose is long, aquiline and pointed, while the mouth is slightly smiling. The cheeks are generally, but not on all Type I dies, heavily gashed with creases. The cheek-bones and chin stick out, the 'Adam's apple' is in most cases painfully pronounced. The Type I likenesses seem clearly to follow, with greater or less fidelity, a single model.

In portraits of Type II, which are again all wreathed, the starkness of Type I is somewhat toned down, although the ugliness of the neck in particular is hardly modified at all. These portraits occur on obverses of Lucius Aemilius Buca, issued in 44 BC, with the legends CAESAR IM P(*ontifex*) M(*aximus*) and CAESAR DICT PERPETVO and sometimes with a crescent behind the head;[18] also on obverses of Publius Clodius, struck in 42 BC, with

24, 25   C. Julius Caesar: obverses of bronze coins struck at Nicaea, 48–47 BC, and at Corinth, 46–44 BC.

26–28   C. Julius Caesar: obverses of denarii struck respectively by M. Mettius, 44 BC; L. Mussidius Longus, 42 BC; and P. Sepullius Macer, 44 BC.

the legend CAESAR IMP (*Ill. 29*);[19] and on other 44 BC denarii of Marcus Mettius, where there are a bowl and a *lituus* behind the head and the legend CAESAR IMP.[20] Still more Type II portraits are to be seen on obverses of Quintus Voconius Vitulus variously dated to 40 or 37 BC (see below), which have a *lituus* behind the head and carry the legend DIVI IVLI, but which show features closer to those of Type I portraits than do other Type II likenesses;[21] and again on obverses of Tiberius Sempronius Gracchus, dated to 40 BC by Sydenham, but

29–31 C. Julius Caesar: obverses of denarii struck respectively by P. Clodius, 42 BC; C. Cossutius Maridianus, *c.*44 BC; and L. Flaminius Chilo, *c.*44 BC.

possibly struck as late as 37 BC (cf. p. 54), where the neck is thicker and sometimes flanked by the letters S C.[22] Realistic posthumous portraits of Caesar, with the legend CAESAR DIC and a jug behind the head, were struck on aurei and denarii issued by Mark Antony in Gaul in 43 BC.[23]

The Type III portraits of category A occur on the denarii struck in *c.*44 BC by Caius Cossutius Maridianus (*Ill. 30*) and on those of Publius Sepullius Macer also issued in *c.*44. These are wreathed, but with a veil drawn over the back of the head, and are very realistic, showing a creased neck, an 'Adam's apple', an enormous nose, and large eyes and mouth. The legends read CAESAR DICT PERPETVO.[24]

Of the more monumental portraits belonging to category C there are two types. Type I is represented by other denarii of Cossutius Maridianus, also issued in 44 BC, which show Caesar veiled and wreathed, with a neat, lean face, large eyes, a pointed nose, and slightly curving lips. Under the chin there is a *lituus* and behind the head an *apex* (augur's spiked cap). The legend reads CAESAR PARENS PATRIAE.[25] Similar are other obverse portraits struck in 44 BC by Sepullius Macer with the legend CAESAR PATER PATRIAE and also with a *lituus* below the chin and an *apex* behind the head.[26] The Type II portraits are on denarii of Flaminius Chilo, issued *c.*42 BC; these show a massive head with large and powerful features and a very broad and thick laurel-wreath, almost turban-like. The cheek-bones and 'Adam's apple' are still prominent, but the neck differs from die to die, being sometimes long and thin, with the transverse folds of skin, at other times shorter and stockier. On some dies the cheeks are vertically creased.[27] No legends accompany these portraits (*Ill. 31*).

Among the idealizing category B coin portraits of Caesar three types may be distinguished. On the obverses of some of the denarii of Q. Voconius Vitulus issued in *c.*40 BC, again without a legend, we have a youthful head with a well-shaped nose, a pleasant mouth, long, curly locks of hair that escape from beneath the much less obtrusive laurel-wreath onto the brow.[28] Apart from some transverse creases on the neck, all the harsh and veristic details have been omitted. The general effect is one of harmony and peacefulness. The reverses of bronze sestertii struck by Octavian in 37 BC and assigned to an Italian mint carry a head, with the legend DIVOS IVLIVS, which is clearly recognizable as Caesar, but again with all the ugly realistic features drastically toned down. The neat hair provides a good covering for the crown of the head and nape of the neck, but does not emerge from beneath the narrow, diadem-like laurel-wreath. A small 'Adam's apple' can be seen below the chin, which is pointed and protruding, and a slightly sardonic smile plays about the mouth.[29] Finally, there is the type of portrait that shows no individual traits and could not be recognized as Caesar, were it not for the comet with four rays and a tail above the head. These heads were struck *c.*17 BC on aurei and denarii of the moneyer Marcus Sanguinius and they present a completely idealized, youthful personage, with abundant hair on the brow, as well as on the crown and neck, encircled by a laurel-wreath, and sometimes with a short beard.[30] This is Caesar as a handsome young god; and it is a type that had already appeared on the obverses of aurei of Marcus Vipsanius Agrippa, issued at a travelling mint in 38 BC.[31] There again the head is laureate and slightly bearded and has a star in front of the brow. Obviously no category B type represents a true historical portrait.

From this survey of the three categories, with their various sub-types, of Caesar's numismatic portraits, it is clear, in view of the very considerable differences between them, that not all of them, by any means – discounting the frankly idealizing types of category B – can represent exactly the Dictator's actual features. A. Alföldi, who has undertaken a minute and systematic study of all Caesar's denarii portraits of 44 BC,[32] has reached the conclusion that of those of category A the issue of Mettius with the title DICT QVART (Type I) – characterized by a squarish face, folded cheeks, creased neck, finely curved nose, and lively eyes – would seem to have reproduced most closely the sculptural prototype used by the mint as a model and to be nearest to Suetonius' description; Mettius' CAESAR IMP portrait (Type II) makes him look too young and sometimes too smooth-cheeked; while the heads of the moneyer's CAESAR IMPER coins are, as we have seen, out and out caricatures, due, Alföldi thinks, to hasty and careless workmanship at the mint. But all are derived from the same prototype and its variants – Buca's CAESAR IM P M portraits (Type II) and those of Macer with CAESAR IMP come fairly close to Mettius' DICT QVART likenesses; whereas Macer's CAESAR IMPER and unveiled CAESAR DICT PERPETVO heads[33] are almost as caricature-like as that of Mettius' CAESAR IMPER.

If only some of Caesar's many numismatic portraits, struck either during his lifetime or in the years immediately following his death, can be accepted as absolutely authentic likenesses, a still greater problem is presented by the sculptural portraits in the round. It has long been recognized that practically all of those that survive are posthumous copies, worked in imperial times, of lost bronze or marble originals. Some of the best of these copies are of Augustan date and could well be based on prototypes made in Caesar's lifetime. But they all differ from the contemporary or near-contemporary coin portraits in that none shows him veiled and only one wearing a wreath, and that a provincial Greek piece, featuring an oak-wreath rather than the laurel-wreath, which is Caesar's constant attribute on the Roman coins. Furthermore, the genuine posthumous copies, taken as a whole, are very far from being uniform, although certain features, such as the treatment of the hair, clearly link them all with the Dictator. Some, when seen from the front, present a somewhat squarish face, others a longer one; some profiles show more idealized, others more realistic, traits. These divergencies do, in fact, suggest that they sometimes depict Caesar, not as his contemporaries actually saw him, but as later generations imagined him to have looked. An extreme instance of such a 'historical portrait', genuinely ancient, but obviously worthless as evidence for Caesar's real appearance, is the latest of his numismatic representations, on Trajan's 'restored' aurei bearing the legends C IVLIVS CAES IMP COS III and DIVVS IVLIVS, where a stocky, solidly built, and unmistakably Vespasianic personage, the contemporary ideal of the strong and worthy ruler, masquerades as the Dictator.[34]

Uncertainties also beset the identification of portraits of Caesar on gems. H. Seyrig has published, as presenting Caesar's portrait, an intaglio in bluish-grey chalcedony acquired in Cairo.[35] Here we have a bust, facing to the right and wearing a laurel-wreath with a wreath of flowers just above it[36] and the ends of the ribbon that hold the two together fluttering on the neck. The face certainly displays Caesarian features – only a slight tuft of hair on the otherwise bald, high and massive brow, deep-set eyes, large nose, hollow cheeks with folds of flesh on them, and an 'Adam's apple'. The style may be described as Ptolemaic; and Seyrig suggests that, in view of this and of the gem's Egyptian provenance, the bust could be related to Caesar's stay with Cleopatra in Egypt in 48–47 BC. The laurel-wreath would in that case be an honorific one, since is was not until 46 BC that his triumphal laurel-wreath was granted to him. If this gem be accepted as truly ancient, it presents us with a lifetime likeness of Caesar as he looked in his early fifties.

It is very doubtful whether the portrait on a large amethyst in the Metropolitan Museum, New York, published as that of Caesar, really represents him.[37] The features are not particularly like his and the personage depicted is anyhow too old to be he. A similar, if less strong, doubt attaches to the bust on a cornelian in the Blatter Collection at Basle, although this does display some stock Caesarian features – scanty hair above the brow, creased forehead, large, deep-set eyes, big nose, and 'Adam's apple'.[38] A white paste gem in Vienna, reproducing the type of a portrait displayed on the gold plate of an iron ring once in the British

Museum but now lost, shows a laureate head, with a jug behind it, which is not at all like Caesar in face, although it presents his large nose and long, scraggy neck with 'Adam's apple'.[39] The head on an amethyst in the Museo Nazionale at Syracuse, while reproducing typical Caesarian features, looks like a modern version based on an ancient coin portrait.[40] More likely to be the Dictator's likeness is the head on a bronze *emblema* from a ring, now in the Louvre. The neck is too thick and the cheeks too full. But there are the broad skull, massive, hairless brow, huge nose, deep-set eyes, and 'Adam's apple'.[41] Undoubtedly the best and most reliable portrait of Caesar on a gem is that on a fragmentary amethyst in the Bibliothèque Nationale (Cabinet des Médailles), Paris (*Ill. 32*).[42] The back of the head and the neck are gone, but most of the front of

32   C. Julius Caesar: portrait gem (Bibliothèque Nationale, Paris).

the head and the face, with its deep-set eyes and creased and hollow cheeks, survive; and they distinctly recall one of Caesar's best authenticated sculptural portraits, the Vatican marble head formerly in the Museo Chiaramonti (opposite).

The most complete and recent study, with detailed documentation and full bibliography, of Caesar's sculptural likenesses is that of F. S. Johansen;[43] in this the Dictator's genuinely antique portraits and those in whose favour strong arguments have been advanced are carefully distinguished both from ancient portraits erroneously identified as representing him and from those that do in fact represent him, but which were made in Renaissance or modern times. Of the sixty portraits of Caesar listed by Bernoulli in 1882[44] only seven or nine can be regarded as authentic, the remaining fifty-three or fifty-one being either post-classical or, if ancient, not portraying Caesar. To Bernoulli's catalogue Johansen adds a list of twenty authentic portraits unknown to Bernoulli, and another of fifty-four modern portraits of which Bernoulli was also unaware. The heart of Johansen's study is the catalogue raisonné, preceding the lists, of Caesar's authentically ancient portraits grouped into three main types, each type being named after the best and best-preserved example that represents it. To these well-defined groups he appends a few pieces of which the authenticity has been much disputed – by some strongly upheld, by others hotly challenged – and a few pieces of provincial origin.

Basic for the study of Caesar's true portraits is the marble head in the Vatican, formerly in the Museo Chiaramonti (No. 107), but now removed to the Sala dei Busti (*Ill. 33*).[45] This is an Augustan copy, probably of a bronze original that may well have been made during the subject's last years, to judge from its general resemblance to Mettius' coin-likenesses. The head is slightly inclined. The hair, if not particularly abundant, is combed forward to form a kind of fringe above the very high, slightly wrinkled brow. The eyes are deep-set, the cheeks are hollow and creased. There is, however, no 'Adam's apple'. The nose and jutting chin are restorations. Of this portrait Johansen lists three replicas and one variant.[46]

Portraits of the second type are grouped round the head in the Campo Santo, Pisa,[47] also an Augustan marble copy of an original probably dating from Caesar's closing years and probably also of bronze. Here the head is erect; and the face is squarer and the eyes more widely open than they are on the Chiaramonti head, while the hair is similarly treated. There are two deep, vertical creases at the root of the nose. The cheeks are again hollow, with hanging folds of skin. There is a slight 'Adam's apple'. Nose and chin are modern restorations. As a work of art it is somewhat inferior to the Chiaramonti head. Aesthetically better, but much mutilated, are two replicas, one a head at Leiden,[48] the other a head in the magazine of the Capitoline Museum.[49] Johansen would assign both replicas to Augustan times. But there is a possibility

33 C. Julius Caesar: marble head (Sala dei Busti, Vatican Museums).

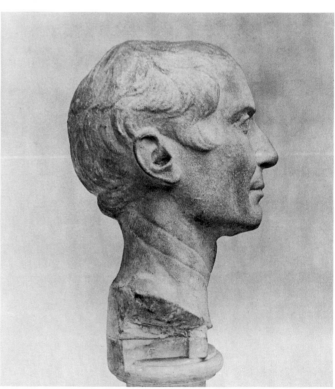

34, 35 C. Julius Caesar: front and
profile views of marble head
(Turin).

that the Leiden head is of Flavian date, since it was found in the *praetorium* of the fortress of Legio X at Nijmegen and could have been carved to adorn that building. Of the Pisa type Johansen enumerates eight replicas and a variant.

The third main type of the Dictator's sculptural portraits is represented by the perfectly preserved marble head, only slightly retouched on the left side, which was unearthed at Tusculum in the early nineteenth century and rediscovered by M. Borda in 1940 in the Castello di Agliè near Turin, in whose Museum of Antiquities it now is (*Ills. 34, 35*).[50] Of all Caesar's likenesses in the round this is certainly the most remarkable and by far the closest to the portraits on Mettius' denarii. The frontal view displays the massive brow, above which the hair recedes, the hollow, creased cheeks, a straight mouth, and the fact that the face is a little asymmetrical, the left side being slightly fuller than the right side. The profile view shows a curious depression between the brow and the back of the head, a large, prominent nose and a rounded chin, and a faintly sardonic smile playing about the lips. There is a long, scraggy, stork-like, heavily creased neck. It is not surprising that Borda[51] and others have seen in this head an original portrait made in Caesar's lifetime; and it certainly presents no features that would rule out this view. On the other hand, some maintain it to be a copy, carved in imperial times, of a contemporary portrait; and the treatment of the hair is, indeed, slightly suggestive of a bronze original. Be that as it may, no one can doubt that we have here the best large-scale piece of evidence for what Caesar really looked like. Among the several heads considered by Johansen to be variants of the Tusculum portrait, that at Woburn Abbey comes nearest to it and displays in addition a very prominent 'Adam's apple'.[52] Other variants listed by Johansen are, however, of doubtful antiquity and do not resemble their alleged model very closely. As for the Woburn head, noted in 1882 by Bernoulli and Michaelis,[53] it is difficult to see how this portrait could be a modern forgery, since the Tusculum head is so distinctive and has only comparatively recently been brought to light.

Standing by itself is the much worked-over head in the Museo Torlonia in Rome.[54] It is characterized by a close-fitting cap of hair covering the head and receding slightly above the brow and by large, wide-open eyes with projecting eyeballs. That it is intended to depict Caesar there can be little doubt; and there would seem to be little reason to believe that the large amount of modern over-working that it displays implies that it was originally a portrait of some one else transformed into the Dictator's likeness. None the less this heavy over-working may be held greatly to diminish the claim of the head to represent an independent type. Notable are the heavily creased cheeks and the wide, thin-lipped mouth. If this head is ancient, it would appear to be derived from a posthumous original. But there would seem to be no clinching evidence for accepting E. Simon's idea that it reproduces the portrait set up by Marcus Antonius in 44 BC, just after Caesar's death, and inscribed *parenti optime merito* (cf. footnote 12) – a 'propaganda portrait' intended to discredit the tyrannicides as the murderers of a gentle, mild, *clemens*, and suffering ruler.[55]

Highly controversial pieces are: the Luxburg head, now in Zurich,[56] held by some, e.g. L. Curtius,[57] to be an ancient portrait of Caesar of early Augustan date, by others to be a modern work, by others again to be antique, but not a likeness of Caesar, whose features it can hardly be said to resemble;[58] and the head found near Acireale in Sicily in 1676, championed by E. Boehringer as an ancient likeness of the Dictator,[59] while others claim it as an antique, Julio-Claudian copy of an original dating from 40–30 BC depicting a personage that is not Caesar.

Three more heads of Caesar of Augustan or Julio-Claudian date are in one case probably, in the two other cases certainly, of Greek provincial origin. A head of crystalline white marble in the Ny Carlsberg Glyptotek, Copenhagen, shows the hair receding from the massive, wrinkled brow, the cheeks hollow and heavily creased, and a marked 'Adam's apple'. It was acquired in 1900 from a Venetian art-dealer and has been written off by some as a post-classical work. On the other hand, despite its superifical polishing it has a rusty coloured patina; and if there is truth in the story that it was already in 1600 the property of Frederico Contarini, procurator of the cathedral of San Marco, it could well have reached Venice from Greece.[60]

This appears to be by no means impossible in view of its resemblance to a head of white Greek marble found at Sparta and now in the local museum.[61] Part of the crown of the head is missing and could once have been completed in plaster; and it may have worn a metal wreath. The third piece was found on the island of Thasos and is worked in the local island marble.[62] The nose is lost, but the other Caesarian elements are present – the furrowed brow, the deep-set eyes, the projecting cheek-bones, and the 'Adam's apple' (*Ills. 36, 37*). It has not a little in common with the Pisa type. A neat fringe of hair emerges on the forehead from below the oak-wreath that encircles the head, and is adorned with a medallion in front, and tied by a ribbon behind. It would seem that the sculptor had some knowledge of the lifetime statue of Caesar wearing the *corona civica* on the Rostra in Rome (cf.

36, 37   C. Julius Caesar: profile and front views of marble head (Thasos Museum).

p. 30).[63] Meanwhile, the upward glance suggests the deified Dictator as the Greeks conceived of him.[64]

1 *Julius* 45.
2 Cf. DC, xliii, 43, 1 : καὶ τῷ στεφάνῳ τῷ δελφίνῳ ἀεὶ πανταχοῦ ὁμοίως ἐκοσμεῖτο. According to K. Kraft, the wreath worn by Julius Caesar was not one of real laurel-leaves, but the gold wreath of the Etruscan kings (*Jahrbuch für Numismatik und Geldgeschichte*, iii–iv, 1952–3, p. 77).
3 *Caesar* 17, 2. Marcus Antonius in his funeral speech for Caesar, as reported by Dio Cassius (xliv, 38, 2) describes him as 'the handsomest of men' (περικαλλέστατον ἀνδρῶν). Velleius Paterculus calls Caesar 'forma omnium civium excellentissimus' (ii, 41); and Cicero (*Brutus*, 75, 261) may refer by 'forma' to his handsome looks.
4 *Bellum civile* iii, 105, 6; DC xli, 61, 4.
5 DC, xliii, 14, 6.
6 DC, xliii, 45, 2–4; cf. Cicero, *Ad Atticum* xii, 45, 3; xiii, 28, 3 (=Quirinus temple); Suetonius, *Julius* 76: 'recipit . . . statuam inter reges' (=Capitol).
7 DC, xliv, 4, 4–5.
8 *NH*, xxxiv, 10 (18). Cf. Younger Pliny, *Epistolae* viii, 6, 13, 'statuam loricatam divi Iulii'.
9 *Bellum civile* ii, 106.
10 *JRS*, xliv, 1954, pp. 65–71.
11 Ibid., pp. 71–2.
12 DC, xlv, 7, 1. Cf. Cicero, *Ad Familiares* xii, 3, 1, for the bronze statue set up in the Rostra by Marcus Antonius soon after Caesar's death, inscribed 'parenti optime merito'.
13 *BMCGC Pontus, etc.*, 1889, p. 153, nos. 8, 9, pl. 31, no. 13; Vessberg 1941, pl. 8, no. 1; Toynbee 1957, pl. 1, no. 1; Herbig 1959, pl. 4, fig. 2; Johansen, 1967, p. 8, fig. 1.
14 *BMCGC Corinth, etc.*, 1889, p. 58, nos. 485–9, pl. 15, no. 2; Vessberg 1941 pl. 6, no. 9; Toynbee 1957, pl. 1, no. 2; Herbig 1959, pl. 4, fig. 3; Johansen 1967, p. 12, fig. 2.
15 Vessberg 1941, pl. 6, nos. 1, 4, pl. 7, no. 5; Sydenham 1952, pp. 176–7, nos. 1055, 1057, pl. 28; Toynbee 1957, pl. 1, no. 5; Michel 1967, pl. 23, fig. 1; Crawford 1974, no. 480, 2, 17, pl. 57.
16 Vessberg 1941, pl. 6, no. 2, pl. 7, no. 2; Sydenham 1952, p. 181, no. 1096; Toynbee 1957, pl. 1, no. 8; Crawford 1974, no. 494, 39, pl. 60.
17 Vessberg 1941, pl. 6, no. 3, pl. 7, no. 4; Sydenham 1952, p. 178, nos. 1070–1073a; Michel 1967, pl. 21, fig. 4; Crawford 1974, no. 480, 5, 9, 10, 11, 18, pl. 57.
18 Vessberg 1941, pl. 6, no. 5, pl. 7, nos. 1, 3; Sydenham 1952, p. 177, nos. 1060–3, pl. 28; Toynbee 1957, pl. 1, no. 6; Michel 1967, pl. 21, fig. 5, pl. 25, fig. 2; Crawford 1974, no. 480, 4, 6, 7, 8, pl. 57.
19 Vessberg 1941, pl. 6, no. 7; Sydenham 1952, p. 184, no. 1123; Crawford 1974, no. 494, 16, pl. 59.
20 Vessberg 1941, pl. 6, no. 6; Sydenham 1952, p. 177, no. 1056; Crawford 1974, no. 480, 3, pl. 56.
21 Grueber 1910, iii, pl. 58, no. 15; Sydenham 1952, p. 185, no. 1132; Toynbee 1957, pl. 1, no. 7; Crawford 1974, no. 526, 2, pl. 63.
22 Grueber 1910, iii, pl. 58, nos. 19, 20; Sydenham 1952, p. 185, nos. 1128, 1129, pl. 28; Crawford 1974, no. 525, 3, 4, pl. 68.
23 Sydenham 1952, pl. 89, nos. 1164–6, pl. 29; *Numismatica e antichità classiche*, 1974, pp. 72, 73, figs. 6, 7; Crawford 1974, no. 488, pl. 58.

24 Vessberg 1941, pl. 6, no. 8; Sydenham 1952, p. 178, nos. 1067–8 (Maridianus); ibid., p. 178, no. 1074; Grueber 1910, iii, pl. 54, no. 21 (Macer); Crawford 1974, no. 480, 13, 15, 16, pl. 57.

25 Vessberg 1941, pl. 7, no. 6; Sydenham 1952, p. 178, no. 1069, pl. 28; Toynbee 1957, pl. 1, no. 3; Crawford 1974, no. 480, 19, pl. 57.

26 Grueber 1910, i, p. 549 with fig.; Sydenham 1952, p. 179, no. 1075; Crawford 1974, no, 480, 20, pl. 57.

27 Vessberg 1941, pl. 7, nos. 7–9; Sydenham 1952, p. 180, no. 1089, pl. 28; Toynbee 1957, pl. 1, no. 10; Crawford 1974, no. 485, 1, pl. 58.

28 Vessberg 1941, pl. 8, no. 2; Sydenham 1952, p. 185, no. 1133; Crawford 1974, no. 526, 4.

29 Vessberg 1941, pl. 8, no. 3; Sydenham 1952, p. 208, no. 1335; Toynbee 1957, pl. 1, no. 11; Crawford 1974, no. 535, 1, pl. 63.

30 *BMCCRE*, i, 1923, p. 13, nos. 69–73, pl. 2, nos, 19, 20, pl. 3, no. 1; Vessberg 1941, pl. 8, nos. 4, 5 (dated *c.* 12 BC on p. 259); Toynbee 1957, pl. 1, no. 12; Michel 1967, pl. 21, fig. 6. Cf. note 12.

31 Grueber 1910, iii, pl. 105, no. 8; Sydenham 1952, p. 207, no. 1329; Crawford 1974, no. 534, 1.

32 'The Portrait of Caesar on Denarii of 44 B.C.', in *Centennial Publication of the American Numismatic Society*, 1958, pp. 27–44, pls. 1–5); Alföldi 1959.

33 Grueber 1910, iii, pl. 54, nos. 15, 18–20.

34 *BMCCRE*, iii, 1936, p. 142, pl. 23, nos. 17–19.

35 H. Seyrig, 'Un portrait de Jules César, in *RN*, ser. 6, 1969, pp. 53–4, fig. 1.

36 Cf. DC, xliii, 22, 1 : Caesar garlanded with flowers at his triumphal entry into Rome in 46 BC.

37 G. M. A. Richter, *Catalogue of the Engraved Gems*, 1956, p. 103, no, 469, pl. 57; cf. Vollenweider 1960, pp. 81–8, pl. 12, nos. 7, 8; pl. 13, no. 4; Vollenweider 1964, pp. 508–18, pl. 14, nos. 2, 3; pl. 15; Vollenweider 1966, p. 59.

38 Johansen 1967, p. 19, fig. 6.

39 F. H. Marshall, *Catalogue of Fingerrings, Greek, Roman and Etruscan, in the British Museum*, 1907, no, 1469, fig. 33; Johansen 1967, p. 23, fig. 9.

40 Johansen 1967, p. 21, fig. 7.

41 Ibid., p. 22, fig. 8.

42 Ibid., p. 17, fig. 5.

43 Ibid., pp. 7–68, pls. 1–27.

44 J. J. Bernoulli, *Römische Ikonographie*, i, 1882, pp. 145–81.

45 Johansen 1967, pp. 25–6, pl. 1; Herbig 1959, pl. 5, fig. 2.

46 Johansen 1967, p. 28, pls. 5 a, b; Herbig 1959, pl. 3, fig. 3.

47 Johansen 1967, pp. 28–9, pl. 6; Herbig 1959, pl. 6, figs. 1, 3; Toynbee 1957, frontispiece.

48 Johansen 1967, p. 30, pl. 8.

49 Ibid., p. 31, pl. 9.

50 Ibid., pp. 34–5, pl. 16; E. Simon, 'Das Caesarporträt im Castello di Agliè', in *AA*, 1952, cols. 123–38; Herbig 1959, pl. 2, figs. 3–5; Toynbee, 1957, pl. 2, a, b; Michel 1967, pl. 24, fig. 1, pl. 25, fig. 1.

51 M. Borda, 'Il ritratto tuscolano di Giulio Cesar', in *Atti della Pontificia Accademia Romana di Archeologia*, ser. iii, *Rendiconti*, xx, 1943 (1945), pp. 347–82.

52 Johansen 1967, pp. 35–6, pl. 17.

53 A. Michaelis, *Ancient Marbles in Great Britain*, 1882, p. 739, no. 143.

54 Johansen 1967, pp. 39–40, pl. 21; Herbig 1959, pl. 5, figs. 1, 3; Toynbee 1957, pl. 2, c, d; Michel 1967, pl. 24, fig. 2.

55 E. Simon, 'Das Caesarporträt im Museo Torlonia', in *AA*, 1952, cols. 138–52.

56 Johansen 1967, p. 58.

57 *RM*, xlvii, 1932, p. 213, fig. 10, pls. 47, 48.

58 J. Charbonneaux, *L'art au siècle d'Auguste*, 1948, fig. 11.

59 Johansen 1967, pp. 52–3; E. Boehringer, *Der Caesar von Acireale*, 1933.

60 Johansen 1967, pp. 24, 42, pl. 25.

61 Ibid., pp. 24, 42, pl. 26.

62 Ibid., pp. 24, 43, pl. 27; Herbig 1959, pl. 3, fig. 4; F. Chamoux, 'Un portrait de Thasos: Jules César', in *Monuments Piot*, xlvii, 1953, pp. 131–47.

63 DC, xliv, 4: ἐπί γε τοῦ βήματος δύο, τὸν μὲν ὡς τοὺς πολίτας σεσωκότος, τὸν δὲ ὡς τὴν πόλιν ἐκ πολιορκίας ἐξῃρημένου, μετὰ τῶν στεφάνων τῶν ἐπὶ τοῖς τοιούτοις νενομισμένων ἱδρύσαντο.

64 The controversial portrait in Berlin, worked in dark-green slate and said to have come from Egypt, is rejected as being a modern work by Johansen (1967, pp. 49, 50), but is accepted by J. C. Balty (in *Festoen*, 1976, pp. 52, 53, pl. 2, fig. 2) as being an ancient likeness.

MARCUS PORCIUS CATO UTICENSIS (95–46 BC)
Ills. 38, 39

No coin portraits of Cato have come down to us, but in 1944 there came to light in a late Roman house, the 'Maison des Bustes' at Volubilis in Mauretania Tingitana, a bronze bust on the breast of which is inscribed, in letters of silver incrustation, the name CATO (*Ill. 38*).[1] The portrait bust is just larger than life-size – 18½ in. (0·47 m.) high – and was found *in situ*, set up on a stuccoed brick pillar of inferior workmanship. The house, owned by a certain Vincentius, appears to have been built during the first half of the third century AD; and it was just about this time, when the ancient palace of Juba II of Mauretania might have been repaired and remodelled as the residence of the Roman provincial governor, now given the title of *praeses*, that the bust could have been removed from the king's one-time collection of Greek and Roman art and installed in a private house.

In his resistance as a 'Pompeian' to Caesar in Africa, Cato had had as his ally and friend Juba II's father, Juba, I, who, like Cato himself, committed suicide after Caesar's victory in 46 BC. Stylistically the bust is of late-republican or of very early Augustan date; and it might well be, or at any rate be based upon, a portrait made in Africa in Cato's lifetime. The arguments that have been adduced for assigning it, on the ground of the shape of the bust, to Neronian or Flavian or even to Trajanic times are not convincing; and even if a portrait of Cato were invented or copied from an original as an inspiration to 'republicans' in Italy during these periods, its appearance in western Mauretania then or later is not easy to explain.

On the other hand, Juba II (*c.* 50 BC–*c.* AD 23; q.v.) was sent to Rome for Caesar's triumph in 46

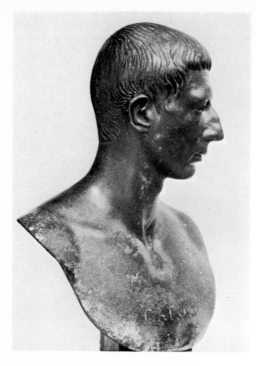

BC and was brought up in Italy, where he received the Roman citizenship and the patronage of Augustus, who reinstated him in Mauretania, probably giving him Volubilis as one of his capitals. He was a man of great learning and culture, noted, as has been said, for his collection of works of Greek and Roman art, in which a first-class original portrait of his father's friend, still extant among Juba I's onetime possessions, or an excellent copy of such a portrait, could well have constituted an important item.

The features of the Volubilis bust are distinctively individual – thick, neatly combed hair, furrowed upper brow, projecting lower brow, very large aquiline nose, parted lips, rounded, jutting chin, and a vivacious, if somewhat disdainful expression. Cato, himself a patron of the arts, was forty-seven when he came to Africa; and if the Greek artist responsible for the portrait did depict him there from the life, he made him look younger than he really was. However, it is of course possible that the portrait of Cato was made in Italy, when he actually was younger, and was taken thence by Juba II to Mauretania at the time of his reinstatement in his kingdom.

So far as the present writer is aware, the Volubilis bust is the only known 'labelled' portrait of Cato. But C. Picard has made the very plausible suggestion that a marble head, found in the socalled 'Villa of Domitian' at Castel Gandolfo and now in Florence, is an Augustan or early JulioClaudian copy of a bronze likeness of Cato. This head has been published as the portrait of an unknown personage.[2] But, well preserved apart from the tip of the nose, it shares many features with the 'labelled' portrait – the thick, neat hair, the bulging lower portion of the brow, the pronouncedly aquiline nose, the slightly parted lips, the rounded, jutting chin, and the somewhat disdainful mien. There would seem to be a good case for believing that the Volubilis bronze and the Florence marble (*Ill. 39*) were intended to portray the same individual.[3]

The only ancient literary record that we have of a portrait of Cato is Plutarch's mention of a statue of him, sword in hand, erected on the beach at Utica.[4] This could well have been the fruit of a late 'republican' cult of Cato in, or not long before, Plutarch's own time.

38, 39 M. Porcius Cato Uticensis: bronze bust from Volubilis; and (*below*) marble head from Castel Gandolfo (Museo Archeologico, Florence).

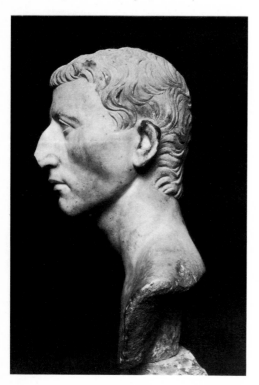

1 C. Picard, 'La date du buste en bronze de Caton d'Utique trouvé à Volubilis, Maroc', in *Festschrift Bernhard Schweitzer*, 1954, pp. 334–40, pl. 73, where the earlier literature on the bust is quoted; G. C. Picard, *L'art romain*, 1962, pl. 26.
2 Archaeological Museum; see *Bollettino d'Arte*, xxx, 1936, pp. 374–6, figs. 6–8.
3 For a bronze copy of early imperial date, found at Pompeii and now in the Naples Museum, see *AA*,

1973, p. 284, fig. 9. For a not very convincing attempt to identify as Cato the elderly man (without a tunic under his cloak or toga and with his left hand clenched and raised to his chin in the orator's gesture) depicted on thirty-one glass pastes and five gems, see ibid., pp. 272–87, figs. 1–8.

4 *Cato* 71: παρὰ τὴν θάλασσαν, οὗ νῦν ἀνδριὰς ἐφέστη-κεν αὐτοῦ ξιφήρης.

MARCUS ANTONIUS (83–30 BC)
Ills. 40–52

Marcus Antonius' appearance is described for us by Plutarch,[1] who writes of him as possessing a 'noble dignity of form' (προσῆν δὲ καὶ μορφῆς ἐλευθέριον ἀξίωμα), a 'not unsightly beard' (πάγων τις οὐκ ἀγεννής), a 'broad forehead' (πλάτος μετώπου), and an 'aquiline nose' (γρυπότης μυκτῆρος): he was held to display the 'virile quality' (τὸ ἀρρενωπόν) peculiar to the painted and sculptured representations of Hercules. Plutarch gives the impression that a beard was a permanent feature of Antonius' appearance. But we are fortunate in having an almost continuous series of coin portraits of him on aurei and denarii from the time of Julius Caesar's death in 44 BC until not long before the battle of Actium in 31 BC;[2] and from this numismatic evidence it is clear that Antonius' beard was worn from 44 BC as one of mourning for Caesar and that he abandoned it in 42 BC, when the defeat of the 'tyrannicides' at Philippi brought his vendetta against them to an end.

Antonius' earliest coin portraits, on denarii issued in Rome in 44 BC by P. Sepullius Macer, show him as augur, veiled and with a *capis* (sacrificial jug) behind his head and a *lituus* (augural staff) beneath his chin. Here we have a fairly youthful, but mature, face, characterized by realistic features – a thick cap of hair above the brow, large eyes, a large, aquiline nose, and a short beard edging cheeks and chin (*Ill. 40*).[3] There would seem to be little reason to doubt that Antonius looked just like that at the time of Caesar's murder.

Denarii struck by Antonius in Gaul, probably at Lugdunum, in 43 BC depict him without a veil, but with a *lituus* behind his head and the legend ANTO or ANTON IMP. His face, somewhat heavier and fleshier than on Macer's portrait, contrasts with Caesar's lean likeness, accompanied by a jug and the legend CAESAR DIC, on the other side (*Ill. 41*).[4] Also issued by Antonius in Gaul, but perhaps a little later, when negotiations for forming the Triumvirate were taking place, are denarii with the same portrait and legend of Caesar on one side and on the other a very similar likeness of Antonius, but with a more jutting chin and RPC added to his legend.[5]

In 42 BC, aurei and denarii were struck in Rome by P. Clodius with Antonius' head and his full

triumviral title – M ANTONIVS IIIVIR RPC – on the obverses and a winged Genius and a standing figure of Mars on the reverses.[6] Here the portrait of Antonius is dignified, square-faced, and monumental, as it also is on aurei and denarii struck in Rome in the same year by C. Vibius Varus. His aurei bear the obverse legend M ANTONIVS IIIVIR RPC and two right hands joined on the reverses,[7] while the denarii portrait, a particularly fine and noble one, is not accompanied by any legend and has as its reverse type a standing Fortuna with the moneyer's name (*Ill. 42*).[8] Other Roman aurei

40–42 M. Antonius: obverses of denarii struck respectively in Rome, 44 BC; in Gaul, 43 BC; and Rome, 42 BC.

issues of 42 BC with the M ANTONIVS IIIVIR RPC legend and the same style of obverse portrait of Antonius are those of L. Mussidius Longus, with Mars and cornucopias reverse types,[9] and of L. Lavineius Regulus, with the hero Anteon or Hercules on the reverse.[10]

Further denarii of 42 BC, struck by Antonius at a travelling mint, show a small, youngish, but realistic portrait of him with the legend M ANTONI IMP on the obverse and on the reverse a medallion carrying a full-face, radiate bust of Sol and inserted into a temple façade, with the legend IIIVIR RPC.[11] Yet again struck in 42 BC are the probably eastern denarii of Antonius and P. Ventidius Bassus, with a somewhat crudely worked and thickly bearded portrait of Antonius, accompanied by M ANT IMP IIIVIR RPC and a *lituus* behind the head, on the obverse, and a standing, nude male figure with a sceptre and a branch on the reverse;[12] and the aurei struck in Gaul conjointly by Antonius and Octavian, with the former's portrait and legend M ANTONIVS IMP IIIVIR RPC AVG(*ur*) on the obverse and Octavian's slightly bearded portrait and titles on the reverse.[13] Probably struck in Rome to celebrate the victory at Philippi are the denarii of Antonius showing on the obverses an excellent legendless portrait with a *lituus* behind it, and on the reverses the rayed, profile head of Sol with the legend M ANTONIVS IIIVIR RPC (*Ill. 43*).[14]

43   M. Antonius: obverse of denarius, probably struck in Rome, 42 BC.

So far, all the coin portraits of Antonius have been bearded. But he appears beardless for the first time – and beardless he remains from now onwards – on denarii of greatly inferior workmanship struck by him at a travelling mint to commemorate the same victory, since again a rayed, profile head of Sol with the legend M ANTONIVS IIIVIR RPC occupies the reverses, while a small head of Antonius, accompanied by a *lituus* behind it and the legend IMP forms the obverse type.[15] Likely still to belong to 42 BC are the aurei of Antonius and M. Aemilius Lepidus, probably struck in Gaul, with the same obverse legend and a small, neat beardless head of

Antonius with a *lituus* behind it;[16] and those of Antonius and Octavian displaying a very similar beardless portrait of the former with a *lituus* behind it and the same legend once more.[17]

Passing to the year 41 BC, we find aurei and denarii issued in the East by Antonius conjointly with M. Cocceius Nerva and Octavian, and with Nerva and Lucius Antonius. Here the head of Marcus is solid and massive and provides our first example of the slightly cynically smiling mouth. The accompanying obverse legend is M ANT IMP AVG(*ur*) IIIVIR RPC M NERVA PROQ(*uaestor*) P(*rovincialis*) and the reverse types are heads of Octavian and L. Antonius (*Ill. 44*).[18] Other aurei and denarii dated to 41 BC by their references to Antonius' consulship show either a small neat head of him with the legend M ANTONIVS IMP IIIVIR RPC, or a larger, less well executed, one with the legend ANT AVG(*ur*) IMP IIIV RPC. The reverses of these coins carry a standing figure of Pietas with the legend PIETAS COS: with the first obverse, probably struck at a travelling mint, she holds a cornucopia on which two storks are perched; with the second obverse, perhaps to be attributed to a north Italian mint, a stork stands at her feet.[19]

Aurei and denarii struck at a travelling mint in 40 BC by Antonius conjointly with Cn. Domitius Ahenobarbus (q.v.), with a prow on the reverse, display a fine portrait on the former – with a *lituus* behind the head – in which the 'nut-cracker' features, namely the sharply down-turned nose and projecting chin with the mouth receding between them, and the smile, are strongly accented; the obverse legend reads ANT IMP IIIVIR RPC.[20] Contemporary with these are the denarii, with much the same portrait, issued also at a travelling mint by Antonius alone with two cornucopias and a *caduceus* as reverse type; the reverse legend reads M ANT IMP IIIVIR RPC.[21] Contemporary again is a unique aureus in Berlin, perhaps struck at a travelling mint, with a bust of Octavia (q.v.; cf. *Ill. 54*) on the reverse and on the obverse a similar, but slightly less 'nut-crackerish', type of portrait of Antonius with the legend M ANTONIVS IMP IIIVIR RPC (*Ill. 45*).[22] Towards the close of 40 BC, or possibly at the very beginning of 39 BC, three series of aurei and denarii of travelling mintage bear obverse portraits of Antonius belonging to the same class as those just cited. One, of rather inferior workmanship, has the head of Octavian (q.v.) on the reverse; the obverse legend is M ANTON IMP IIIVIR RPC, sometimes with AVG(*ur*) added at the end.[23] The second series shows a much better executed portrait head with a jug behind it and the legend M ANT IMP AVG(*ur*) IIIVIR RPC L GELL Q(*uaestor*) P(*rovincialis*): it was issued conjointly with L. Gellius Publicola and Octavian and has the latter's head as reverse type.[24] The third series, which brings out still more clearly

Antonius' smile and 'nut-cracker' face, presents an excellent portrait and was struck conjointly with M. Barbatius Philippus. The obverse legend reads M ANT IMP AVG(ur) IIIVIR RPC M BARBAT Q(uaestor) P(rovincialis) and the reverse shows the portrait either of Octavian or of L. Antonius. Here the contrast between the solid, heavy head of Antonius

To later on in 37 BC Bernareggi ascribes the Antonius/Octavia cistophoroi, minted either at Ephesus or at Pergamon, for the reasons that they suggest a recognition of the part played by Octavia as mediatrix in the negotiations between Antonius and Octavian which ended in the treaty of Tarentum in the spring of that year; and that Antonius

44–48   M. Antonius: (*top left*) obverse of denarius, 41 BC; (*centre*) obverse of aureus, 40 BC; (*top right*) obverse of aureus, 40–39 BC; (*below left*) reverse of aureus, 37 BC; (*below right*) obverse of cistophoros, 37 BC.

and the much lighter, slimmer portraits of the reverses is strongly marked (*Ill. 46*).[25]

It would seem that no coin portraits of Antonius can be dated either to the rest of 39 BC or to 38 BC. In 38 BC, on 31 December, the Triumvirate, as defined in the *lex Titia*, had lapsed; and the legends that now, in early 37 BC, accompany Antonius' and Octavian's portraits on aurei and denarii, possibly struck at a travelling mint, are simply ANTONIVS IMP and CAESAR IMP. Antonius' very realistic portraits here are very close to those of 40–39 BC and on the denarii a winged *caduceus*, with one or other of the legends just cited, forms the reverse type (*Ill. 47*).[26]

bears the titles COS DESIG ITER ET TERT, accorded to him by the Tarentum pact; while the reverse legend IIIVIR RPC points to the Triumvirate's renewal. One cistophoros type has on the reverse the bust of Octavia surmounting a *cista mystica*, while the obverse displays a splendidly realistic likeness of Antonius crowned with ivy as the Neos Dionysos, with head and neck heavier and stockier than before; portrait and legend are both encircled by an outer ivy-wreath (*Ill. 48*). The second type depicts the jugate heads of Antonius, again ivy-crowned, and Octavia, while on the reverse a figure of Dionysos himself stands on the *cista mystica*.[27]

Dated to 36 BC by the mention of Antonius' third acclamation as *imperator* are aurei and denarii of travelling mintage with a profile head of Sol on the reverse and a full-length standing portrait of Antonius either as augur, veiled and holding a *lituus*, or in military dress on the obverse. The legends are M ANTONIVS M F M N AVGVR IMP TER (obverse) and COS DESIG ITER ET TERT IIIVIR RPC (reverse).[28] Contemporary aurei show an obverse portrait of Antonius very similar to that of the first cistophoros type and a head of Octavia on the reverse.[29] To 35 BC, the year in which Octavia joined Antonius in Greece and was then ignominiously sent back by him to Italy, no Roman coin portraits of Antonius can be assigned. After repudiating Octavia, Antonius would appear to have summoned Cleopatra (q.v.) to Antioch and to have married her there. And it may well have been for that occasion that a Greek silver tetradrachm was struck by Antonius, probably at Antioch, with his portrait on the obverse and that of Cleopatra (cf. *Ill. 142*) on the reverse.[30] It displays a fine, monumental head of Antonius with a very thick neck, a very jutting chin, a receding mouth, a markedly hooked nose, and a thick cap of hair.

In 34 BC, the year of Antonius' successful Armenian campaign, three series of denarii, struck at travelling mints, recorded his triumph in Cleopatra's company at Alexandria. One series, which carries on its reverses a trophy of arms and the legend IMP TER shows a very well executed likeness of Antonius with thick neck and square jaw, quite close to the Antiochene(?) tetradrachm portrait; the obverse legend is ANT AVGVR IIIVIR RPC.[31] The second series depicts an Armenian tiara with the legend IMP TERTIO IIIVIR RPC, while the obverse has a square, but rather less realistic, portrait of Antonius.[32] There can be no doubt that these coins belong to 34 BC, the year of the Armenian war, although the obverse legend describes Antonius as COS DES ITER ET TERT, whereas in 34 BC he was already COS ITER and no longer COS DES

ITER. The third series, probably issued at Alexandria, carries on the obverses Antonius' head with an Armenian tiara behind it and the legend ANTONI ARMENIA DEVICTA; and on the reverses a bust of Cleopatra with the legend CLEOPATRAE REGINAE REGVM FILIORVM REGVM.[33] Here, in Antonius' 'nutcracker' features a definite element of caricature can be detected. The neck is very thick in proportion to the slightly shrunken face; the chin protrudes further and the nose is more downturned and pointed than ever before. Antonius is beginning to look somewhat senile. Aurei of this year show the same type of portrait as the one just described. On these, which bear on the reverse the head of M. Antonius junior, Antonius is entitled COS ITER DESIGN TERT or COS DES III.[34]

To 33–32 BC may be ascribed two denarii issues which carry on the obverses a very distinctive portrait of Antonius. He is still COS DES III, but his creeping senility is now evinced in the swollen, flabby cheeks that give his countenance an extremely heavy, squarish look, with the chin even more prominent than before and with staring eyes. The reverse types consist of two-line inscriptions – M SILANVS AVG(*ur*)/Q(*uaestor*) PRO(*vincialis*) COS and ANTONIVS/AVG(*ur*) IMP III (*Ill. 49*).[35]

But Antonius' final stage of decadence and degradation is shown in the portrait struck on denarii in conjunction with D. Turullius just before the battle of Actium. The reverse type is a Victory holding a wreath and a palm and encircled by a laurel-wreath – a false prophecy of the outcome of Antonius' final confrontation with Octavian. On the obverses the former is described as IMP IIII and COS TERT and his portrait is even more grotesque than that of the previous year, with its bull-like neck, still heavier and squarer jowl, inane smile, and huge, wide-open eyes (*Ill. 50*).[36] This is Antonius' last numismatic likeness; and it is indeed a far cry from the handsome, dignified, and controlled personage portrayed earlier on the denarii of 44–42 BC.

49, 50   M. Antonius: obverses of denarii struck respectively in 33–32 and 31 BC.

51 M. Antonius: limestone
statue (Cairo Museum).

No portrait in the round of Antonius that is well authenticated by an ancient inscription has come down to us, but in a recent, comprehensive study of his sculptural likenesses O. C. Brendel has listed five – (1) Cairo, (2) Bologna, (3) Berlin, (4) Narbonne, (5) Kingston Lacy, Dorset – that have been generally identified as he.[37] Of these Brendel eliminates (2) on account of its colossal size, unlikely in the portrait of a human individual in pre-imperial times,[38] and (3) on account of its deviation from the coin portraits.[39] Of the remaining three, the Cairo (*Ill. 51*)[40] and the Narbonne[41] portraits are obviously variant renderings of the same personage with a heavy square head, a swollen, receding brow, a massive chin and side whiskers in front of the ears that are to be distinguished from the beard of mourning which fringes both cheeks and chin. The Cairo portrait statue, which is carved in limestone, depicts Antonius in the guise of Zeus. The Narbonne marble head, originally inserted in a statue, is very realistic, with its heavy, flaccid cheeks, wrinkled brow, large, angry eyes, and protruding chin; the nose is lost. The Kingston

Lacy portrait, carved in green basalt of Egyptian origin, represents a different, more idealizing tradition (*Ill. 52*).[42] It has Antonius' very aquiline nose and jutting chin; but its neck is slenderer than in the other likenesses and its face more elongated and it lacks side whiskers. Its nobility of expression recalls that of the early coin portraits of 44–42 BC.

Dubious as authentic likenesses of Antonius are two which Brendel adds to his list – a head of Egyptian green schist in the Brooklyn Museum, New York,[43] and a sardonyx cameo in the Bibliothèque Nationale, Paris.[44] More acceptable is H. Möbius' identification as Antonius of the Triptolemus figure on the silver dish from Aquileia, now in Vienna,[45] where the massive square head and the heavy, muscular forms of the torso remind us of the phrase *gladiatoria totius corporis firmitas* applied by Cicero to Antonius' portraits.[46] Unconvincing is H. von Heintze's attempt to interpret as depicting Antonius the colossal marble Hellenistic Hercules in the Palazzo dei Conservatori.[47] More recently still, G. Grimm has suggested that the marble head in the Cleveland Museum of Art,

Ohio, found in the Nile delta and depicting a very powerful and strong personality with a very heavy, protruding chin, must be either C. Cornelius Gallus, prefect of Egypt in 30 BC, or Antonius himself.[48]

1 *Antony* 4.
2 Bernareggi 1973.
3 Vessberg 1941, pl. 10, nos. 1, 2; Sydenham 1952, p. 179, no. 1077: Michel 1967, pl. 31, fig. 3; Bernareggi 1973, p. 65, fig. 1; Crawford 1974, no. 480, 22, pl. 57.
4 Sydenham 1952, p. 189, nos. 1164–5, pl. 29; Bernareggi 1973, p. 72, fig. 6; Crawford 1974, no. 488, 1, pl. 58 (see also p. 551, no. 103).
5 Sydenham 1952, p. 189, no. 1166; Bernareggi 1973, p. 73, fig. 7; Crawford 1974, no. 488, 2.
6 Sydenham 1952, p. 184, nos. 1118, 1121, pl. 28; Bernareggi 1973, p. 75, fig. 9; Crawford 1974, no. 494, 5, 17, pl. 59.
7 Sydenham 1952, p. 186, no. 1141; Crawford 1974, no. 494, 11, pl. 59.
8 Vessberg 1941, pl. 10, no. 4; Sydenham 1952, p. 186, no. 1144, pl. 29; Bernareggi 1973, p. 76, fig. 10; p. 103, fig. 37; Crawford 1974, no. 494, 32, pl. 60.
9 Vessberg 1941, pl. 10, no. 3; Sydenham 1952, p. 182, nos. 1097, 1100; Crawford 1974, no. 494, 8, 14, pl. 59.
10 Sydenham 1952, p. 182, no. 103, pl. 28; Crawford 1974, no. 494, 2, pl. 58.
11 Sydenham 1952, p. 190, no. 1168; Bernareggi 1973, p. 77, fig. 11; Crawford 1974, no. 496, 1, pl. 60.
12 Sydenham 1952, p. 190, no. 1175, pl. 29; Bernareggi 1973, p. 77, fig. 12; Crawford 1974, no. 531, 1, pl. 63 (dates 39 BC).
13 Sydenham 1952, p. 189, no. 1167; Crawford 1974, no. 493, pl. 58.
14 Vessberg 1941, pl. 10, no. 5; Sydenham 1952, p. 190, no. 1170; Bernareggi 1973, p. 80, fig. 13; Crawford 1974, no. 496, 2, pl. 60.
15 Sydenham 1952, p. 190, no. 1169, pl. 29; Michel 1967, pl. 31, fig. 2; Bernareggi 1973, p. 80, fig. 14; Crawford 1974, no. 496, 3, pl. 66.
16 Sydenham 1952, p. 189, no. 1161, pl. 29; Crawford 1974, no. 492, 2, pl. 58 (dates 43 BC).
17 Sydenham 1952, p. 189, no. 1162, pl. 29; Crawford 1974, no. 492, 1, pl. 58 (dates 43 BC).
18 Vessberg 1941, pl. 10, no. 6; Sydenham 1952, pp. 191–2, nos. 1183–6, pl. 29; Bernareggi 1973, p. 81, fig. 15; Crawford 1974, no. 517, 4–6, pl. 62.
19 Sydenham 1952, p. 190, nos. 1171–4; Bernareggi 1973, p. 82, figs. 16, 17; Crawford 1974, no. 516, 1–5, pl. 62.
20 Sydenham 1952, p. 191, nos. 1178–9, pl. 29; Bernareggi 1973, p. 84, fig. 18; Crawford 1974, no. 521, pl. 62.
21 Sydenham 1952, p. 192, no. 1189; Bernareggi 1973, p. 85, fig. 19; Crawford 1974, no. 520, pl. 62.
22 Vessberg 1941, pl. 10, no. 7; Sydenham 1952, p. 193, no. 1196; Crawford 1974, no. 527, pl. 63 (dates 39 BC). This coin must have been struck at the time of Antonius' marriage with Octavia.
23 Sydenham 1952, p. 192, nos. 1192–4; Bernareggi 1973, p. 85, fig. 20; Crawford 1974, no. 528, pl. 63.
24 Sydenham 1952, p. 192, nos. 1187–8; Bernareggi 1973, p. 87, fig. 22; Crawford 1974, no. 517, 7, 8, pl. 62.
25 Sydenham 1952, p. 191, nos. 1180–2; Michel 1967, pl. 31, fig. 4; Bernareggi 1973, p. 87, fig. 23, pl. 103, fig. 38; Crawford 1974, no. 517, 1–3, pl. 62 (dates 41 BC).

26 Sydenham 1952, p. 207, nos. 1327–8; Bernareggi 1973, pp. 89–90, fig. 25; Crawford 1974, no. 529, 1–3, pl. 63 (dates 39 BC).
27 Sydenham 1952, p. 193, nos. 1197–8, pl. 29; Michel 1967, pl. 31, fig. 1; Bernareggi 1973, p. 90–1, figs. 26, 27.
28 Sydenham 1952, p. 193, no. 1199; Bernareggi 1973, p. 92, fig. 28; Crawford 1974, no. 533, 1, 2, p. 63 (dates 35 BC).
29 Sydenham 1952, p. 193, nos. 1200–1, pl. 29; Crawford 1974, no. 533, pl. 63 (dates 38 BC).
30 *BMCGC Galatia, etc.*, 1899, p. 158, nos. 53–6, pl. 19, no. 3; Richter 1965, fig. 1859; Davis and Kraay 1973, pl. 44; ΑΝΤΩΝΙΟC ΑΥΤΟΚΡΑΤΩΡ ΤΡΙΤΟΝ ΤΡΙΩΝ ΑΝΔΡΩΝ (obverse); and ΒΑCΙΛΙCCΑ ΚΛΕΟΠΑΤΡΑ ΘΕΑ ΝΕΩΤΕΡΑ (reverse).
31 Sydenham 1952, p. 194, nos. 1202–4; Bernareggi 1973, pp. 93–4, fig. 29; Crawford 1974, no. 536, pl. 64 (dates 37 BC).
32 Sydenham 1952, p. 194, no. 1205; Bernareggi 1973, pp. 94–5, fig. 30; Crawford 1974, no. 539, pl. 64 (dates 36 BC).
33 Sydenham 1952, p. 194, no. 1210, pl. 29; Bernareggi 1973, p. 95, fig. 31; Crawford 1974, no. 543, pl. 64 (dates 32 BC).
34 Vessberg 1941, pl. 10, no. 8; Sydenham 1952, p. 194, nos. 1206–7, pl. 29; Crawford 1974, no. 541, pl. 64.
35 Sydenham 1952, p. 194, nos. 1208–9; Bernareggi 1973, p. 98, figs. 32, 33; Crawford 1974, no. 542, pl. 64.
36 Sydenham 1952, p. 195, no. 1211; Bernareggi 1973, p. 100, fig. 34, p. 103, fig. 39; Crawford 1974, no. 545, pl. 64.
37 O. C. Brendel, 'The Iconography of Marc Antony', in *Hommage à Albert Grenier*, i, 1962, pp. 359–67.
38 Ibid., p. 361, pl. 76, figs. 3, 4.
39 Ibid., p. 361, pl. 77, figs. 5, 6.
40 Ibid., pls. 74, 75, figs. 1, 2; Michel 1967, pl. 26, fig. 2; pl. 27; figs. 1, 2.
41 Brendel, op. cit., pl. 78, figs. 7, 8.
42 Ibid., pl. 79, figs, 9, 10; Michel 1967, pls. 29, 30.
43 Brendel, op. cit., pl. 81, figs. 14, 15.
44 Ibid., pl. 82, fig. 16.
45 H. Möbius, 'Der Silberteller von Aquileia', in *Festschrift F. Matz*, 1962, pp. 80–97, pls. 24–7: see especially fig. 2 on pl. 27; Michel 1967, pl. 33.
46 *Philippics* ii, 25, 63.
47 Helbig, *Führer*, 4th ed., 1966, pp. 414–16, no. 1610.
48 G. Grimm, 'Zu Marcus Antonius und C. Cornelius Gallus', in *JDAI*, lxxxv, 1970, pp. 158–70, figs. 1–12.

FULVIA (?–40 BC)

Ill. 53

Fulvia, the daughter of Marcus Flavius Bambalio, had been the wife first of Publius Clodius and then of Caius Scribonius Curio junior before she married Marcus Antonius in *c.*45 BC. A woman of great ambition and strong personality, she played a leading part in the campaign against Octavian which led to the Perusine war. After the fall of Perusia in 40 BC she escaped to Greece, where she died in the same year.

Of the four Roman obverse coin types displaying a winged female bust with contemporary coiffure –

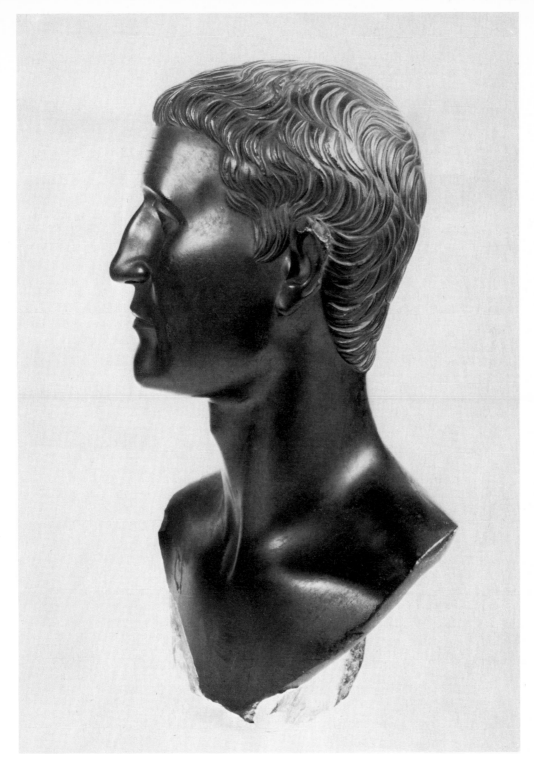

52 M. Antonius: green basalt head (Kingston Lacy, Dorset).

that is, with the hair combed back at the sides and puffed out or looped in front above the brow and then carried back over the crown of the head to join the side hair in a braided coil or 'bun' at the back – only one can be regarded with reasonable certainty as an authentic likeness of Fulvia. This occurs on gold quinarii struck by Marcus Antonius in Gaul in 43–42 BC, as the reverse legends A(*nno*) XL and XLI, referring to Antonius' age, indicate (*Ill. 53*).[1] It shows a determined looking person, facing right, with large eyes, long, pointed nose, firm mouth, full cheeks, and long, slender neck. The face is very definitely portrait-like; while the wings of Victory might suggest Antonius' hopes, after the formation of the Triumvirate, for victory over the tyrannicides. To the same date may be assigned the bronze coins of the city of Fulvia (= Eumeneia?) in Phrygia which carry on the obverses winged busts, facing to the right, with Fulvia's hair-style and features, and ΦΟΥΛΟΥΙΑΝΩΝ on the reverse.[2] Doubtful as a portrait of Fulvia is the bust of Victory, again facing right, on aurei struck in Rome by C. Numonius Vaala, with, as reverse type, a soldier attacking a *vallum*, which two soldiers are defending.[3] Its date is controversial. If minted in Rome in 43 BC, it could hardly have been sponsored by Antonius before the November of that year, when he was reconciled with Octavian by the formation of the Triumvirate, after having been forced to spend the earlier months of that year in Gaul. Until November, Octavian, with whom Antonius had quarrelled, controlled the Roman mint. The features of the Victory on the obverse differ somewhat from those of the Gaul quinarii: for instance, its 'bun' is much larger; but it has the same full cheeks and determined mouth. This type too might have been issued in anticipation of the triumvirs' victory over the tyrannicides. The same date, late 43 or early 42 BC, and meaning might also be applied to the Roman denarii of L. Mussidius Longus, on the

obverse of which appears a bust of Victory facing right, similar to that of Vaala's aurei; a Victory in a *biga* occupies the reverse.[4]

No portraits in the round can be identified with any confidence as portraits of Fulvia.

1 Vessberg 1941, pl. 13, no. 7; Sydenham 1952, p. 189, nos. 1160, 1163. No. 1160 was struck before no. 1163, which has IIIVIR RPC on the reverse and must date from after the actual formation of the Triumvirate; Crawford 1974, no. 489, 5, 6, pl. 58.
2 *BMCGC Phrygia, etc.* 1906, p. 213, nos. 20, 21; pl. 27, nos. 4, 5.
3 Vessberg 1941, pl. 13, no. 8; Sydenham 1952, p. 180, no. 1086; Crawford 1974, no. 514, 1, pl. 62 (dates 41 BC).
4 Vessberg 1941, pl. 13, no. 6; Sydenham 1952, p. 181, no. 1095; Crawford 1974, no. 494, 40, pl. 60. For a full discussion of these coin types, see H. Bartels, *Studien zum Frauenporträt der augusteischen Zeit: Fulvia, Octavia, Livia, Julia*, n.d. (1963?), pp. 12–14.

OCTAVIA MINOR (?–11 BC)
Ills. 54–6

Octavia Minor was the sister of Octavian/Augustus and the third wife of Marcus Antonius, whom she married after the death of her first husband, Caius Marcellus, in 40 BC. She was with Antonius in Athens during the winters of 39–38 BC and 38–37 BC and was largely instrumental in bringing about the treaty of Tarentum in 37 BC, when Antonius and Octavian agreed to renew the Triumvirate. But when in 35 BC she travelled eastwards with supplies and reinforcements for Antonius, he, having tired of her, sent her ignominiously back to Italy – an act that was tantamount to repudiation of her. She was an essentially noble, loyal and kindly character, who looked after her stepchildren in Rome even after Antonius had formally divorced her. She was unreservedly respected and admired for her patience under very trying circumstances.

53 Fulvia: obverse of denarius, 43–42 BC.

54 Octavia Minor: reverse of aureus, 40 BC.

The earliest completely authentic portrait of Octavia that we possess is her head facing right (as in all her numismatic likenesses) and without a legend, on the reverse of a unique aureus in Berlin, with Antonius' portrait on the obverse (cf. *Ill. 45*) – a coin which must have been struck to commemorate her marriage with Antonius in 40 BC (*Ill. 54*).[1] Here her coiffure is basically the same as that of Fulvia. But the side hair, instead of being combed back, is worn in a roll round each side of the head, while the front hair is formed into a puff above the brow and then carried in a plait across the crown of the head to join the side rolls in a neat 'bun' on the nape of the neck; short curls escape down the sides of the neck behind the ears. She has a straight nose, mild eyes, a kindly mouth, and rounded cheeks and chin.

Cistophoroi minted in Asia Minor in 37 BC show either Octavia's bust surmounting a *cista mystica* on the reverse or her bust conjoined with Antonius' portrait on the obverse.[2] In the first case her coiffure is identical with that on the Berlin aureus, but her features are less refined; and on the second cistophoros type the puff of hair above the brow is flatter and the throat fuller. On the reverses of eastern aurei of 36 BC, with the head of Antonius and his title IMP TERT on the obverse (cf. *Ill. 48*),[3] is a fine head of Octavia, again fuller in the face than on the Berlin aureus and with the central puff of hair, rising above the brow and drawn across the crown, more loop-like, after the manner of portraits of Fulvia (q.v.), while the side hair is combed back towards the 'bun' (which is higher up the head), without being gathered in a roll above the temples and cheeks. The locks that hang down the side of the neck behind the ears are long and more luxuriant; and here Octavia wears a large ear-ring. Some dies show horizontal folds of flesh on the neck below the chin.

Datable to 37 or 36 BC by their description of Antonius as COS DESIG ITER ET TER are bronze coins struck by him in Italy conjointly with L. Sempronius Atratinus, L. Calpurnius Bibulus, and M. Oppius Capito. Most of these carry either confronted or conjoined portraits of Antonius and Octavia. In the first case Octavia's puff of hair above the brow, her neat 'bun' and neck-locks, closely resembling those on the Berlin aureus, can be clearly distinguished.[4]

No anciently inscribed sculptural portraits of Octavia in the round are so far known. It is, however, very likely, in view of her high reputation both in life and after death, that many sculptured likenesses of her were made. Heads and busts representing her are not always easy to distinguish from those of Livia, whose earliest coiffures are the same as hers. For example, the green basalt head in the Louvre, at one time identified as Octavia, is now generally believed, largely on the score of its aquiline nose (which is, however, much restored), to depict not her, but Livia.[5] On the other hand, quite a number of portraits featuring Octavia's hair-style have a good chance of depicting her, on account of the close resemblance of the features to those of her brother, Octavian/Augustus. Among such portraits are those in: the von Bergen Collection in Rome (*Ill. 55*);[6] the Museo Nazionale Romano, found at Velitrae,

55 Octavia Minor: marble head (von Bergen Collection, Rome).

Augustus' birth-place;[7] and the National Museum in Athens, found at Smyrna.[8] A portrait statue in the Museo Nazionale at Naples, with the tip of the nose restored, probably shows Octavia at an advanced age; she is veiled.[9] Another head in the National Museum in Athens, found in Crete, also veiled and with a fairly straight nose, may be hers.[10] Also very likely to be a portrait of her is the colossal head in the museum at Seville, found in the amphitheatre of Italica and clearly the pendant of the head of Augustus from the same site (*Ill. 56*).[11] Other portraits ascribed to Octavia come from Carthage and Butrinto in Albania,[12] but the Carthage head could well be Livia. Still further possible sculptural portraits of her are those in the

56 Octavia Minor: marble head (Museo Arqueologico,
Seville).

National Gallery in Oslo;[13] in the Dresden Alberti-
num;[14] and in the Archaeological Museum in
Istanbul.[15]

The cameo in the Cabinet des Médailles in the
Bibliothèque Nationale, Paris, described as portraying Octavia,[16] might in reality depict Livia,
since the nose is quite remarkably aquiline.

1   Vessberg 1941, pl. 13, no. 9; Sydenham 1952, p. 193,
    no. 1196; Crawford 1974, no. 527, pl. 63.
2   Sydenham 1952, nos. 1197, 1198, pl. 29; Bernareggi
    1973, p. 91, figs. 26, 27.
3   Vessberg 1941, pl. 13, no. 10; Sydenham 1952, p.
    193, nos. 1200, 1201, pl. 29; Crawford 1974, no. 533,
    3, pl. 63 (dates 38 BC).
4   Monuments Piot, xlv, 1951, pp. 82–3, fig. 2, nos. 6–12;
    Sydenham 1952, pp. 197–9.
5   CAH, vol. iv of plates, 1934, pp. 166–7; Die Antike,
    xiv, 1938, p. 264, fig. 9; RM, liv, 1939, pl. 18; Bartels,
    op. cit., pp. 18, 82–3, n. 115.
6   Die Antike, xiv, 1938, pls. 28, 29.
7   Monuments Piot, li, 1960, p. 63, figs, 8, 9.
8   Inv. no. 547; Bartels, op. cit., p. 16 and n. 101.
9   Bollettino d'arte, xxv, 1931–2, pp. 445–54, figs. 1–3.
10 Inv. no. 355; RM, liv, 1939, p. 80, pl. 22.
11 A. García y Bellido, Esculturas romanas de España y
    Portugal, 1949, pp. 40–2, no. 32, pl. 28.
12 RM, liv, 1939, pls. 19 (Carthage), 20 (Butrinto).
13 Die Antike, xiv, 1938, pp. 255–63, figs. 1, 2.
14 Bartels, op. cit., p. 82, n. 103.
15 Inv. no. 4668.
16 Monuments Piot, xlv, 1951, pp. 77–87, pl. 10.

Marcus Aemilius Lepidus
(triumvir; c.89–13/12 BC)
Ills. 57, 58

Marcus Aemilius Lepidus was praetor urbanus in
49 BC and consul in 46 BC. After the murder of
Caesar he supported Marcus Antonius and in 43 BC
was appointed triumvir with Antonius and Octavian. He held the governorships of Gallia Nar-
bonensis and of the two Spains until after the battle
of Philippi, when he was deprived of those provinces. But he was given Africa and Numidia as a
reward for supporting Octavian in the Perusine
war of 41 BC. In 36 BC he was forced to retire from
public life, but remained pontifex maximus until
his death.

Three main types of coin portrait of Lepidus can
be distinguished. One type shows him as fairly
young, facing to the right, with a long, pointed
nose, large mouth with full lips, and abundant,
freely growing locks of hair. This portrait appears
on the obverses of aurei, issued in Rome by L.
Livineius Regulus in 42 BC, with the legend M
LEPIDVS IIIVIR RPC,[1] and on the reverses of provincial aurei struck by him conjointly with Marcus
Antonius in 43 BC, with the same legend and a
simpulum (ladle) and sprinkler behind the head (*Ill.
57*).[2] In the second type Lepidus' head faces to the
left and is more elderly in look, with a heavier face,
but with the same thick cap of hair. This likeness
occurs on aurei struck in Rome by L. Mussidius
Longus in 42 BC, with the same legend again (*Ill.
58*):[3] one die shows him with a double chin.
Slightly later, c.41 BC, are the leftward-facing
heads on the obverses of aurei of P. Clodius and C.
Vibius Varus, issued in Rome.[4] These, too, carry
the legend M LEPIDVS IIIVIR RPC. A third type depicts
Lepidus as considerably older, with a thin neck and
'Adam's apple', two vertical creases of flesh on the
cheeks on some dies, and straight hair brushed
back. This portrait, facing right, is found on the
reverses of denarii struck by Lepidus conjointly
with Octavian and bearing the legend LEPIDVS
PONT MAX IIIVIR RPC.[5] He was pontifex maximus
from 44 BC onwards. But these denarii must have
been issued in Italy before his retirement from
public life in 36 BC, perhaps in 40 BC.

No epigraphically attested portraits in the round
of Lepidus have so far come down to us. But three
have been identified as he, with some reason, by
Ludwig Curtius.[6] A bronze bust at Naples, depicting a personage in his forties, has the long, pointed
nose and cap of hair that are to be seen in Lepidus'
coin portraits of the first and second types.[7] The
head of a marble statue from Velleia, now at
Parma, presents what may be the same individual
about ten years older and veiled like a priest.[8]
Finally, in a colossal marble head in the Ny
Carlsberg Glyptotek, Copenhagen, we have a like-

57, 58 M. Aemilius Lepidus: reverses of aurei struck respectively at a travelling mint, 43 BC, and in Rome, 42 BC.

ness that might be that of Lepidus in his seventies, taken shortly before his death, with wrinkled brow, hanging folds of flesh on the cheeks, and crow's feet at the corners of the eyes.[9]

1 Vessberg 1941, pl. 9, no. 9; Sydenham 1952, p. 182, no. 1105, pl. 28; Crawford 1974, no. 494, 1, pl. 58.
2 Sydenham 1952, p. 189, no. 1161, pl. 29; Crawford 1974, no. 492, 2, pl. 58.
3 Vessberg 1941, pl. 9, nos. 7, 8; Sydenham 1952, p. 182, nos. 1099, 1102; Crawford 1974, no. 494, 7, 13, pl. 59.
4 ZfN, vi, 1879, p. 19, pl. 1; Sydenham 1952, p. 184, no. 1120 (Clodius); p. 186, no. 1143 (Varus); Crawford 1974, no. 494, 4, 10, pls. 58, 59.
5 Vessberg 1941, pl. 9, no. 10; Sydenham 1952, p. 206, no. 1323, pl. 30; Crawford 1974, no. 495, 1, 2, pl. 60.
6 RM, xlvii, 1932, pp. 242–68.
7 Ibid., figs. 21, 23.
8 Ibid., pl. 59.
9 Ibid., figs. 22, 24.

Caius Octavianus
(63 BC–AD 14); from 27 BC Augustus
Ills. 59–76

According to Dio Cassius, Octavian wore a beard of mourning for Julius Caesar until 39 BC.[1] But a beard is actually found on some of his coin portraits

as late as 36 BC; and he is occasionally depicted as beardless in numismatic likenesses before 39 BC. Suetonius,[2] who describes him as 'unusually handsome' ('forma fuit eximia'), implies that Octavian/Augustus seems to have been indifferent as to whether he was clean-shaven or bearded ('modo tonderet modo raderet barbam'). He had clear, bright eyes ('oculos habuit claros ac nitidos'). His teeth were small and had gaps between them ('dentes raros et exiguos'). His hair was slightly curly and rather yellow ('capillum leviter inflexum et subflavum'). His eyebrows met ('supercilia coniuncta'); his ears were of moderate size ('mediocres aures'); his nose jutted out and then bent slightly inwards ('nasum et a summo eminentiorem et ab imo deductiorem'). His complexion was neither dark nor fair ('colorem inter aquilum candidumque'). He was short of stature ('staturam brevem').

Not all of Octavian's coin portraits (nearly all of which are rightward-facing) can claim to represent him as he actually was at the time of their striking. The most youthful of all his numismatic representations was issued on aurei and denarii at a travelling mint by Marcus Antonius, M. Barbatius Philippus, and Octavian conjointly in 40–39 BC (cf. *Ill. 46*). These present him with almost childish features – a *retroussé* nose (on some dies), a thick mop of hair, a very slender neck and a beardless chin, but with a short side-burn in front of each ear.[3] This extreme rejuvenation of Octavian may well have had a propagandist purpose, to emphasize by contrast Antonius' creeping senility; and Octavian's head is obviously not a likeness in the true sense here.

Another youthful, but much less boyish, type of portrait occurs on the obverses of aurei struck in Rome by M. Mussidius Longus in 42 BC. The legend reads C CAESAR IIIVIR RPC and the head is square, with a close-fitting cap of hair, a straight, but rather thick and blunt, nose, a somewhat pouting mouth, a slight chin-beard and a stocky neck (*Ill. 59*).[4] Octavian still looks rather less than his age in 42 BC, which was twenty-one years; and the same obverse portrait with the same legend was rendered in the same year in Rome on aurei of C. Vibius Varus (*Ill. 60*).[5]

On the other hand, denarii struck by this same C. Vibius Varus show a more mature type of obverse likeness, legendless, with slightly freer locks of hair, a sharper and more pointed nose, sometimes with, at other times without, a chin-beard (*Ill. 61*).[6] These portraits could well reflect Octavian's actual looks in 42 BC and succeeding years. Close to them are the contemporary heads of Octavian on aurei and denarii of L. Livineius Regulus, with the legends C CAESAR IIIVIR RPC or CAESAR IIIVIR RPC (*Ills. 62, 63*).[7] Similar again, accompanied by the same legends and of the same date, are the obverse portraits of Octavian on aurei and denarii of P. Clodius, on some dies with a slight beard, on others without (*Ill. 64*).[8]

Further examples of this portrait type are on aurei and denarii struck in Gaul and Italy in 43–42 BC, with or without a slight beard, by Octavian alone (*Ill. 65*)[9] or (*Ill. 66*) with M. Aemilius Lepidus (q.v.).[10] Denarii of a travelling mint, issued by Octavian and M. Vipsanius Agrippa show on their obverses the same type of Octavian portrait, but facing to the left and confronting a rightward-facing Julius Caesar (*Ill. 67*).[11] These

are dated to 38 BC by the reverse legend M AGRIPPA COS DESIG, as are also – by their use of the same reverse legend, and of the obverse legend IMP CAESAR DIVI IVLI F – denarii struck by Octavian conjointly with Agrippa, with Octavian's head facing to the right as obverse type;[12] Octavian assumed the *praenomen* IMPERATOR in 38 BC. Bearded heads of Octavian on denarii struck by him alone at a travelling mint are dated by their obverse legend IMP CAESAR DIVI F IIIVIR ITER RPC to *c.* 36 BC, the Triumvirate having been renewed towards the end of 37 BC.[13] Yet further examples of this type of

59–64   C. Octavianus, coin obverses: (*top left*) aureus of M. Mussidius Longus, 42 BC; (*top right*) aureus of C. Vibius Varus, 42 BC; (*centre left*) denarius of C. Vibius Varus, 42 BC; (*centre right*) aureus of L. Livineius Regulus, 42 BC; (*below left*) denarius of L. Livineius Regulus; (*below right*) denarius of P. Clodius, 42 BC.

likeness, so far as one can tell from the background position of Octavian's head, are to be found on non-Roman bronze coins struck in *c.* 36 BC, where the conjoined heads of Marcus Antonius and Octavian face the head of Octavia;[14] on the reverses of aurei and denarii struck at a travelling mint in 40–39 BC, with Marcus Antonius' head on the obverse and with Octavian shown wearing a slight beard;[15] and on the aurei and denarii that were struck at a travelling mint in *c.* 40 BC by Marcus Antonius, L. Gellius Publicola and Octavian conjointly, where Octavian has distinctly

woolly hair, a very slight beard, and a *lituus* behind the head (*Ill. 68*).[16]

A less common type of Octavian coin portrait shows a slightly older face, with large eyes, rather thinner cheeks, a slight beard, and a markedly long, thin neck, with a small 'Adam's apple' below the chin. It occurs on the obverses of aurei and denarii issued in Rome by Q. Voconius Vitulus, dated by Sydenham to 40 BC, but more likely to have been struck in 37 BC: the legends read DIVI IVLI F or DIVI F (*Ill. 69*).[17] Probably also struck in 37 BC, although again dated by Sydenham to

65–70 C. Octavianus, coin obverses: (*top*) aurei struck in Gaul or Italy, 43–42 BC (*left*), and conjointly with M. Aemilius Lepidus (cf. *Ill. 57*), 43 BC; (*centre*) denarii struck at travelling mints in, respectively, 38 and 41 BC, with (*left*) Octavian confronting Julius Caesar; (*below*) aurei issued respectively by Q. Voconius Vitulus, and by Ti. Sempronius Gracchus, both 37 BC(?).

40 BC (cf. p. 32), are the Roman aurei and denarii of Tiberius Sempronius Gracchus with the same type of portrait (*Ill. 70*).[18] And this type occurs again on the obverses of bronze coins struck in Italy by Octavian in 38(?) BC with the legends CAESAR DIVI F and DIVI F, coins with the latter legend displaying a star in front of Octavian's head.[19]

A most unusual coin portrait of Octavian, if, indeed, it is intended to represent him, appears on the obverses of denarii issued by the moneyer M. Arrius Secundus, which are, in that case, likely to be as early as 43 BC, the date assigned to them by Sydenham.[20] This personage has lanky locks of hair, large eyes, a pointed nose, and a chin-beard, and he is distinguished by a fat neck thrown so far forward that the head appears to be retreating. It is strange that Octavian's name does not appear; and the military reverse motifs would be appropriate to Quintus Arrius (q.v.), praetor in *c.* 72 BC.[21]

The latest coin portraits of Octavian, before he received the title of Augustus, are those on aurei and denarii issued at an eastern mint between 31 and 29 BC (*Ills. 71, 72*).[22] All carry the reverse legend

the right eye which characterizes all his sculptural portraits in the round that were carved both before and after he became Augustus. The heads and busts that have been identified as Octavian or 'the young Augustus' are very numerous;[23] and only a few examples of special interest can be discussed and illustrated here.

The earliest of Octavian's likenesses in the round is a very fine marble head (in private hands in Rome) with very youthful, boyish features.[24] He is veiled as a pontifex, an office conferred upon him in 48 BC, when he was not quite fifteen years old. Here he has already grown side-burns, but is beardless; and the portrait was therefore most probably carved before Caesar's death, between 48 and 44 BC. The hair is flat and grows low on the brow, as on the pre-Actium coin portraits.[25] The eyes are deep-set, and the mouth is small and straight. Only the tip of the nose is lost.

With hair very similar to that of this early portrait, but with more mature features, is a very well preserved marble head found in the Crypto-porticus at Arles and now in the Arles Archaeological Museum (*Ill. 73*). The eyes are again

71, 72   C. Octavianus: obverses of coins struck at an eastern mint, 31–29 BC.

CAESAR DIVI F, while the legendless obverses show heads of Octavian facing now to the left, now to the right. These heads are more youthful and idealized than the great majority of those on coins struck before Actium. All are beardless and have longer and more untidy hair than before, with luxuriant locks on the nape of the neck. The brow is higher than on earlier portraits and the lower part of it protrudes, the nose is larger, thinner and more pointed, and the very large eyes are deeply set. To what extent these heads are true likenesses of Octavian as he looked at this period remains in doubt. There is about them a quite distinct touch of Hellenistic ruler iconography.

On none of Octavian's profile coin portraits was it possible to render the famous 'fork' of locks above

deep-set, but the mouth is larger and the cheeks somewhat thinner; and the slight beard indicates a date after Caesar's murder.[26] A bearded marble head in the Roman Theatre Museum at Verona could be of much the same date as the Arles likeness, with its similar hair-style (*Ill. 74*). The tip of the nose is lost.[27] Very close to these, with the same compact hair growing low on the brow, deep-set eyes, and largish mouth, is a marble head in the British Museum, which may just antedate 44 BC, since it has short side-burns, but no beard. Again the tip of the nose is missing.[28]

Still with the same flat hair, falling low over the brow, and slight side-burns is a marble head with mutilated nose in the Aquileia Archaeological Museum. But the face is older, with the twist of the

73   C. Octavianus: marble head (Arles).

74   C. Octavianus: marble head
          (Verona).

head towards the left giving it a somewhat 'pathetic' touch.[29] The absence of a beard suggests a post-39 BC dating.

A marble head in the Villa Albani in Rome shows neat, cap-like hair again, but the brow is higher and the locks above the temples do not fall so low as on the portraits described above; and the face has a still more mature look.[30] Here we would appear to have a type of portrait that links the youthful likenesses with those on the eastern aurei and denarii of 31–29 BC.[31] The latter are paralleled in sculpture by such heads as that in the Metropolitan Museum of Art, New York,[32] and by the splendid Capitoline Museum head (*Ill. 75*),[33] where the lower portion of the lofty brow protrudes and the locks of hair on the head are much looser and more picturesquely untidy than on any of the sculptured heads so far discussed. Both of these portraits would appear to have been carved during the last years in which Octavian bore that name. A marble head with damaged nose, found at Fondi and now in the Naples museum, is a portrait of Octavian of Hellenistic type, probably carved soon after Actium, with the lower part of the brow slightly jutting out and loose, tortuous locks of hair covering the skull (*Ill. 76*).[34]

1 DC, xlviii, 34, 3: ἀμέλει τὸν πάγωνα ὁ Καῖσαρ τότε πρῶτον ξυράμενος . . . καὶ ὁ μὲν καὶ ἔπειτα ἐπελειοῦτο τὸ γένειον.

2 *Augustus* 79.

3 Sydenham 1952, p. 191, nos. 1180, 1181; Bernareggi 1973, p. 87, fig. 23; Crawford 1974, no. 517, 12, pl. 62 (date 41 BC).

4 Vessberg 1941, pl. 11, no. 1; Sydenham 1952, p. 182, nos. 1098, 1101; Crawford 1974, no. 494, 9a, 15, pl. 59.

5 Sydenham 1952, p. 186, no. 1142, pl. 28; Crawford 1974, no. 494, 12, pl. 59.

6 Sydenham 1952, p. 186, nos. 1145, pl. 29 (=Crawford 1974, no. 494, 33, pl. 60); 1146 (=Grueber 1910, i, p. 589 =hybrid).

7 Vessberg 1941, pl. 11, nos. 2, 3; Sydenham 1952, pp. 182, 183, nos. 1104, 1107; Crawford 1974, no. 494, 3, 25, pl. 58, 59.

8 Sydenham 1952, p. 184, nos. 1119, 1122–4, pl. 28; Crawford 1974, no. 494, 6, 16, 18, 19, pl. 59.

9 Sydenham 1952, p. 206, e.g. no. 1321, pl. 30: legend C CAESAR COS PONT(*ifex*) AVG(*ur*); no. 1324, legend C CAESAR IIIVIR RPC = *NZ*, xxviii, 1896, pl. vi, no. 140; Crawford 1974, no. 490, 1–4, pl. 58.

10 Sydenham 1952, p. 206, no. 1323, pl. 30: legend CAESAR IMP IIIVIR RPC; Crawford 1974, no. 495, pl. 60.

11 Sydenham 1952, p. 207, no. 1330, pl. 30: obverse legend DIVOS IVLIOS DIVI F; Crawford 1974, no. 534, 2, pl. 63.

12 Grueber 1910, ii, pp. 412–13, nos. 103, 104; iii, pl. 105, no. 7; Sydenham 1952, p. 207, no. 1331; Crawford 1974, no. 534, 3, pl. 63.

13 Grueber 1910, ii, p. 415, no. 116; iii, pl. 105, nos. 14, 15; Sydenham 1952, p. 208, no. 1334; Crawford 1974, no. 538, 1, pl. 64.

14 *NZ*, xxxvii, 1905, pl. 1, nos. 2, 8; Sydenham 1952, pp. 197–8, nos. 1256, 1262, 1266.

15 Sydenham 1952, p. 192, nos. 1192–4; Bernareggi 1973, p. 85, fig. 20; Crawford 1974, no. 528, pl. 63.

16 Sydenham 1952, p. 192, nos. 1187–8, pl. 29; Bernareggi 1973, p. 87, fig. 22; Crawford 1974, no. 517, 7, 8, pl. 62.

17 Vessberg 1941, pl. 11, no. 4; Sydenham 1952, p. 185, nos. 1130, 1131, pl. 28; Crawford 1974, no. 526, 1, 3, pl. 63 (dates 40? BC or later).

18 Sydenham 1952, pp. 184–5, nos. 1126, 1127, pl. 28; Crawford 1974, no. 525, pl. 63 (dates 40? BC or later).

19 Grueber 1910, ii, pp. 412–13; iii, pl. 105, nos. 9–11; Sydenham 1952, p. 208, nos. 1335, 1336; Crawford 1974, no. 535, pl. 64.

20 Sydenham 1952, p. 180, nos. 1084, 1085, pl. 28; Crawford 1974, no. 513, 2, 3, pl. 62 (dates 41 BC).

21 For other pre-Actium coin portraits of Octavian, see (1) Sydenham 1952, pp. 205–6, nos. 1316–19, pl. 30 (Cisalpine Gaul, *c.*41 BC, aurei and denarii of Octavian); (2) ibid., p. 206, no. 1322 (Gaul, 40–36 BC, denarii of Octavian); (3) ibid., pp. 206–7, nos. 1325–7 (Gaul, 40–36 BC, aurei and denarii of Octavian and L. Cornelius Balbus, Q. Salvius Salvienus Rufus, and Marcus Antonius); (4) ibid., p. 189, no. 1167 (Gaul, *c.*42 BC, aurei of Octavian and Marcus Antonius). (1) = Crawford 1974, no. 490, 3, no. 318, 2, no. 498, 1, no. 497, 1; (2) = Crawford no. 497, 2; (3) = Crawford no. 518, 1, no. 523, 1a, no. 529, 1, 2; (4) = Crawford no. 493, 1; revised dates and mints.

22 *BMCCRE*, i, 1923, pp. 97–9, nos. 590–608, pl. 14, nos. 10–13, 15–19, pl. 15, nos. 1, 2; Vessberg 1941, pl. 11, nos. 5–7.

23 See O. Brendel, *Ikonographie des Kaisers Augustus*, 1931, an unillustrated analysis of types and catalogue of examples; L. Curtius, 'Zum Bronzekopf von Azaila und zu den Porträts des jugendlichen Augustus', in *RM*, lv, 1940, pp. 36–64, figs. 1–15, pls. 1–8.

24 Curtius, op. cit., pl. 1, pl. 2, fig. 1.

25 Vessberg 1941, pl. 11, nos. 1–4.

26 H. Kähler, *Rome and her Empire*, 1963, colour-plate on p. 80. The fact that this head comes from the same site as a marble copy of the golden shield hung up in the Curia in Rome at the time at which Octavian became Augustus does not prove that the portrait was carved at that time. His features, as coin portraits show, were familiar in Gaul before his visit to the province in 27 BC; and the beard definitely militates against a post-Actium dating.

27 Curtius, op. cit., pl. 2, fig. 2.

28 No. 1885: ibid., p. 61, fig. 15.

29 Ibid., p. 41, figs. 5, 6.

30 Ibid., p. 51, figs. 9, 10; P. Zankler, *Studien zu den Augustus-Porträts I. Der Actium-Typus*, 1973, pp. 21, 22, pl. 19a, dates it to the time of Tiberius. Cf. the marble head found in 1929 in the theatre at Butrinto (Buthrotum) in Albania: *Bollettino del Museo dell'Impero Romano*, i, 1930, pp. 113–15, pls. 1, 2.

31 See note 22.

32 Curtius, op. cit., pp. 38, 39, figs. 2, 4.

33 Ibid., pl. 7; Zankler, op. cit., pp. 15, 16, pls. 6b–8.

34 E. Buschor, *Das hellenistische Bildnis*, 2nd ed., 1971, no. 226, pl. 75; Zankler, op. cit., pp. 29–31, pls. 22–4, believes it to be post-Augustan.

CNAEUS POMPEIUS IUNIOR
Ill. 77

In 49 BC Cnaeus Pompeius, the elder son of Cnaeus Pompeius Magnus (q.v.), acquired an Egyptian fleet, which he used for destroying Caesar's transports before the battle of Dyrrachium. During the African war he occupied the Balearic islands and

75 C. Octavianus: marble head
(Capitoline Museum, Rome).

76 C. Octavianus: marble head
from Fondi (Museo Nazionale,
Naples).

went to Spain, where he was joined after the battle of Thapsus by his brother and Labienus, raised thirteen legions, and seized most of the southern province. But he was defeated in 45 B C by Caesar at Munda, captured and put to death.

Cnaeus' portrait appears on the reverses of aurei struck in Sicily by his younger brother. Sextus, between 42 and 38 B C. His bust faces to the left and confronts that of his father (cf. p. 25). Behind his head is a tripod and the reverse legend reads PRAEF(ectus) CLAS(sis) ET ORAE MARIT(imae) EX SC (*Ill. 77*).[1] Cnaeus has a square head and small face topping a thick neck. His thick hair forms a mat of locks, arranged in tiers, on the back of the head and nape of the neck. He has a beard, presumably in mourning for his father, a low brow, a very prominent nose, and a somewhat negroid mouth.

Asia Minor, but was captured there and executed in 35 B C.

Sextus' likeness, facing to the right and encircled by an oak-wreath, appears on the obverses of aurei, with his father's and brother's portraits shown on the reverses (cf. p. 25), which he struck in Sicily between 42 and 38 B C (*Ill. 78*).[1] He has an even squarer head than his brother, the same tiered locks of hair on the back of the head and the nape of the neck, and a still thicker neck, with horizontal folds of flesh below the chin. He, too, wears a beard of mourning for his father, whose bulbous nose he also displays. The legend reads MAG PIVS IMP ITER.

1 Vessberg 1941, pl. 5, no. 7; Sydenham 1952, p. 210, no. 1346, pl. 30; Crawford 1974, no. 511, 1, pl. 61 (dates 42–40 B C).

77 Cn. Pompeius Iunior (facing left, confronting Cn. Pompeius Magnus): reverse of aureus struck in Sicily, 42–38 B C.

78 Sextus Pompeius Magnus Pius: portrait with oak-wreath on obverse of aureus (cf. *Ill. 77*) struck in Sicily, 42–38 B C.

This posthumous portrait was no doubt based upon a lifetime original.

1 Vessberg 1941, pl. 5, nos. 8, 9; Sydenham 1952, p. 210, no. 1346, pl. 30; Crawford 1974, no. 511, 1, pl. 61 (dates 42–40 B C).

SEXTUS POMPEIUS MAGNUS PIUS
Ill. 78
After the battle of Pharsalus in 48 B C, Sextus Pompeius, the younger son of Pompeius Magnus (q.v.), travelled to Egypt with his father; and when the latter was murdered he went to Africa and joined his brother in Spain after the battle of Thapsus. In 43 B C he was appointed commander of the fleet by the Senate, but was outlawed under the *lex Pedia*. He used his fleet to occupy Sicily and to raid and blockade the Italian coast. In 40 B C he supported Marcus Antonius against Octavian and under the treaty of Misenum was made governor of Sicily, Sardinia and Achaia. At the battle of Naulochus in 36 B C he escaped with some ships to

LUCIUS ANTONIUS
(younger brother of Marcus Antonius)
Ill. 79
Lucius Antonius was quaestor in Asia in 50 B C and as tribune in 44 B C he carried a law giving Caesar special powers and an agrarian law under which he served as a commissioner. He was legate to his brother Marcus in the Mutina war and as consul in 41 B C opposed Octavian. In 40 B C he surrendered at Perugia and was sent as Octavian's legate to Spain, where he seems to have died soon afterwards.

Lucius' likeness, facing right, is to be found on the reverses of aurei and denarii issued conjointly by him, Marcus Antonius and M. Cocceius Nerva at a travelling mint in 41 B C (*Ill. 79*).[1] The legend is L ANTONIVS COS. Lucius is bald on the top of the head, while at the back the hair grows quite luxuriantly. The lower part of his brow protrudes, his eyes and ears are very large, his nose is straight, his mouth small and rather compressed, with the lower lip slightly jutting out; he has a double chin;

and on his long, thick neck there are horizontal creases of flesh.

1 Vessberg 1941, pl. 10, no. 9; Sydenham 1952, pp. 191–2, nos. 1184–6, pl. 29 (p. 191, no. 1182 appears to be either false or a hybrid); Crawford 1974, no. 517, 3–6, pl. 62.

Marcus Antonius Iunior
Ill. 80

In 47 BC, at the treaty of Misenum, Marcus Antonius Iunior, elder son of Marcus Antonius and Fulvia, was betrothed to Octavian's daughter Julia. He assumed the *toga virilis* after Actium; and he was put to death after the capture of Alexandria by Octavian.

Rightward-facing portraits of Marcus Iunior occur on the reverses of aurei struck by him at a travelling mint in association with his father in 34 BC. The reverse legends read COS ITER DESIGN TERT IIIVIR RPC referring to his father, and M ANTONIVS M(*arci*) F(*ilii*) F(*ilius*), referring to himself (*Ill. 80*).[1] Marcus Iunior has a narrower head than either his father or his uncle, a mop of thick, curly hair covering the whole skull, large eyes, a straight, pointed nose, a small, slightly smiling mouth, a projecting chin like his father's, and a long neck. Since in 34 BC the young Marcus was only about nine years old, these heads can hardly be said to represent true likenesses.

1 Vessberg 1941, pl. 10, nos. 10, 11; Sydenham 1952, p. 194, nos. 1206–7, pl. 29; Crawford 1974, no. 541, pl. 64.

Caius Numonius Vaala (mid-first century BC)
Ill. 81

The moneyer C. Numonius Vaala is only known from aurei and denarii minted in Rome *c.*43 BC. The reverse types show a soldier attacking a *vallum*, which two other soldiers defend, with the legends C NVMONIVS VAALA or just VAALA.[1] The head facing to the right on the obverses of the denarii (*Ill. 81*) with the reverse legend VAALA is labelled C NV-MONIVS VAALA and can hardly depict Julius Caesar, as Sydenham suggests, since it shows neither veil nor wreath and has quite different features. Nor can it be a portrait of the moneyer himself. It is most likely to portray the moneyer's father, note-worthy for some military exploit otherwise unre-corded.

The head is distinctly portrait-like, with straight locks of hair receding from the temples, a very high brow, a very large, aquiline nose, a small, set mouth, hollow cheeks with prominent cheek-bones

on some dies, and a very long, thin neck with a small 'Adam's apple'.

1 Vessberg 1941, pl. 8, nos. 6, 7; Sydenham 1952, p. 180, no. 1087, pl. 28; Crawford 1974, no. 514, 2 (dates 41 BC). For reverse type, cf. p. 48.

Lucius Livineius Regulus
(praetor and friend of Cicero?)
Ill. 82

Aurei and denarii issued in Rome by the moneyer L. Livineius Regulus in 42 BC carry on their obverses the head, facing right, of a man well

79 L. Antonius: reverse of denarius struck at a travelling mint. 41 BC.

80 M. Antonius Iunior: reverse of aureus struck at a travelling mint, 34 BC.

81 C. Numonius Vaala: obverse of denarius struck in Rome, *c.*43 BC.

advanced in middle age, with abundant straight hair, a furrowed brow, large eyes, a very aquiline nose, a small mouth, fat cheeks, a full, receding chin, and a thick neck. The expression is somewhat arrogant; and the features are highly individual (*Ill. 82*).[1] Some dies bear the legend REGVLVS PR, while others are legendless; and there can be little doubt that the personage portrayed is the praetor Regulus, father of the moneyer. He might be identical with the Livineius Regulus described by Cicero as 'familiarissimus meus'.[2]

1 Vessberg 1941, pl. 5, nos. 10, 11; Sydenham 1952, p. 183, nos. 1108–13, pl. 28; Crawford 1974, no, 494, 26–31, pl. 59.
2 Cicero, *Ad Familiares* xiii, 60.

82   L. Livineius Regulus: obverse of denarius, 42 BC.

LUCIUS and CNAEUS DOMITIUS AHENOBARBUS
(Lucius consul 54 BC; Cnaeus consul 32 BC)
Ills. 83, 84

On the obverses of aurei struck at a travelling mint in 40 BC by Cnaeus Domitius Ahenobarbus is a most remarkably life-like and veristic portrait head, facing to the right, of a grossly fat, elderly man, bald on the top of the head, with deep-set eyes, a large nose, full, flabby cheeks, a hard mouth, a double chin, and a great bull-like neck: the legend reads AHENOBAR (*Ill. 83*).[1] This head can hardly depict the moneyer himself, who was not consul until 32 BC; at the date at which he issued these coins he could have been no more than in his early thirties, and would obviously have been much younger than the personage here portrayed. Most probably it is Cnaeus' father, Lucius Domitius Ahenobarbus, who is depicted – the opponent of the First Triumvirate, consul in 54 BC, granted the governorship of Gaul by the Senate in 49 BC, but spared by Caesar when he surrendered at Corfinium. He fell at Pharsalus in 48 BC, fighting for the Pompeian cause. Cnaeus might well have possessed a gem portrait, taken not long before his father's death, from which the coin portrait was made. On the reverse we have the moneyer's name, CN DOMITIVS L F IMP and a temple labelled NEPT, which Cnaeus must have either built or restored.

On the obverses of denarii issued at the same date by Cnaeus and also at a travelling mint we find the legend AHENOBAR and the head of a considerably younger man. He, too, faces to the right. He has a high brow, is thinnish in the face, has a long, straight nose and a fairly slender neck. He wears a short beard. (*Ill. 84*).[2] Vessberg holds that this is a 'fancy' portrait of a mythical ancestor of the Domitii Ahenobarbi family.[3] But the features are portrait-like and might well depict the moneyer

himself, who held an independent *imperium* at this time. Cnaeus, brought up as a Pompeian, had commanded a fleet in the Adriatic against the members of the Second Triumvirate. But before the treaty of Brundisium between the triumvirs in October 40 BC he had joined Marcus Antonius (q.v.) and was appointed governor of Bithynia. Although Antonius had dropped his beard of mourning in 42 BC, Cnaeus might just conceivably

83   L. Domitius Ahenobarbus: obverse of aureus struck at a travelling mint, 40 BC.

84   Cn. Domitius Ahenobarbus(?): obverse of denarius struck at a travelling mint, 40 BC.

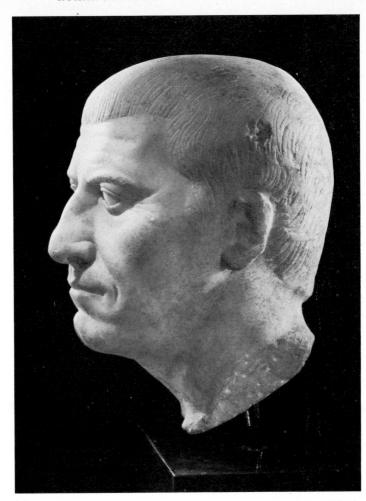

85 C. Cassius Longinus(?):
marble head (Museum of Fine
Arts, Montreal).

have adopted one as a token of his retrospective
association with Caesar through his new alliance
with Antonius; more probably it represents a
personal taste (cf. p. 63). On the reverses Cnaeus is
again described as CN DOMITIVS IMP; and the reverse
type, a trophy on a prow, may allude to the
victorious fleet with which he joined Antonius. On
the aurei and denarii which Cnaeus and Antonius
issued conjointly, with the latter's portrait on the
obverse (cf. p. 42), a prow with the legend CN
DOMITIVS AHENOBARBUS IMP occupies the reverse.[4]

CAIUS CASSIUS LONGINUS(?) (90/85–42 BC)
Ill. 85
If the very fleshy man on the obverses of Cnaeus
Domitius Ahenobarbus' aurei is rightly identified
as Lucius Domitius Ahenobarbus (q.v.), the personage featured in the group of so-called 'Corbulo'
portraits cannot be he, as has been suggested by H.
Jucker in an article on the very fine marble head,
belonging to this group, which has recently been
acquired by the Museum of Fine Arts, Montreal
(*Ill. 85*).[1] The best-known variant in the group is
the marble head in the Museo Nuovo of the
Palazzo dei Conservatori on the Capitol;[2] but from
the point of view of trying to establish the man's
identity two other marble variants, both in the
Louvre, are of greater importance.[3] Both of these
were found at Gabii in 1793 in a species of hall,
which an inscription of AD 140[4] states to have been
built and furnished by two freedmen in honour of

1 Vessberg 1941, pl. 9, no. 4; Sydenham 1952, p. 191,
   no. 1176, pl. 29; Crawford 1974, no. 519, 1, pl. 62.
2 Vessberg 1941, pl. 2, nos. 7, 8; Sydenham 1952, p.
   191, no. 1177, p. 29; Crawford 1974, no. 519, 2, pl.
   62.
3 Vessberg 1941, p. 123.
4 Sydenham 1952, p. 191, nos. 1178–9, pl. 29; Crawford 1974, no. 521, pl. 62.

the family of Domitia Longina, daughter of Cnaeus Domitius Corbulo, the famous Julio-Claudian general, and the Augusta (and finally the widow) of the Emperor Domitian. In such honorific buildings it was customary to erect portraits of distinguished ancestors, sometimes more than one portrait of the same ancestor, of the person or persons that such a structure honoured. Domitia was descended from Lucius Domitius Ahenobarbus through her father, while on her mother's side (as her name Longina suggests) she was probably descended from the tyrannicide Caius Cassius Longinus, who is Jucker's alternative, and (if I am right about the Ahenobarbus coin-portraits) more acceptable, candidate for 'Corbulo's' identity.

There is, then, some ground for believing that we have in this group copies of a contemporary likeness, made between 50 and 40 BC, of Cassius, the Montreal copy dating from *c.*AD 100, the Capitoline copy from the second half of the first century BC. Characteristics of all these heads are the neat hair combed forward onto the brow, the lined forehead, the concentrated gaze, the long, straight nose (on the Montreal head and on one of the Louvre heads the original noses are preserved and are identical), the lean cheeks, deeply creased on either side of the nostrils, the wide, set, thin-lipped, ruthless mouth, and the pointed chin. Unfortunately we have no coin-portraits of the tyrannicide nor any literary description of his physiognomy by which to check the claim of these heads to represent him.

1 H. Jucker, 'A Republican Ancestor of the Empress Domitia Longina', *Apollo*, May 1976, pp. 350–7, figs. 1–5.
2 Ibid., figs. 6, 7.
3 Ibid., figs. 8–11.
4 *CIL*, xiv, 2795.

QUINTUS ATIUS LABIENUS PARTHICUS
(died 39 BC)
Ill. 86
Quintus Labienus Parthicus was sent to Parthia by Crassus to obtain help against Antonius and Octavian. Held up in Parthia by the battle of Philippi, he managed to invade Syria in the winter of 41–40 BC with Parthian help and defeated Antonius' governor Decidius Saxa, whose troops he used for overrunning Asia Minor. At an eastern mint he struck coins on which he styled himself 'Parthicus Imperator'. But in 39 BC he was defeated and killed by Antonius' supporter Publius Ventidius.

Labienus' coins bear on the legendless reverses a Parthian horse standing to the right, saddled and bridled and carrying a bow-case. On the obverses is his portrait with the legend Q LABIENVS PARTHICVS

IMP (*Ill. 86*).[1] He has a pointed, triangular face, with a thick mop of hair that forms a regular row of small locks fringing the brow. He has large eyes and

86 Q. Atius Labienus Parthicus: obverse of denarius struck at an eastern mint, *c.*40 BC.

a long, hooked nose, which gives him a somewhat Semitic look. His upper lip protrudes slightly. He has side-burns and a short beard. The die-engraver was possibly a Syrian.

1 Vessberg 1941, pl. 9, nos. 5, 6; Sydenham 1952, p. 212, nos. 1356–7, pl. 30; Crawford 1974, no. 524, pl. 63.

MARCUS IUNIUS QUINTUS CAEPIO BRUTUS
(the tyrannicide; 88(?)–42 BC)
Ills. 87, 88
Portraits of Marcus Iunius Brutus, all facing to the right, appear on aurei and denarii issued by him conjointly with three different moneyers at a travelling mint in 43–42 BC. Those struck with Pedanius Costa show a 'fancy' head of the consul Lucius Brutus on the obverses and one, on a small scale, of Iunius Brutus on the reverses with the legend BRVTVS IMP COSTA LEG, all in an oak-wreath.[1] Brutus has a thick mop of hair growing low down on the nape of the neck, a rather weak chin, a bony face with prominent cheek-bones and arched eyebrows, thick lips, side-burns and a slight beard; there is a small 'Adam's apple' below the chin. The general impression is one of lack of self-confidence and of weakness of character. On the obverses of aurei issued conjointly with Casca Longus, Brutus, accompanied by the legend BRVTVS IMP, appears on a rather larger scale and here the encircling wreath is of laurel, while the features are much the same as before.[2] The best and largest portrait is that on the obverses of denarii of Brutus and L. Plaetorius Cestianus. It, too, is bearded and has still more prominent cheek-bones, with creases of flesh near the nose and mouth, while

the expression is slightly more forceful. Brutus is described as BRVT IMP; and the famous EID MAR legend, with a cap of Liberty between two daggers,

87 M. Iunius Quintus Caepio Brutus: obverse of denarius struck at a travelling mint, 43–42 BC.

occupies the reverse (*Ill. 87*).[3] The beard could be explained as due to personal taste (cf. p. 61).

A bearded head facing to the right, with thick hair, lean cheeks and a pointed chin, on denarii struck in Rome in 41 BC by Servius Rufus, may possibly depict Brutus.[4]

Probably a sculptural portrait of Brutus in the round is a marble head in the Prado, Madrid. No ancient inscription identifies it, but it shows some of Brutus' physical characteristics. The face is rather narrow, with a low brow, prominent cheek-bones, a slightly negroid mouth, a projecting lower lip, and a short chin-beard. It could be an imperial-age, perhaps Hadrianic, copy of a contemporary original (*Ill. 88*).[5]

1 Vessberg 1941, pl. 9, no. 3; Sydenham 1952, p. 202, no. 1295, pl. 30; Crawford 1974, no. 506, 1, pl. 61.
2 Vessberg 1941, pl. 9, no. 1; Sydenham 1952, p. 203, no. 1297, pl. 30; Crawford 1974, no. 507, 1, pl. 61.
3 Vessberg 1941, pl. 9, no. 2; Sydenham 1952, p. 203, no. 301, pl. 30; Crawford 1974, no. 508, 3, pl. 61.
4 Sydenham 1952, p. 179, no. 1082, pl. 28; Crawford 1974, no, 515, 2, pl. 62.
5 M. Möbius, *Studia Varia*, 1967, pp. 210–15, pl. 45, figs. 3, 4.

MARCUS VIPSANIUS AGRIPPA (*c*.63–13/12 BC)
Ills. 89–94

Marcus Vipsanius Agrippa was the friend, supporter and collaborator of Octavian/Augustus from the time of Julius Caesar's murder onwards. Consul in 37 BC, he organized Octavian's first fleet and became its admiral, his naval successes culminating at Actium. He held a second consulship in 28 BC and a third in 27 BC and was then sent on a mission to the East, from which he was recalled to Rome in 21 BC. During the next two years he dealt with troubles in Gaul and Spain, after which he shared in Augustus' *proconsulare imperium, tribunicia potestas*, and, from either 18 or 13 BC, *imperium maius*. He went on a second mission to the East in 16–13 BC. In the latter year he was sent to Pannonia, where a revolt was feared, and he died soon after his return to Italy in 13 or 12 BC. He was closely associated with Augustus' religious and building programmes in Rome.

No literary descriptions of Agrippa's looks have come down to us. But his portraits certainly reflect his character as later Roman writers assessed it. Velleius Paterculus states that he combined great readiness to obey in the single case of Augustus with a passion for commanding others;[1] and Pliny describes him as being closer to a countryman than to a dandy – 'rusticitati propior quam deliciis' – and remarks upon his sternness (*torvitas*).[2]

Agrippa's earliest numismatic likenesses are on the obverse of a large bronze coin struck by him in 37–36 BC, after the treaty of Tarentum, possibly at the military post of Puteoli where his appointment

Left
88 M. Iunius Quintus Caepio Brutus(?): marble head (Prado, Madrid).

as admiral was marked by a great scheme for harbour construction close by (*Ill. 89*).[3] The obverse legend reads M AGRIPPA ORAE [*maritimae et*] CLAS(*sis*) PRAE(*fectus*) C(*os?*) and the type shows Agrippa's bare head facing to the left and already

89   M. Vipsanius Agrippa: obverse of bronze coin, 37–36 BC.

displaying all the distinctive physical traits that consistently characterize his portraiture almost throughout: a thick, close-fitting mop of hair, growing low over the centre of the brow, while receding at the sides; a projecting lower portion of the brow, with transverse furrows just above it, producing a slightly frowning and definitely stern effect; a long and slightly hooked nose; quite remarkably deep-set eyes; a firm, tightly set mouth; rather full cheeks; a full and double chin; and a strong, thick neck. On the reverse is a *triskele*, referring, not to the place where the coin was minted, but rather to Agrippa's naval campaigns in Sicilian waters; and the legend in this case is CAESAR IIIVIR RPC.

A much defaced bronze coin minted at Parium in Asia Minor, probably in 29 BC, has Octavian's portrait on the obverse and that of Agrippa facing to the right on the reverse with the legend M AGRIPPA. The head is somewhat tilted up. The characteristic hair, eyes, nose, mouth and neck are all to be distinguished, although the chin is badly worn.[4]

A series of very large bronze coins, convincingly attributed by Grant to Gades in Hispania Baetica, show Agrippa's head, again slightly tilted up, but facing to the left, on the obverses with the inscription AGRIPPA.[5] The various reverse legends

read: MVNICIPI PATRONVS; MVNICIPI PARENS; MV-NICIPI PATRONVS PARENS; and M AGRIPPA COS III MVNICIPI PARENS. The phrase COS III indicates that these coins cannot be earlier than 27 BC; and since Agrippa was proconsul in Spain in 19 BC, the reverse titles must record the foundation in that year of Gades as a *municipium*.[6]

Another bronze coin portrait of Agrippa this time struck in Asia Minor, almost certainly at Apamea, shows a posthumous representation of him, since the reverse bears the small head of Agrippa Postumus, his third son by Julia, born in 12 BC after his father's death. Agrippa's head faces to the right and presents his usual facial features.[7] Much less like him, and in fact in no sense a true likeness, is the head, also facing to the right, on the reverses, labelled AGRIPPA COS III IMP, of bronze coins issued at the same mint in Agrippa's lifetime, in 27 BC. On the obverses is the head of Octavian described as COS VII.[8]

The most interesting bronze provincial coinage with portraits is from the Nemausus (Nîmes) mint. The reverse type is the famous crocodile-cum-palm-tree, alluding to Actium and the annexation of Egypt, with the legend COL NEM. These coins were not merely local currency, but circulated widely, and over a long period of years, throughout the West.[9] Some coins of the series, believed to have been issued from 28/27–20 BC, bear on their obverses twin heads back to back, that on the right, facing right, being Octavian's portrait; while the leftward-facing head on the left must be intended for Agrippa, since it wears the admiral's rostral crown. Although the features are his, there is a beard, which never appears on any other of his portraits (*Ill. 90*).[10] Later issues with the two heads, minted in *c.* 15–12 BC, show Agrippa's distinctive

90   M. Vipsanius Agrippa (facing left, with Octavian): obverse of bronze coin, 28/27 BC.

91, 92   M. Vipsanius Agrippa: reverse of denarius, 13 BC; and obverse of as, posthumously minted.

ward facing head is bare and the features are heavier and older.[15] On the reverses of denarii issued in 12 BC by the moneyer Cossus Lentulus he is still depicted facing to the right and wearing the combined mural and rostral crown, and looks considerably older, with a rather drawn face and cheek-bones showing (*Ill. 91*).[16] But the best of all the Roman coin portraits of Agrippa is that on the obverses of bronze asses struck posthumously, under either Gaius (Caligula) or Claudius,[17] but clearly modelled on a contemporary original sculptural likeness. Here we have an outstandingly powerful head, facing to the left, wearing a rostral crown and with all his characteristic traits – particularly his deep-set eyes, stern mouth, and strong neck – excellently rendered (*Ill. 92*).[18] The legend reads M AGRIPPA L F COS III; and the reverse type is, appropriately enough, a standing figure of Neptune. These coins were copied by Titus' and Domitian's die-engravers for their 'restored' coin series.[19]

To turn to Agrippa's sculptural likeness – two profile portraits in relief are to be identified as his from their close correspondence with the coins. One is the very well-known veiled personage, facing to the left and with a child clutching his toga, who walks behind the axe-bearer and *flamines* in the processional scene of the imperial family on the south side of the precinct wall of the Ara Pacis Augustae.[20] Whether Agrippa functions here as deputy for Lepidus, the disgraced and banished pontifex maximus, whose place (according to Festus' *ordo sacerdotum*) was immediately behind the *flamines*, or simply in his capacity as *quindecimvir sacris faciundis*, there can be no doubt at all that we have his portrait here, made to look somewhat younger than he was on 4 July 13 BC, when this ceremony for the altar's foundation took place. The distinctive brow, furrowed and with its lower portion projecting, the deep-set eyes, firm mouth, full throat and somewhat flabby cheeks are all characteristic of him. The nose is restored.

Much less familiar is the fragment of a historical relief, 13½ in. (34.5 cm.) high, found in Athens and now in the Museum of Fine Arts, Boston, which carries Agrippa's rightward-facing head.[21] The bare head is almost perfectly preserved and presents most vividly all his familiar traits as seen at an age somewhat younger than that of the Ara Pacis *velatus*. Here are the close-fitting cap of hair, receding above the temples, the projecting lower part of the brow with the transverse furrows above it, extremely deep-set eyes, a large, aquiline nose, a set mouth and a full throat. Since Agrippa was well known in Greece, his portrayal there on some public monuments need cause no surprise.

Of the genuine portraits of Agrippa in the round, one is the finest and best preserved, and perhaps

features without a beard;[11] others again are posthumous, dating from *c*. 11–9 BC, and have on some specimens excellent likenesses of him.[12] Quite a number of these twin-headed pieces were struck as late as Julio-Claudian times.[13] Agrippa's important activities in Gaul and his very considerable contribution to the naval victory at Actium and subsequent incorporation of Egypt into the Roman Empire readily explain his continuing prominent appearance beside Octavian in this long-lived COL NEM series.

Agrippa's naval and military achievements are further commemorated on coins of Roman mintage. On aurei struck by the moneyer C. Sulpicius Platorinus in 13 BC, Augustus' head appears on the obverse and Agrippa's head on the reverse, facing to the right and wearing a combined mural and rostral crown. His name, M AGRIPPA, is inscribed beside him, along with that of the moneyer; and although the face is youngish, the eyes, nose, mouth and chin are all distinctive of Agrippa.[14] On the same moneyer's denarii, however, Agrippa's right-

93 M. Vipsanius Agrippa:
marble head from the Roman
theatre at Butrinto.

the earliest that we possess, is the marble head, broken off from a statue, that was found in the Roman theatre at Butrinto (Buthrotum), in modern Albania, in 1929 (*Ill. 93*).[22] It is a youngish likeness, comparable to that on the Puteoli(?) coin (cf. *Ill. 89*), and perhaps carved about 35 BC. It is rather fuller in the face than most of the sculptural representations of him, with his characteristic hair-style, brow, eyes, mouth (here slightly less firmly set than elsewhere) and throat. The piece is 14 in. (35·5 cm) high.[23]

Among the fairly numerous other marble and bronze portrait heads in the round that have been identified, many of them obviously quite in-correctly, as Agrippa's likenesses, three stand out as unquestionably genuine representations of him. The magnificent marble bust, found at Gabii in the eighteenth century and now in the Louvre, is a copy – probably Claudian – of an original dating from *c.* 30–27 BC, since it presents him as older than he was at the time when the Puteoli(?) coin portrait was engraved and already arrived at the height of his powers (*Ill. 94*).[24] Only the tip of the nose is restored; and all the facial traits are superbly rendered – in particular, the frowning brows above the deep-set eyes, the slightly scornful mouth, the double chin and the thick, creased neck.

The colossal marble head, probably once let into a cuirass-statue, now in the Capitoline Museum,[25] is said to have been found near the Pantheon; and it could possibly be the original head of the statue of himself that Agrippa set up, along with one of Augustus, in the vestibule of the Pantheon;[26] or it could be a replacement of the original head, since some, at any rate, of the Pantheon statues were struck by lightning in 22 BC.[27] All the familiar Agrippan features are present, but the cheeks have fallen in somewhat, so that the cheek-bones are visible, and there are 'crow's feet' at the outer corners of the eyes. In this likeness Agrippa is older, sadder, and in less good health than he was when the Louvre portrait's original was carved; and the Capitoline head must date from not so very long before his death, say *c.* 25–15 BC. The statues in the Pantheon vestibule could have been erected some years after the building itself was completed; and the replacements for the damaged statues need not have been made at once.

Thirdly, the Ny Carlsberg Glyptotek, Copen-hagen, possesses the remnant of a first-rate original portrait of Agrippa, worked in Pentelic marble.[28] Agrippa wears a mural crown, his brow is heavily furrowed, and his face is pinched and pointed, with the cheek-bones showing through the skin. The

94 M. Vipsanius Agrippa:
marble bust from Gabii (Louvre,
Paris).

nearest numismatic parallel is the portrait on Cossus Lentulus' denarii, issued in 12 BC, around the time of Agrippa's death (cf. p. 65).

An onyx cameo in Vienna shows a head with a number of Agrippa's standard traits – projecting brow, deep-set eyes, aquiline nose, set mouth, double chin and thick neck.[29]

1 ii, 79: 'parendi, sed uni scientissimus, aliis sane imperandi cupidus'.
2 *NH*, xxxv, 4 (26).
3 Grant 1946, pp. 46–7, pl. 1, no. 13; Sydenham 1952, p. 214, no. 1367; DC, xlviii, 50.
4 Grant 1946, p. 249, pl. 9, no. 2.
5 Ibid., pp. 171–2, pl. 5, no. 29.
6 For a bronze coin portrait of Agrippa, facing right, probably struck at Saguntum not long after Actium, see ibid., p. 159, pl. 6, no. 8.
7 Ibid., pp. 255, 258, pl. 8, no. 17.
8 Ibid., p. 255, pl. 8, no. 16.
9 Ibid., pp. 70–9.
10 Ibid., pp. 73–4, pl. 2, nos. 17, 18.
11 Ibid., p. 74, pl. 2, nos. 19, 23.
12 Ibid., p. 74, pl. 2, nos. 20–22.
13 Ibid., pp. 75–6, pl. 2, no. 24, pl. 3, nos. 1–12. Cf. H. Mattingly, *Roman Coins*, 2nd ed., 1960, pl. 48, no. 3; also *NC* ser. 7, vi, 1966, pp. 95–124; *American Numismatic Society Museum Notes*, xix, 1974, pp. 65–86.
14 Grueber 1910, ii, p. 96, no. 4653; iii, pl. 71, no. 7; *BMCCRE*, i, 1923, p. 23, nos. 110, 111, pl. 4, no. 6.
15 Grueber 1910, ii, p. 97, nos. 4654–6; iii, pl. 71, no. 8; *BMCCRE*, i, p. 23, nos. 112–14, pl. 4, no. 7.
16 Grueber 1910, ii, p. 101, no. 4671; iii, pl. 72, no. 1; *BMCCRE*, i, p. 25, no. 121, pl. 4, no. 12.
17 Ibid., i, p. cxxxiii. Cf. *NC* and *American Numismatic Society Museum Notes* (see note 13 above).
18 Ibid., i, pp. 142–3, nos. 161–8, pl. 26, no. 7.
19 Ibid., ii, 1930, pp. 285, 416, nos. 281, 510, pl. 54, no. 9, pl. 83, no. 1.
20 L. M. Ugolini, 'L'Agrippa di Butrinto' in *R. Istituto d'Archeologia e Storia dell'Arte*, iv, 1932, pl. 6 (on right).; G. Moretti, *Ara Pacis Augustae*, 1948, p. 15, figs. 3, 4, p. 228, fig. 171, pl. A; J. M. C. Toynbee, 'The Ara Pacis Reconsidered, etc.', in *Proceedings of the British Academy*, xxxix, 1953, pp. 83–4, pl. 17).
21 C. Vermeule, *Roman Imperial Art in Greece and Asia Minor*, 1968, p. 176, fig. 108; *Greek and Roman portraits 470 B.C.–A.D. 500: Boston Museum of Fine Arts*, 1972, pl. 41.
22 Ugolini, op. cit., pls. 1–3.
23 For what is probably another somewhat youthful and idealized portrait head of Agrippa of eastern provenance, from Magnesia-on-the-Maeander, see C. Blümel, *Staatliche Museen zu Berlin: römische Bildnisse*, 1933, pp. 7–8, no. R 15, pl. 10.
24 *RM*, xlviii, 1933, pls. 30, 31; Ugolini, op. cit., pls. 4 (on left), 6 (on left).
25 *RM*, xlviii, 1933, pls. 40, 41.
26 DC, liii, 27: ἐν δὲ τῷ προνάῳ τοῦ τε Αὐγούστου καὶ ἑαυτοῦ ἀνδριάντας ἔστησε.
27 Ibid., liv, 1.
28 *RM*, xlviii, 1933, pls. 42, 43.
29 Ugolini, op. cit., p. 9, fig. 8.

PUBLIUS SITTIUS

Ill. 95

P. Sittius, an equestrian friend of Cicero, was suspected of sympathy with Catiline; he then established himself as an adventurer in Mauretania, where he exerted influence over Kings Bocchus and Bogud. In the civil war he supported Caesar, creating with Bocchus in 46 B C a diversion in Numidia. Caesar gave him the best portions of Masinissa's and Juba's territories;[1] and there he settled with his followers, the Sittiani. He was assassinated in 44 B C; and the bronze coins that he struck date from the last few months of his life (*Ill. 95*).[2]

On the obverses of these coins Sittius' head, slightly tilted upwards, faces to the right. He has crisp hair, a short nose, a long upper lip, a small mouth with slightly parted lips, a protruding chin, and a thin neck with a small 'Adam's apple'. Sittius issued his coins on his property, which was probably Simitthu, and on them he describes himself as IIIIVIR [*Quattuorvir*] DECR(*eto*) DECUR(*ionum*), striking at his own expense, D(*e*) S(*ua*) P(*ecunia*). His other title, MVCONIANVS, has been ingeniously interpreted by Grant as MU(*nicipi*) CON(*stitutor*) I(*ulii*) A(*ntonii*) NV(*midici*) S(*imitthensium*). Sittius was, then, a local magistrate and the actual founder of a *municipium* that had been planned by Caesar and Antonius.

1 Appian, *Bell. Civ.* iv, 54.
2 Grant 1946, pp. 178–81, pl. 6, nos. 15, 16.

QUINTUS HORTENSIUS HORTALUS

Ill. 96

Q. Hortensius Hortalus was a republican and the uncle of Brutus, to whom he was subordinate. In a speech delivered on 16 March 44 B C Brutus promised to confirm Julius Caesar's grants of land, hence Hortensius' appointment as *praefectus* with a *provincia* that included Achaia, Macedonia and part of Illyria, in order to carry out his nephew's conciliatory schemes of colonization. Colonial coinage shows that he established both Dium and Cassandrea before he was killed at Philippi. The reverse types of the bronze coins that Hortensius struck in Macedonia are a plough, a *vexillum*, and a yoke, all symbols of colonial foundations; and Hortensius is described in his legend as PRAEF(*ectus*) COLON(*iis*) DEDV(*cendis*) (*Ill. 96*).[1]

Hortensius' portrait shows a very square head facing to the right. He has a tuft of hair above the brow, a long, hooked nose, a small, firm mouth and a square jaw. His glance is directed slightly upwards.

1 Grant 1946, pp. 33–5, pl. 2, nos. 7, 8.

95   P. Sittius: obverse of denarius, 44 B C.

96   Q. Hortensius Hortalus: reverse of bronze coin struck in Macedonia, *c.* 44 B C.

97   C. Caninius Rebilus: obverse of bronze coin struck at Cephaloedium, *c.* 43 B C.

Caius Caninius Rebilus
Ill. 97

This Rebilus must be the proscribed man of that name who in 43 BC joined Sextus Pompeius in Sicily. His bronze coins bear the reverse legend ΚΕΦΑ and were struck at Cephaloedium, of which *municipium* they were probably foundation issues (*Ill 97*).[1] He had served under Caesar against Vercingetorix (52 BC), fought in Africa under Curio and at Thapsus, and later at Munda. Caesar appointed him consul suffectus for a few hours during the last day of 45 BC.

Rebilus' head faces rightwards and is again tilted upwards. He has a thick mat of hair on the nape of the neck, a straight nose, and a jutting chin.

1   Grant 1946, pp. 30, 192–3, pl. 12, no. 28.

Marcus Sempronius Rutilus
Ill. 98

This M. Sempronius Rutilus can be identified with the Caesarian who was second-in-command to T. Labienus in his campaign against the Sequani in 59 BC.[1] The bronze coins struck by him, executed in a manner strongly suggestive of an Asia Minor mint, have as their obverse legend M RVTILVS PROCOS COL(*oniam*) IVL(*iam*) [*deduxit*], with the reverse type of a colonist ploughing with a pair of humped oxen.[2] In Asia Minor the humped ox is commonly found in Caria, Lycaonia, and neighbouring areas; and therefore the colony which Rutilus founded is likely to have been in those parts, which, however, passed out of Roman hands in 38–36 BC. Of all the colonies in that region Lystra alone bore the title of *Iulia*, not *Iulia Augusta*; and, moreover, a later coin inscribed LYSTRA has the same ploughing-with-humped-oxen motif.[3] Lystra would seem, therefore, to have been the colony that Rutilus founded or colonized;[4] and the most probable date for his proconsulship there is the early months of 43 BC, when P. Cornelius Dolabella was governor of Asia and must have left a deputy proconsul behind him when he himself departed for Syria, whose governorship he was intending to seize.[5]

The portrait head, facing right, on the obverses of Rutilus' coins (*Ill. 98*) presents an amazingly veristic likeness. He is grossly fat, with a large fleshy face. He has cropped hair, a low brow, mean eyes, an aquiline nose, a weak mouth with parted lips, a sagging double chin, and a thick neck. He looks stupid and bloated, as well as far advanced in years.

1   Caesar, *Bellum Gallicum* vii, 90, 4.
2   Grant 1946, p. 238, pl. 8, nos. 8, 9.
3   Ibid., pl. 8, no. 10.
4   Ibid., pp. 239–40.
5   Ibid., p. 242.

Lucius Sempronius Atratinus
Ill. 99

A Greek incription found at Hypata in Thessaly shows that L. Sempronius Atratinus was *legatus propraetore* of Marcus Antonius in Achaia.[1] His governorship must have been held between 39 and 37 BC, before the Sicilian campaign. After the treaty of Tarentum he took an Antonine squadron to help Octavian against Sextus Pompeius (36 BC). When Antonius abdicated the consulship on 1 January 34 BC, Atratinus became consul suffectus for six months. Later he went over to Octavian and became proconsul of Africa, receiving a triumph on his return (21 BC). He committed suicide in AD 7.

The obverse of a bronze coin struck by him at Sparta bears his name – ΑΤΡΑΤΙΝΟϹ – and realistic portrait head, facing to the right. He has a turned-up nose, a slightly smiling mouth and a square jaw (*Ill. 99*).[2]

1   *Inscriptiones Latinae Selectae*, no. 9461: ἡ πόλις Ὑπάτα Λ[ο]ύκιον Σενπρ[ώ]νιον Βηστία υἱὸν ᾿Ατρατῖνον πρεσβωτὰν καὶ ἀντιστάτηγον, τὸν ἴδιον εὐεργέταν.
2   Grant 1946, p. 382, pl. 12, no. 3.

98   M. Sempronius Rutilus: obverse of bronze coin, *c.*43 BC.

99   L. Sempronius Atratinus: obverse of bronze coin, *c.*39–37 BC.

Marcus Tullius Cicero Iunior
Ill. 100

M. Tullius Cicero Iunior was the only son of the orator and Terentia. He served in Greece under Brutus, but after Philippi he joined Sextus Pompeius. He was Octavian's colleague in the consulship of September 30 BC and was proconsul of Asia and governor of Syria under Augustus. A bronze coin struck at Magnesia-ad-Sipylum has on the obverse the Younger Cicero's rightward-facing head with the legend ΜΑΡΚΟΣ ΤΥΛΛΙΟΣ ΚΙΚΕΡΩΝ (*Ill. 100*).[1] He has deep-set eyes, a straight nose, a firm mouth and a rather square jaw. This pleasant, but not particularly intelligent, face corresponds with the Elder Seneca's assessment of him.[2]

1 Grant 1946, p. 385, pl. 9, no. 32.
2 *Suasoriae* vii, 13: 'cum M. Tullius, filius Ciceronis, Asiam obtineret, homo qui nihil ex paterno ingenio habuit praeter urbanitatem'.

Thorius Flaccus
Ill. 101

Thorius Flaccus was proconsul of Bithynia, 29–28 BC. Bronze coins struck at Nicaea bear on their reverses the legend ΕΠΙ ΑΝΘΥΠΑΤΟΥ ΘΩΡΙΟΥ ΦΛΑ and on the obverses ΝΙΚΑΙΕΩΝ, with Flaccus' portrait facing to the right (*Ill. 101*).[1] It shows him with head and neck slightly thrust forward, a prominent lower brow, a long, straight nose, a small mouth and large ears.

1 Grant 1946, pp. 384, 396, pl. 12, no. 9.

Publius Vedius Pollio (died 15 BC)
Ill. 102

P. Vedius Pollio, the wealthy son of a freedman, was made a knight by Octavian. This friend and helper of Augustus was cruel and luxurious: he is said to have punished slaves by throwing them alive to his lampreys. The obverses of bronze coins of Tralles show Pollio's head facing right and the legends ΠΟΛΛΙΩΝ or ΟΥΗΔΙΟΣ ΚΑΙΣΑΡΕΩΝ (*Ill. 102*).[1] After Actium Tralles had been refounded as a stipendiary city, with a nucleus of Roman residents and the name Caesarea. Of two inscriptions both from Ephesus mentioning Pollio, one is a pronouncement *ex constitutione Vedi Pollionis*.[2] As Grant points out, such a decree by a mere knight would have been impossible after proconsular government in Asia had been restored in 29–28 BC. His post at Tralles must therefore have been held between 31 and 29 BC.

Pollio is depicted with hair growing low on a long, thin neck. His eyes and ears are large and his nose is up-turned.

1 Grant 1946, pp. 382–3, 385, pl. 9, no. 31.
2 *Corpus Inscriptionum Latinarum* iii, 7124.

100   M. Tullius Cicero Iunior: obverse of bronze coin struck at Magnesia ad Sipylum.

101   Thorius Flaccus: obverse of bronze coin struck at Nicaea, *c.* 29–28 BC.

102   P. Vedius Pollio: obverse of bronze coin struck at Tralles, *c.* 31–29 BC.

VALERIUS MESSALA POTITUS (*c.* 75–17 BC)
Ill. 103

Valerius Messala Potitus was the son of Marcus Valerius Messala Niger, consul in 61 BC, by his first marriage and the half-brother of the more famous Valerius Messala Corvinus, Niger's son by his

103 V. Messala Potitus: obverse of bronze coin struck at Aezani, *c.* 28/24 BC.

104 Appius Claudius Pulcher: obverse of bronze coin struck at Apamea(?), 27 BC.

105 Cn. Statius Scribonius Libo: obverse of bronze coin struck at Saguntum(?), *c.* 28 BC.

second marriage with Pola, who served first under Marcus Antonius and then under Octavian at Actium and was patron of a literary circle. Potitus was consul suffectus in 29 BC and proconsul of Asia either *c.* 28 BC (if M. Grant is right in assuming that infractions of the *Lex Pompeia*, requiring a five-year interval after consulships, were frequent during this period)[1] or *c.* 24 BC.

A bronze coin struck at Aezani in Phrygia and known from three examples shows on the obverse Potitus' portrait facing left (*Ill. 102*).[2] He has a high brow, a narrow face, an aquiline nose, a firm mouth and a remarkably long, thin and creased neck. The obverse legend reads ΜΕΣΣΑΛΑΣ ΠΟΤΙΤ, that on the reverse ΕΖΕΑΝΙΤΩΝ.

1 Grant 1946, p. 385.
2 *British Museum Quarterly*, xxii, pp. 72, 74, pl. 23, no. 9; H. Hommel, 'Porträtmünze des Valerius Messala Potitus, Proconsul der Provinz Asia ca. 24 v. Chr.' in *Congresso internazionale di numismatica, Roma Settembre 1961, vol. ii Atti*, 1965, pp. 301–5, pl. 22, nos. 1, 2.

APPIUS CLAUDIUS PULCHER (consul 38 BC)
Ill. 104

Appius Claudius Pulcher, a nephew of the consul of 54 BC who had supported Pompeius, was one of the early aristocrats to join the young Octavian: he held a triumph from Spain in 33–32 BC. He is described on the obverse of a bronze coin struck in Asia Minor, probably at Apamea (*Ill. 104*),[1] with his rightward-facing portrait, as PROCOS. This coin, and others of the same group, with Augustus' head and titles on the obverse and no portrait of Pulcher, refer to a refoundation of the colony – C(*oloniam*) R(*estituit*): and Pulcher must have been entrusted with this task. But Pulcher himself does not bear any city-founder title (e.g. *deductor* or *conditor*), since by 27 BC, when he was proconsul, the function of founding colonies was in theory reserved to Augustus.

Pulcher, who faces to the right has thick, curly hair, a large nose, a set mouth, and a heavy chin, apparently bearded.

1 Grant 1946, pp. 255–8, pl. 8, no. 14.

CNAEUS STATIUS SCRIBONIUS LIBO
Ill. 105

Cnaeus Statius Scribonius Libo, otherwise unknown to history, has his portrait on the obverse of a bronze coin probably struck at the *municipium* of Saguntum in Spain in *c.* 28 BC (*Ill. 105*).[1] Described as PRAEF(*ectus*) and SACERDOS, he seems to have held an exceptional position in connection with the foundation of the town as a Roman municipality: as sole *praefectus iure dicundo* he acted for Augustus who had accepted the duovirate of the city for a year. The portrait is a remarkably realistic one, with a long, straight nose, a set mouth, flesh hanging in folds on the cheeks, and a long, thin neck.

1 Grant 1946, pp. 158, 162–3, pl. 6, no. 9.

106 M. Atius Balbus: obverse of bronze coin struck at Uselis, c. 37 B C.

MARCUS ATIUS BALBUS
Ill. 106

Otherwise unknown to history, M. Atius Balbus must have been the son of the man with the same name who was praetor in 59 B C, and thus a brother of Atia, Octavian's mother. Bronze coins bearing on their obverses his name and title, M ATIVS BALBVS P R, were issued at Uselis in Sardinia, probably in the years immediately after Octavian's occupation of the island in 38 B C (*Ill. 106*).[1] The initial letters P R could then stand for P(*atronus*) R(*eipublicae*) and in that case Atius would have been patron and founder of the *municipium* of Uselis.

Atius' head faces to the left. It is squarely built and he has very large eyes, short, thick hair receding at the sides, heavy, fat cheeks, nose and brow forming a continuous straight line, a weak chin and a thick neck.

1 Grant 1946, pp. 150–2, pl. 6, no. 4.

107 T. Statilius Taurus: obverse of bronze coin struck at Lipara, 36 B C.

TITUS STATILIUS TAURUS
(consul suffectus 37 B C; consul II 26)
Ill. 107

T. Statilius Taurus was a Lucanian *novus homo* and Octavian's greatest military leader after Agrippa, distinguishing himself particularly in the Sicilian war in 36 B C. After the conquest of Sicily he secured Africa and held a triumph in 34 B C. He commanded the land forces at Actium and led operations in Spain in 29 B C and was *praefectus urbi* in 16 B C. The date of his death is not known.

On bronze coins struck in 36 B C at Lipara (a naval base of Octavian) bearing his name, STATI, and that of Trebonius, who may have been his quaestor, Taurus is sometimes entitled IMP (*Ill. 107*).[1] He was first saluted *imperator* after Naulochus in 36 B C. His portrait, facing to the right, on the obverse is encircled by an oak-wreath and shows distinctive features – a very square head, a large nose, a small mouth and a heavy jaw.

1 Grant 1946, pp. 52–4, pl. 2, no. 13.

LUCIUS RUFINUS
Ill. 108

A bronze coin struck at Chalcis in Euboea by the procurator of Achaia, probably c. 28 B C, bears the obverse legend Λ ΡΟΥΦΙΝΟΣ ΑΝΘΥΠΑΤΟΣ and Rufinus' portrait facing to the right: on the reverse is the legend ΧΑΛΚΙΣ (*Ill. 108*).[1] As proconsul he would have governed Achaia either before or after Agrippa's eastern command, i.e. close to 18 or 13 B C. Rufinus, whose head is slightly tilted up, has thick, lanky hair, a very large aquiline nose, a small, determined mouth, and a long, very thin neck.

1 Grant 1946, pp. 385–7, pl. 12, no. 1.

MESCINIUS
Ill. 109

Again on a bronze coin of Chalcis in Euboea is an obverse head, labelled ΜΕΣΚΙΝΙΟΣ ΣΤΡΑ [τηγός]. The man in question was thus a praetorian *legatus*,

108 L. Rufinus: obverse of bronze coin struck at Chalcis, *c.*28 BC.

109 Mescinius: obverse of bronze coin struck at Chalcis, *c.*16–13 BC.

an agent of Agrippa, in virtue of the latter's large *provincia*, which gave him authority in Achaia (*Ill. 109*).[1] Mescinius has a straight nose forming an unbroken line with his brow, large eyes, a small mouth, and a long neck.

1 Grant 1946, pp. 385–7, pl. 12, no. 2.

Marcus Pompeius Macer
Ill. 110
M. Pompeius Macer was Augustus' librarian[1] and proconsul of Asia early in his principate. As an *amicus principis* his portrait appears on the obverse of a bronze coin of Priene, with the legend … ΟΣ ΜΑΚΕΡ and ΠΡΙΗΝΕΩΝ on the reverse (*Ill. 110*).[2] This unusual grant of the right of portraiture to a knight illustrates the prestige which members of this order could enjoy when favoured by Augustus. Macer has a thick cap of hair, a receding brow, an aquiline nose, a thin, pointed face, with a slight beard and a long neck.

1 Suetonius, *Iulius* 56: 'Pompeium Macrum, cui ordinandas bibliothecas delegaverat [sc. Augustus]'.
2 Grant 1946, pp. 388–9, pl. 9, no. 34.

110 M. Pompeius Macer: obverse of bronze coin struck at Priene, *c.*27 BC.

Aulus Ambatus
Ill. 111
On the reverse of a large bronze coin struck at the *municipium* of Zama Regia in Africa, with Augustus' head and name on the obverse, is the portrait head of A. Ambatus, with the legend A AMBATVS PRAEF(*ectus*) ITER(*um*) IVLIA SAMARE (*Ill. 111*).[1] The issue must date from 27–26 BC, since Octavian is already Augustus and the city is still 'Iulia'. Ambatus acted as *adsignator* of the new *municipium* both for the governor of Africa (the *constitutor*) and as representative of Augustus who was *duovir*: since he remained in office for a second year (*praefectus*

111 A. Ambatus: reverse of bronze coin struck at Zama Regia, 27–26 BC.

iterum) the *municipium* must have been founded in
29–28 BC. About the same time portraits were
allowed to two other special *adsignatores*, Cn.
Statius Scribonius Libo and Appius Claudius Pulcher (qq.v.).

Ambatus' portrait faces to the right and is on a
large scale – larger than that of Augustus' head. He
has a very square head, with an upstanding tuft of
hair above the brow. The face as a whole is heavy
and slightly up-turned. The eyes are large and the
nose is aquiline, the mouth small and somewhat
pursed up, the chin, which carries a beard, juts out,
and the neck is very thick. Ambatus looks, in fact,
like the Berber that he was: but his name is Celtic.

1 Grant 1946, pp. 182–4, pl. 6, no. 13.

AFRICANUS FABIUS MAXIMUS
Ill. 112

A bronze coin struck at Hadrumetum in Africa
bears on its obverse the legend AFR(*icanus*) FA(*bius*)
MAX(*imus*) PROCOS VIIVIR EPVLO and the head of
Africanus (consul in 10 BC) facing to the right: on
the reverse is an African elephant trampling on a
serpent. Africanus' proconsulship can be dated to
*c.*6–5 BC. He was related to Augustus by marriage.
This portrait shows him with a thick cap of hair, an
aquiline nose, and a rather stern mouth.[1] Another
coin from the same mint carries on the reverse a
very similar portrait of Africanus, on a larger scale,
and with the legend AFRIC(*anus*) FABIVS MAX(*imus*)
COS PROCOS VIIVIR EPVL(*o*).[2] Yet a third bronze coin
portrait of Africanus, issued at Hippo Diarrhytus,
with the head of Claudius Nero (Tiberius) on the
reverse, depicts him on the obverse facing to the left
and with lankier hair, a more projecting nose, and
a small 'Adam's apple' below the chin, while the
neck is thinner than on either of the other likenesses. The accompanying legend is FABIO AF-
RICANO (*Ill. 112*).[3]

1 Grant 1946, pp. 139–40, pl. 4, no. 28.
2 Ibid., p. 228, pl. 7, no. 28.
3 Ibid., p. 224, pl. 6, no. 24.

PAULLUS FABIUS MAXIMUS (11 BC)
Ill. 113

Paullus Fabius Maximus, brother of Africanus, was
consul in 11 BC and governor of Asia, possibly in 9
or 5–4 BC, and belonged to Augustus' circle of *amici*.
This patron of literature was characterized by the
orator Cassius Severus as 'quasi disertus es, quasi
formosus es, quasi dives es; unum tantum es non

quasi, vappa' (Seneca, *Controversiae* ii, 4, 11). He
showed favour to Ovid and perhaps to Horace (e.g.
Ovid, *Ex ponto* i, 2, 1; iii, 3, 2; in his *Odes* Horace
dedicated Book IV, no. 1, to him: 'centum puer
artium'). Bronze coins of Hierapolis show his
portrait on the obverses, facing to the right with
hair and features very similar to those on the first

112 Africanus Fabius Maximus: obverse of bronze coin
struck at Hadrumetum, *c.*6–5 BC.

113 Paullus Fabius Maximus: obverse of bronze coin
struck at Hierapolis, *c.*9 or 5–4 BC.

two coin series of his brother, but with a more
unpleasant mouth and a long scraggy neck, on
which appears a small 'Adam's apple': the legend
reads ΦΑΒΙΟΣ ΜΑΞΙΜΟΣ (*Ill. 113*).[1]

1 Grant 1946, pp. 229, 387, pl. 11, no. 58.

LUCIUS VOLUSIUS SATURNINUS
Ill. 114

A bronze coin of L. Volusius Saturninus was struck
at Achulla in Africa probably sometime before 6–5

BC.[1] It bears the reverse legend L VOLVSIVS SATVRN and displays the head of the proconsul facing to the right. He has a very large nose, full, slightly parted lips, a jutting chin, and a slender neck. The obverse legend is ACHVLLA.

1 Grant 1946, pp. 228, 230, pl. 7, no. 29.

114 L. Volusius Saturninus: reverse of coin struck at Achulla, before 6–5 BC.

PUBLIUS QUINCTILIUS VARUS (consul 13 BC)
Ill. 115

Favoured by Augustus, P. Quinctilius Varus became proconsul of Africa probably *c.* 7–6 or 4–3 BC, and was then legate of Syria. He is best known for his disastrous defeat, with the loss of three legions, and suicide in the Teutoberger Forest in AD 9.

115 P. Quinctilius Varus: reverse of bronze coin struck at Achulla, *c.* 7–6 or 4–3 BC.

A bronze coin issued at Achulla bears on the reverse the legend P QVINCTILI VARI ACHVLLA and the head of the proconsul facing right (*Ill. 115*).[1] Varus' likeness vividly illustrates Velleius Paterculus' characterization of him as 'sluggish in mind and body, fitter for leisurely camp-life than for warfare'.[2] His head is tilted upwards, with a vacant expression in his eyes. He has broad cheeks, a pointed nose that thickens at the tip, a heavy jowl, a weak, inane-looking mouth, and a thick, squat neck.

1 Grant 1946, pp. 228, 230, pl. 7, no. 30.
2 ii, 117, 2: 'ut corpore ita animo immobilior, otio magis castrorum quam bellicae adsuetus militiae'.

116 C. Asinius Gallus: obverse of bronze coin struck at Temnus, *c.* 6–5 BC.

CAIUS ASINIUS GALLUS (consul 8 BC)
Ill. 116

C. Asinius Gallus, the son of Asinius Pollio, married Vipsania Agrippina (daughter of Agrippa) after Tiberius had been compelled by Augustus to divorce her (12 BC). This friend of the emperor was considered to be sufficiently ambitious to aspire to the principate (Tacitus, *Annals* i, 13). He was governor of Syria 6–5 BC. Later he offended Tiberius and died in AD 33 after three years' imprisonment. His bronze coins struck at Temnus owe their obverse portraits of him, facing to the right, with the legend ΑΣΙΝΙΟΣ ΓΑΛΛΟΣ ΑΓΝΟΣ, to his *amicitia* with Augustus (*Ill. 116*).[1] The term ἁγνός 'gives his position a religious flavour', as Grant points out. Gallus has a thinnish, tapering face, a slightly upturned nose, a small mouth, a pointed chin and a slender neck. A small tuft of hair rises above the centre of his brow.

1 Grant 1946, pp. 387–8, pl. 9, no. 33.

PART II

Foreign Rulers
(3rd century BC – AD 5th century)

Egypt

PTOLEMY II PHILADELPHOS (285–246 BC) and
ARSINOË II PHILADELPHOS
Ills. 117–20
Ptolemy II reigned jointly with his father from 285
BC, and succeeded in his own right in 283 BC; he
married Arsinoë II *c.*276 BC. He was the first
Egyptian king to enter into relations of friendship
with Rome. In 273 BC, after Rome's defeat of
Pyrrhus, he took the initiative by sending envoys to
Rome to establish *amicitia* (φιλία) with her.[1] Appian
tells us that the Carthaginians sent an embassy to
Ptolemy with a view to getting 2,000 talents from
him. But since he enjoyed the friendship of both
Rome and Carthage, he tried to reconcile the two
parties; and, when he failed to do so, declared that
one must fight alongside one's friends against one's
enemies and not against one's friends.[2] The friendship established with Rome on terms of equality
lasted till 204 BC.[3] The statement in Livy's *Epitome*
that Rome had a formal alliance (*societas*) with
Ptolemy[4] thus conflicts both with Livy himself and
with the other ancient authorities. Ptolemy organized the bureaucratic administration of Egypt,

and built much in Alexandria, including the
museum, library and lighthouse (Pharos).

The portraits of Ptolemy II and of his son and
successor Ptolemy III are not always easy to tell
apart. However, a bronze coin, probably minted in
Cyrenaica, shows on the obverse a head, facing to
the right (as in the case of all Ptolemaic royal coin
portraits), with Ptolemy II's characteristic heavy
facial features, jutting chin and small, thick-lipped
mouth. (*Ill. 117*).[5] Portraits with untidy hair encircled by a diadem and sometimes with a lion-skin
knotted tightly round the neck, occurring on silver
tetradrachms, have been variously identified as
Ptolemy II[6] and Ptolemy III.[7] Certain likenesses
of Ptolemy II are on the gold octadrachms and
tetradrachms issued by Ptolemy III with the jugate
heads of Ptolemy I and his queen Berenice I on the
reverse and those of Ptolemy II and his sister/
queen Arsinoë II on the obverse (*Ill. 118*).[8] Here
Ptolemy II's bust is draped and his diademed hair
more neatly arranged. Still neater is the hair of the
draped busts on a coin said to be in Brussels[9] and
a gem in the Ashmolean Museum, Oxford (*Ill.*

117–19   Ptolemy II Philadelphos: obverse of bronze coin, probably minted at Cyrenaica; obverse of gold octadrachm
(Ptolemy and Arsinoë II jugate); and gem portrait.

119),[10] both of which show features closely resembling those of Ptolemy II on Ptolemy III's issues, where he sometimes sports sideburns. No portraits in the round can be firmly identified as Ptolemy II.

Arsinoë II had great influence on Ptolemy and his policies. As seen beside her brother/husband, she is veiled(?), with her hair in stiff waves. Her chin is very similar to his and she has a very long, straight nose with down-turned tip. She died in 270 BC and was honoured after death with her portraits on the obverses of gold and silver coins issued by her

5 *BMCGC Ptolemies*, 1883, pl. 6, no. 12.
6 *JDAI*, xlv, 1930, pl. 2, no. 17, pl. 3, nos. 1–8.
7 *BMCGC Ptolemies*, 1883, pl. 9, nos. 4–6; Newell 1937, p. 89, pl. 15, nos. 6, 7; Richter 1965, fig. 1807.
8 *BMCGC Ptolemies*, 1883, pl. 7, nos. 1–7; *JDAI*, xlv, 1930, pl. 2, nos. 14–16; Newell 1937, pl. 15, no. 3; Richter 1965, figs. 1779, 1781; Davis and Kraay 1973, pls. 15, 16, 18, 19.
9 Richter 1965, fig. 1801.
10 Ibid., fig. 1784.
11 BMCGC Ptolemies, 1883, pl. 8, nos. 1–10; *JDAI*, xlv, 1930, pl. 3, no. 17; Newell 1937, pl. 15, no. 2, and p. 91, fig. 11; Richter 1965, figs. 1802, 1836; Davis and Kraay 1973, pls. 20–22.
12 *AJA*, lix, 1955, pp. 199–206, pls. 54, 55.

PTOLEMY III EUERGETES (246–221 BC) and BERENICE II
Ills. 121–3

Ptolemy III maintained his father's friendly relations with Rome, but showed his independence by declining an offer of assistance against Antiochus of Syria which is alleged to have been made, at the end of the First Punic War, by a Roman embassy.[1]

We have already noted the coin portraits variously attributed to Ptolemy II (q.v.) and Ptolemy III. Bronze coins show the latter laureate and draped in the aegis of Zeus.[2] Silver coins depict him with diademed hair, a lion's skin knotted tightly round his throat, and thick folds of flesh on his neck (*Ill. 121*).[3] Most striking are the gold octadrachm portraits, probably struck at the beginning of his successor's reign, where he wears a radiate crown and an aegis and is accompanied by a trident (*Ill. 122*).[4] The cheeks and neck are very heavy and fleshy, but the features – eyes, nose and mouth – are finely cut. The attributes betoken his successes in war (the Third Syrian War, 246–241 BC) through the aid of Helios, Zeus and Poseidon.

120 Arsinoë II: obverse of silver coin, posthumously minted.

husband and son (*Ill. 120*).[11] Here the queen is veiled and wears a diadem in her stiffly waved hair, which is gathered in a coil under the veil at the back of the head. The tip of a sceptre projects above the top of her head and a ram's horn can be seen beneath the ear. Again we note the long, straight, pointed nose, set mouth and firm chin. A small basalt head in a private collection in Athens has been recognized by D. B. Thompson as a portrait of Arsinoë II on the score of the ram's horn below the ear. But the facial features are too much mutilated to be identified as hers.[12]

1 Eutropius ii, 15: 'C. Fabio Licinio C. Claudio Canino consulibus anno urbis conditae quadringentesimo sexagesimo primo legati Alexandria a Ptolemaeo missi Romam venere et a Romanis amicitiam, quam petierant, obtinuerunt.' Cf. DC frag. 41.
2 *Sic.*, 1.
3 Livy xxvii, 4, 10 (210 BC): 'Alexandream ... legati ad commemorandam renovandamque amicitiam missi'.
4 *Epit.*, 14: 'cum Ptolemaeo Aegypti rege sociates iuncta est'.

121 Ptolemy III Euergetes: obverse of silver coin with laureate head.

122 Ptolemy III Euergetes: obverse of gold octadrachm showing radiate crown, probably struck posthumously.

123 Berenice II: obverse of silver dodecadrachm showing coiffure similar to that of Arsinoë II (*Ill. 120*).

Ptolemy III's wife, Berenice II, daughter of King Magus of Cyrene, is portrayed on the obverses of gold decadrachms and silver dodecadrachms (*Ill. 123*).[5] Her coiffure is much the same as that of Arsinoë II (cf. *Ill. 120*). She is diademed and either unveiled or veiled. Her cheeks and throat are full, her eyes large, and she has a delicately chiselled profile. An unveiled marble head at Benghazi, with the same 'melon' hair-style, a kiss-curl in front of each ear, full cheeks, and fine facial features, may well represent Berenice;[6] as may also a head found in Egypt and now in the Musée Mariemont in Brussels.[7] Ptolemy named a star 'The

Lock of Berenice' after her, as recorded by Callimachus and Catullus.

1 Eutropius iii, 1: 'finito igitur punico bello ... Romani ... legatos ad Ptolemaeum, Aegypti regem, miserunt auxilia promittentes, quia rex Syriae Antiochus bellum ei intulerat. ille gratias Romanis egit, auxilia non accepit.'
2 *BMCGC Ptolemies*, 1883, pl. 12, no. 2; *JDAI*, xlv, 1930, pl. 3, no. 13.
3 Ibid., pl. 3, no. 9; Richter 1965, fig. 1813.
4 *BMCGC Ptolemies*, 1883, pl. 12, nos. 3–5; *JDAI*, xlv, 1930, pl. 3, nos. 10–12; Newell 1937, pl. 15, no. 8; Richter 1965, fig. 1814; *JDAI*, lxxxviii, 1973, p. 201, fig. 4; Davis and Kraay 1973, pls. 23, 24, 27.
5 *BMCGC Ptolemies*, 1883, pl. 13, nos. 2–10; *JDAI*, xlv, 1930, pl. 3, no. 18; Newell 1937, pl. 15, no. 5; Richter 1965, figs. 1820–1; Davis and Kraay 1973, pls. 25, 26, 28.
6 Richter 1965, figs. 1822–3.
7 *L'Antiquité Classique*, xxxviii, 1969, pp. 89–100, pls. 1–4.

PTOLEMY IV PHILOPATOR (222–205 BC) and ARSINOË III

Ills. 124–7

Ptolemy IV continued to maintain his predecessor's *amicitia* with Rome. In 210 BC Rome begged from him a supply of corn to relieve her distress during the Second Punic War. It was on this or a separate occasion that M. Atilius and M' Acilius were sent to renew the friendship between Rome and Egypt (cf. p. 80, note 3) and to present the king and his consort with gifts – a toga, a purple tunic, and an ivory throne for him, an embroidered robe (*palla*) and a purple mantle (*amiculum*) for her.[1]

Silver coins depict Ptolemy IV as Dionysus, wearing a diadem entwined with ivy-leaves and with a *thyrsus* behind his shoulder (*Ill. 124*).[2] Other portraits on gold and silver coins show him with a thick cap of short curls, a diadem, and side-burns (*Ill. 125*).[3] The king has fat, heavy cheeks, a full

124 Ptolemy IV Philopator: obverse of silver coin depicting Ptolemy as Dionysos.

125   Ptolemy IV Philopator: obverse of silver coin.

127   Arsinoë III: obverse of gold octadrachm.

throat, and a slightly *retroussé* nose; his upper lip is short and his small mouth rather scornful. A diademed portrait head at Boston, which displays just these features, may well be a representation of Ptolemy (*Ill. 126*).[4]

Arsinoë III married her brother Ptolemy in 217 BC. In her gold octadrachm portraits she is shown wearing a diadem, ear-rings, and a necklace, and has her side locks gathered back into a thick role on the nape of the neck. She presents a somewhat

126   Ptolemy IV Philopator: marble head with features resembling this king's coin portraits (Museum of Fine Arts, Boston).

proud and disdainful expression. Her eyes are large, her cheeks full and fat, her nose straight, but her small mouth is not unlike that of her brother/husband. Folds of flesh ring her throat. A sceptre appears, now behind her head, now below the roll of hair at her neck (*Ill. 127*).[5] Arsinoë is said to have been murdered either shortly before or just after Ptolemy IV's death; and Livy must therefore be wrong in giving Cleopatra as the name of his queen to whom the Romans sent gifts (see above).[6]

1   Polybius ix, 44; Livy xxvii, 4, 10. Details of Livy's account are suspect: see F. W. Walbank, *Commentary on Polybius*, ii, 1967, pp. 9–10, 137.
2   *BMCGC Ptolemies*, 1883, pl. 14, nos. 6, 7, pl. 20, no. 6, pl. 27, no. 12.
3   Ibid., pl. 14, nos. 9, 10, pl. 15, nos. 1, 2; *JDAI*, xlv, 1930, pl. 3, no. 14; Newell 1937, pl. 15, no. 9; Richter 1965, fig. 1827; Davis and Kraay 1973, pls. 29, 30, 33; H. Kyrieleis, 'Die Porträtmünzen Ptolemaios V. und seine Eltern: zur Datierung und historischen Interpretation', in *JDAI*, lxxxviii, 1973, pp. 213–46, figs. 20–7, 30–2, where evidence is produced to show that these coin portraits, and those of Arsinoë III, were all issued during the early years of Ptolemy V's reign.
4   Richter 1965, figs. 1829–30.
5   *BMCGC Ptolemies*, 1883, pl. 15, nos. 6, 7; *JDAI*, xlv, pl. 3, no. 20; Richter 1965, fig. 1828; Davis and Kraay 1973, pls. 31, 32, 34; *JDAI*, lxxxviii, 1973, p. 239, figs. 33, 34.
6   See note 1 above.

PTOLEMY V EPIPHANES (205/4–180 BC)
Ills. 128, 129

Ptolemy V was only five or six years old when his father died. His accession (Polybius xv, 25) was followed by a time of internal strife and external threats. It is probable that the boy's guardians renewed Egypt's friendship with Rome in his name; and Rome sent various embassies to Egypt.[1]

But the story that one of the Roman ambassadors, M. Aemilius Lepidus, assumed the guardianship (*tutela*) of Ptolemy is almost certainly legendary.[2] Rome demanded that Philip of Macedon and Antiochus III of Syria should stop their aggression against Egypt.[3] In 193 BC Ptolemy married a Syrian princess, Cleopatra I, but remained friendly to Rome in her war against Antiochus. In 190 BC the king and queen sent ambassadors to Rome to congratulate her on Antiochus' defeat at Thermopylae.[4]

Coin portraits show Ptolemy V's draped bust with youthful features. He has a straight nose, large eyes, a small mouth, a pointed chin, full cheeks, and quite a pleasant expression. On some gold octadrachms he wears a radiate crown with a diadem, on others a diadem alone encircles his neat, thick hair (*Ills. 128, 129*).[5] On the radiate portraits a spear emerges from behind his shoulder. No coin portraits that certainly depict Cleopatra I survive.

1 Livy xxxi, 2, 3; xxxii, 33, 4.
2 E.g. Valerius Maximus vi, 6, 1; Tacitus, *Ann.* ii, 67. Lepidus, however, continued to have close and friendly relations with the Ptolemaic dynasty. This is illustrated on a much later Roman denarius: Sydenham 1952, p. 137, no. 831, pl. 24.
3 Polybius xviii, 33, 34.
4 Livy xxxvii, 3, 9–11.
5 *BMCGC Ptolemies*, 1883, pl. 16, no. 1, pl. 17, nos. 1, 2, 5; *JDAI*, xlv, 1930, pl. 3, no. 15; Newell 1937, pl. 15, no. 10; Richter 1965, fig. 1832 a, b; Davis and Kraay 1973, pls. 35, 36, 39; *JDAI*, lxxxiii, 1973, pp. 213–46, figs. 1, 2, 3 (with radiate crown), 5, 6, 7, 8–11, 17–19, 28, 29 – the writer demonstrates that all Ptolemy V's coin portraits were struck before his coming of age in 197 BC (cf. p. 82, note 3) and he also suggests that the corn-ears which sometimes adorn the young king's diadem were intended to equate him with Harpocrates-Triptolemus as bestower of wealth and prosperity.

PTOLEMY VI THEOS PHILOMETOR
(180–146/5 BC)
Ill. 130

Ptolemy VI also was still a child when he came to the throne. In 170 BC his ministers made war on Antiochus Epiphanes of Syria, who defeated the Egyptians and the young king fell into his hands. Antiochus advanced on Alexandria, but was twice (169 and 168) forced to withdraw by the Roman deputies sent at the request of an Egyptian embassy to Rome – in 170 Rome had recognized Ptolemy as joint king with his brother Ptolemy VIII Euergetes II Physkon.[1] Ptolemy then assumed the title of Theos. Now was the beginning of clientship, as contrasted with mere *amicitia*, in Egypt's relations with Rome, when the Senate told Ptolemy's envoys that he and his brother would find that the full security of their kingdom (*regni sui maximum semper praesidium*) depended on the good faith of the Roman people (*positum esse in fide populi Romani*).[2]

Ptolemy VI's and Euergetes' joint rule lasted till 164, when the latter expelled the former who went to Rome to complain of his brother and appeared in rags as a suppliant before the Senate. The next year Ptolemy VI was accompanied to Egypt by Roman deputies who reinstated him and arranged for him to rule Egypt while his brother ruled Cyrene. In 162 Euergetes went to Rome with a view to getting Cyprus added to Cyrene; and again in 154 with complaints against his brother, displaying to the Senate the knife-wounds which he alleged that Ptolemy had inflicted on him. Five Roman warships escorted Euergetes to Cyprus, but his brother defeated him there and forced him to return to Cyrene; Ptolemy VI remained sole ruler of Egypt until his death in 146/5.

Ptolemy VI never placed his portrait on any coins struck in Egypt. But his likeness appears on a silver tetradrachm minted at Ake-Ptolemaïs in Palestine,

128, 129 Ptolemy V Epiphanes: obverses of gold octadrachms showing the king with diadem and radiate crown and with diadem alone.

where he had gone to intervene in Syrian affairs. This coin is inscribed BASILEOS PTOLEMAIOU THEOU PHILOMETOROS on the reverse, while the obverse depicts his diademed head with curly hair, a long nose, a small mouth, and a rather sharp, jutting chin (*Ill. 130*).[3] This is an attractive face, harmonizing well with Polybius' eulogy of his goodness, kindliness, and courage both in a crisis and on the battlefield.[4]

1 Livy xliv, 19, 10–12 = 169 BC; Polybius xxix, 8, 11. Cf. H. H. Scullard, *Roman Politics 220–150 BC*, 1973, p. 210, n. 2, for details. The most spectacular withdrawal by Antiochus was in 168 BC, when he received the Senate's orders from C. Papillius Laenas, who demanded instant obedience.
2 Livy xlv, 13, 7: 168 BC.
3 Richter 1965, fig. 1838.
4 Polybius xl, 12.

130   Ptolemy VI Theos Philometor: obverse of silver tetradrachm minted in Palestine.

PTOLEMY VIII EUERGETES II PHYSKON (170–116 BC)
Ill. 131

Ptolemy VIII's activities up to the death of Ptolemy VI (q.v.) have been outlined above. In order to secure the goodwill of Rome he had proclaimed in 155 BC that, if he died without legitimate heirs, Cyrene should be left to the Roman people, but in fact he did have heirs.[1] In 144 BC he married his brother's wife, Cleopatra II, but in 142 BC, without divorcing her, took to wife Cleopatra III. Cleopatra II in 132 BC led a revolt against him. He fled to Cyprus and it was not until 127 BC that he recovered Alexandria and in 124 BC settled down peaceably with his two Cleopatras. He kept on good terms with Rome and received with great respect Scipio Aemilianus Africanus when he visited Egypt in the company of Panaetius of Rhodes.

Ptolemy's nickname Physkon ('Pot-belly') is mentioned by Strabo.[2] His portrait appears on rare didrachms struck at Alexandria in 138/7 (*Ill. 131*).[3]

131   Ptolemy VIII Euergetes II: obverse of didrachm struck at Alexandria, 138/137 BC.

He wears a radiate crown and an aegis and has 'bloated cheeks, protruding eye and flaring nostril – the living picture of an abnormally fat man suffering from asthma' – to quote Newell's most apt interpretation of his likeness.

1 *Supplementum Epigraphicum Graecum*, ix, 7.
2 xvii, 795.
3 *JDAI*, xlv, 1930, pl. 3, no. 16; Newell 1937, p. 91, fig. 12; Richter 1965, fig. 1853.

PTOLEMY IX PHILOMETOR SOTER LATHYROS (116–80 BC)
Ills. 132, 133

Ptolemy IX, nicknamed 'Pulse', was the eldest son of Ptolemy VIII Euergetes and the father of Ptolemy XII Auletes. In 107 BC he was forced off the throne by Ptolemy X Alexander but he recovered it in 88 BC. In 86 BC Sulla sent Lucullus to him to seek aid against Mithradates, but the king abandoned the alliance with Rome out of cowardice, although he received Lucullus with great honour.[1]

132   Ptolemy IX Philometor Soter Lathyros: coin portrait after Richter (fig. 1854).

According to Richter, the coin portrait in her fig. 1854 is Soter (*Ill. 132*). This personage has a diademed head, a straight nose, a small mouth, and side-burns. The same features appear on her fig. 1855 (*Ill. 133*), identified by her as Auletes, but who could well be Soter too, if fig. 1854 really represents him.

1 Plutarch, *Lucullus* 2, 2ff.

PTOLEMY XII THEOS PHILADELPHOS NEOS DIONYSOS AULETES (80–58 BC; 55–51 BC)
Ill. 134

Ptolemy XII, nicknamed 'Flute-player', the son of Ptolemy IX, obtained recognition by Rome in 59 BC.[1] It was probably in this year that the king bribed Caesar and Pompey to secure for him the title of 'friend and ally of the Roman people'.[2] In 58/7 BC the Alexandrians revolted against Auletes,[3] who fled to Rome. Both Pompey and Caesar were interested in his reinstatement and Cicero delivered a speech in his favour. Finally he was restored to his kingdom in 55 BC[4] by Gabinius, the proconsul of Syria, who had been bribed to help him.[5] Gabinius gave him a bodyguard (*praesidium*) of Gauls and Germans.[6] In his will he adjured the Roman people to ensure the execution of its provision, namely the succession of his elder son and elder daughter.[7]

Auletes' authentic coin portrait is not easy to identify. As we have noted above, Richter's fig. 1855 is labelled as Auletes and it is quite different from the portrait in her fig. 1856, also labelled Auletes, where the mouth is larger and more curved and the nose notably hooked, not straight. These two portraits of Auletes(?) are again very different from Davis and Kraay's pls. 37 and 40,

identified as he, but which seem to represent an older man; and all three differ from Newell p. 91, fig. 13, identified as Auletes, where the subject, wearing diadem and lion's skin, is remarkable for his enormous protruding nose with down-turned tip. In view of the extraordinary resemblance of this portrait to that of Auletes' daughter Cleopatra

134 Ptolemy XII Auletes: obverse of bronze coin (after Newell).

VII (q.v.) it would seem to have the best claim to be his true likeness (*Ill. 134*).[8]

1 Not in 63 BC, in Caesar's aedileship, as Suetonius states: *Julius* 11.
2 Suetonius, *Julius* 54, 3; Caesar, *Bellum Civile* iii, 107, 2.
3 Again not in Caesar's aedileship, as according to Suetonius, *Julius* 11: 'Alexandrini regem suum socium atque amicum a senatu appellatum expulerant, resque vulgo improbabatur'.
4 Cicero, *Ad Atticum*, iv, 10.
5 DC xxxix, 55, 1, 2, 3; Plutarch, *Antonius*, 3, 4, 5; Appian, *Syr.* 51; Cicero *Pro Rabirio Postumo* ii, 4.
6 Caesar, *Bellum Civile* iii, 4, 4.
7 Ibid., iii, 108, 4–6.
8 *AJA*, xli, 1937, p. 460, figs. 3, 4.

PTOLEMY XV THEOS PHILOPATOR PHILOMETOR KAISARION (47–30 BC)
[No illustration]

Ptolemy XV was reputedly the son of Julius Caesar and Cleopatra VII, born in 47 BC. He was associated with his mother as joint ruler in 44 BC, and in 34 BC at the 'Donations of Alexandria' he was proclaimed by Marcus Antonius as Julius' legitimate son and 'King of Kings'. After Actium he was killed by Octavian, who could not allow the survival of a potential rival. No coin portraits of him are known, but Richter has made a good case for identifying as him a marble head in Oslo which is certainly that of a Hellenistic prince and dates stylistically from the last years of the Republic.[1] The age of the boy portrayed would fit Kaisarion. He wears a wreath of leaves entwined with a ribbon.

1 Richter 1965, fig. 1860 a, b.

133 Ptolemy IX(?): coin portrait after Richter (fig. 1855: Auletes) possibly portraying Ptolemy – cf. *Ill. 132*.

CLEOPATRA VII PHILOPATOR (51–30 BC)
Ills. 135–43

The facts of the career of Cleopatra VII, by far the cleverest in brain and the most determined in character of all the Ptolemies, are very well known and her life has been written many times.[1] In brief: born in 69 BC, she became joint ruler of Egypt in 51 BC; after expulsion she was restored with her brother Ptolemy XIV by Julius Caesar in 48 BC. In 46 BC she stayed in Rome with her son, probably Caesar's child, and husband, returning to Egypt in 44 BC after Caesar's murder. In 41 BC she met Marcus Antonius and at least by 37 BC had established a political and personal relationship with him. Her ambition to restore the past glories of the Ptolemies culminated in the 'Donations of Alexandria' in 34 BC, when large portions of the East were assigned to her children, thus threatening the unity of the Roman Empire. Rome declared war on her in 32 BC and she was defeated at Actium with Antonius; her suicide followed.

According to Plutarch,[2] 'her beauty was in itself by no means unsurpassed nor such as to dumbfound those who saw her' (καὶ γὰρ ἦν, ὡς λέγουσιν, αὐτὸ μὲν τὸ κάλλος οὐ πάνυ δυσπαράβλητον, οὐδὲ οἷον ἐκπλῆξαι τοὺς ἰδόντας). Her attraction, he continues, consisted in the charm of her manner, the sweetness of her voice, the brilliance of her conversation, and her generally stimulating personality (ἤθους τι κέντρον). We are fortunate in possessing numerous authentic coin portraits issued at six different mints, of this remarkable woman; and these bear out what Plutarch has told us of her looks.

The earliest numismatic portraits that we have from the Alexandrian mint are on bronze coins issued some time between her accession at the age of seventeen in 51 BC and 49 BC, since the portraits of her on silver tetradrachms struck at Askalon in Palestine, which were clearly derived from the Alexandrian likenesses of her, first appeared at the later date (see below). On these Alexandrian pieces we see her draped bust, with her diademed 'melon' coiffure and a 'bun' of hair on the nape of her neck, her high brow, large, deep-set eyes, very projecting nose with down-turned tip, slightly cynical mouth, and determined chin (*Ill. 135*).[3] The same portrait type is found on an Alexandrian silver drachm (*Ill. 136*).[4] The coin portrait that resembles that of her father Ptolemy XII (q.v.) so closely is on a silver drachm in the British Museum, where the head alone is shown and the 'melon' coiffure has no 'bun' behind, and where the nose is particularly large, hooked, and jutting (*Ill. 137*).[5] This coin is dated 47/6 BC, when Cleopatra was 22; and with it would seem to go another bronze coin of Alexandrian mintage, which features the same portrait head (*Ill. 138*).[6]

135 Cleopatra VII: obverse of bronze coin struck at Alexandria, 51/49 BC.

136 Cleopatra VII: obverse of silver drachm struck at Alexandria.

The second important mint for Cleopatra's early portraits is that of Askalon in Palestine. The above-mentioned silver tetradrachms of Askalon with her likenesses, issued in 49 BC (*Ill. 139*),[7] were repeated in 38 BC, the coins of the latter date providing a particularly fine likeness (*Ill. 140*).[8] The diademed 'melon' coiffure is completed with a 'bun' behind, the bust is draped, and the queen, who wears a necklace, looks decidedly more mature and more masterful on the issue of 38 BC. At both of these dates Palestine was in need of Egypt's goodwill and support, as was signified by this striking at a Palestinian mint of Cleopatra's honorific portraits, for which, as we have noted above, the ultimate models were the portraits of herself that she struck at the beginning of her reign in her own capital.

Another early portrait of the queen is on a bronze coin thought to have been struck in Cyprus, where her bust appears with what is almost certainly her infant son by Julius Caesar, Kaisarion, born in 47 BC, in her arms. On her 'melon' coiffure, with a 'bun' behind, she wears both a diadem and a metal *stephane* (upstanding coronet), and a sceptre

137, 138   Cleopatra VII: obverses of coins struck at Alexandria showing 'melon' coiffure without bun.

139, 140   Cleopatra VII: obverses of coins struck at Ascalon in 49 and 38 BC respectively, showing 'melon' coiffure with bun.

141   Cleopatra VII (with Kaisarion): early portrait, c. 47 BC, on bronze coin struck in Cyprus(?).

protrudes from behind her shoulders (*Ill. 141*).[9] Here the features are less attractive, in that the smile that plays about her slightly parted lips is more ironical than on any of the other portraits so far cited.

To pass to Cleopatra's later coin portraits – a silver tetradrachm with Greek inscriptions, probably issued in 35 BC at Antioch-on-the-Orontes to commemorate her marriage there with Marcus Antonius, bears the portraits of Antonius on the obverse (cf. p. 44) and on the reverse the queen's highly realistic, not to say veristic, likeness, shown as a deep bust (*Ill. 142*).[10] Here the 'melon' coiffure is particularly elaborate; she wears a diadem and a small 'bun' of hair behind, and a necklace round her long, rather thin, neck. Her brow is lofty, her nose long and hooked, her mouth set and faintly smiling, her jutting chin firm – a queen if ever there was one, although her youthful bloom has passed: her legend reads ΒΑCΙΛΙCCΑ ΚΛΕΟ-ΠΑΤΡΑ ΘΕΑ ΝΕΩΤΕΡΑ. Very similar as to style, but slightly older in look, is Cleopatra's portrait on the reverse of a Roman denarius struck in 34 BC, with Marcus Antonius' likeness on the obverse. Here again we have a draped bust with diadem, small 'bun', and necklace. Her face is thin and her

142, 143 Cleopatra VII: reverses of silver tetradrachm struck at Antioch(?), c. 35 BC, and Roman denarius. 34 BC, probably struck at Alexandria.

neck almost scraggy; but her proud legend runs CLEOPATRAE REGINAE REGVM FILIORVM REGVM (*Ill. 143*).[11] This coin was probably engraved and struck at Alexandria, when Antonius and Cleopatra were there together, by the personnel of a travelling Roman mint.

Cleopatra's latest coin portraits, struck in 31 BC, occur on relatively poor bronze pieces issued at Berytus. These carry a draped bust of the queen on the obverse and on the reverse either a Nike or a portrait of Marcus Antonius.[12] A unique bronze coin of Berytan mintage at Boston, also of 31 BC, presents a much better likeness of her – a draped bust with a small 'bun' and her face slightly tilted upwards.[13]

As regards Cleopatra's portraits in the round – it is reasonable to identify as her a youthful marble head in the Vatican.[14] The nose of the sculpture is unfortunately restored; but the head has the queen's high brow, deep-set eyes and small mouth. The 'melon' coiffure and the diadem are absolutely right for Cleopatra, while, on the other hand, the expression as we now see it without the true nose is undoubtedly far less determined and characterful than that on any of her numismatic likenesses. A veiled female marble head in the museum at Cherchel (Caesarea) in Algeria has been identified as Cleopatra.[15] The hair-style – loose curls covering the head in front of the veil, instead of the 'melon' coiffure – is wrong for Cleopatra; but, although the mouth is damaged, we can recognize her deep-set eyes, her hooked nose and, above all, her imperious, almost masculine mien. The veil could be explained if this was a posthumous portrait, as has been suggested, erected at Caesarea by her daughter, Cleopatra Selene, and by the latter's husband, Juba II of Mauretania, at the time of, or not long after, their marriage in 20 BC. But to the present writer neither of these sculptural identifications seems wholly convincing.

1 The most recent serious study is that of M. Grant, 1971.
2 *Antonius* 27, 2, 3.
3 *BMCGC Ptolemies*, 1883, pl. 30, nos. 7, 8; *AJA*, xli, 1937, pl. 9, nos. 3, 5.
4 Ibid., pl. 9, no. 9.
5 *BMCGC Ptolemies*, 1883, pl. 30, no. 5; *AJA*, xli, 1937, p. 460, fig. 4, pl. 9, no. 6; Richter 1965, fig. 1857.
6 *AJA*, xli, 1937, pl. 9, no. 4.
7 *BMCGC Ptolemies*, 1883, pl. 31, no. 6; *BMCGC Palestine*, 1914, pl. 12, no. 3; *AJA*, xli, 1937, pl. 9, no. 1.
8 Ibid., pl. 9, no. 2, p. 463, fig. 5; Richter 1965, fig. 1858.
9 *BMCGC Ptolemies*, 1883, pl. 30, no. 6; Davis and Kraay 1973, p. 46.
10 *BMCGC Ptolemies*, 1883, pl. 31, no. 7; *BMCGC Galatia, etc.*, pl. 19, no. 3; Davis and Kraay, 1973, pls. 44, 45, 47.
11 Sydenham 1952, p. 194, no. 1210, pl. 29; Bernareggi 1973, p. 95, fig. 31.
12 *BMCGC Phoenicia*, 1910, pl. 7, nos. 9, 10.
13 Ibid., pl. 40, no. 2; *AJA*, xli, 1937, pl. 9, no. 8.
14 *RM*, xlviii, 1933, pls. 25–7; Richter 1965, figs. 1863–4.
15 *Libyca (Archéologie et Épigrafie)*, ii, 1954, pp. 54–63, figs. 1, 4, 10; Richter 1965, fig. 1861.

Numidia

MASINISSA (*c.* 240–149 BC)
Ill. 144
Masinissa (or Massinissa)[1] was born at Carthage and served with the Carthaginians against Rome in Spain in 212 BC. In 206 BC Scipio Africanus won his friendship and he became Rome's independent ally,[2] joining the Roman forces when they landed in Africa in 204 BC and playing a decisive part in the battle of Zama in 202 BC. Masinissa now became a client of Rome, who recognized his kingship and allowed him gradually to extend his frontiers at Carthage's expense.[3] In Rome's wars with Macedon, Masinissa voluntarily sent her cavalry, elephants and supplies of corn; and in return he received Rome's connivance at his resistance to Carthaginian attacks.[4] Masinissa's loyalty to Rome, Rome's favour to Masinissa, and the latter's persistent attempts to undermine Carthage in Roman eyes enabled him to provoke the Carthaginians to break their treaty with Rome; he thus precipitated the Third Punic War (149 BC). He died in 148 BC. He developed Numidia's resources, making Berber 'nomads into farmers and welding them into a State' (Strabo xvii, 833), and encouraged urban life and Punic culture; he followed the example of Hellenistic monarchy.

a plain diadem. He has large eyes, a straight nose, a firm mouth and he wears a very projecting pointed beard.

Quite uncertain is the identification as Masinissa of a diademed marble head of a man in early middle age (also identified by Richter as Juba II, q.v.), which was found at Cherchel and is now in the Louvre.[6]

1 For recent discussions of Masinissa, see *JRS*, lv, 1965, pp. 149–60; C. Saumagne, *La Numidie et Rome: Massinissa et Jugurtha*, 1966.
2 Appian, *Iber.*, 37: Μασσανάσσης . . . φιλίαν τῷ Σκιπίωνι συνθέμενος ὤμοσε συμμαχήσειν.
3 Livy xxx, 15, 11: 'Masinissam primum regem appellatum'; xxx, 17, 10: 'petere ut regium nomen ceteraque Scipionis beneficia senatus decreto confirmaret'; xlv, 13, 15: 'Masinissam meminisse se regnum a populo Romano partum auctumque et multiplicatum habere'; Polybius xxii, 4: Μασαννάσαν . . . βασιλέα τῶν πλείστων μερῶν τῆς Λιβύης πεποιήκατε.
4 Livy, *Epit.*, 49: 'placuit . . . quod socio populi Romani et amico Masinissae arma intulissent [sc. Carthaginienses] . . . bellum indici'.
5 Mazard 1955, pp. 30–43, pls. on pp. 236–40, nos. 17–72; Richter 1965, fig. 2003; Scullard 1970, pl. 18. Mazard (p. 30, no. 17; pl. on p. 237, no. 17) gives the only coin which bears Masinissa's name and thus provides a portrait with which the extremely numerous and varied later issues can be compared.
6 *AA*, 1970, p. 418, fig. 6.

144 Masinissa: obverse of bronze coin showing laureate head.

Masinissa's likeness is known from the obverses of his bronze coinage (*Ill. 144*).[5] His head faces left and on his thick, curly hair he wears either a laurel-wreath, generally with *taeniae* fluttering behind, or

SYPHAX (*c.* 213–202 BC)
Ill. 145
Syphax, chief of the Numidian tribe of the Masaesyles (or Masaesylii), was an enemy of Carthage and a rival of Masinissa. During the Second Punic War he tried to retain his *amicitia* with Rome, but was won over to Carthage by Sophonisba (the daughter of Hasdrubal, son of Gisgo), whom he married. In 203 BC, while fighting against Rome, he was defeated and captured and died a prisoner in Italy.

Syphax's earlier portraits on the obverses of his bronze coinage are very distinctive.[1] His leftward-facing head, which is slightly tilted up, is bare. His nose is straight; and his lank locks are brushed back from his brow over the crown of his head to form a thick mat at the nape of the neck. This is doubtless a native style of coiffure. His beard is very pointed and projecting. The portraits of his second coin series, also of bronze, are, on the other hand, much more Hellenized (*Ill. 145*).[2] Here his beard is occasionally jutting and pointed, but generally it is short and curly and his curly hair is encircled by a diadem.

1 Mazard 1955, pp. 18–20, pl. on p. 235, nos. 1–9.
2 Ibid., pp. 20–1, pl. on p. 235, nos. 10–12; Scullard 1970, pl. 20.

145   Syphax: obverse of bronze coin showing later, more Hellenized, portrait style.

VERMINA (202–192 BC)
Ill. 146

Vermina, the son of Syphax, succeeded his father as chief of the Masaesyles. Before Zama he helped Hannibal; but was afterwards left by Rome in possession of his territory as her *socius atque amicus*, according to Livy,[1] to counterbalance Masinissa.

Vermina's portrait-bust, facing right, appears on his coins minted in silver and bronze (*Ill. 146*).[2] Clean-shaven, like a Ptolemy or a Roman, he has straight hair bound by a diadem and neatly combed forward onto his brow and down the nape of his neck. The nose is long and pointed, the lips are full and parted, the chin is prominent and the cheeks are plump and smooth. The ears are markedly large. Here we have a Berber chieftain in the guise of a Hellenistic king.

1 xxxi, 11, 13. In fact Vermina was probably only Rome's 'friend', and Livy's use of *socius* is anachronistic.
2 Mazard 1955, pp. 21–2, pl. on p. 235, nos. 14–16; Scullard 1970, pl. 22.

146   Vermina: obverse of bronze coin with portrait in the manner of a Hellenistic king.

HIARBAS (108–81 BC)
Ill. 147

Hiarbas, who ruled in western Numidia, fought against Pompey when the latter landed in Africa in 81 BC in order to eject the Marian forces; he campaigned under the command of Cnaeus Domitius Ahenobarbus. At first victorious, he was later deserted by fortune and fled for refuge to his capital, Bulla Regis. There he was captured by his enemy, Bocchus I of Mauretania, and was given up to Pompey, who had him killed.

Hiarbas' likeness, very native in character, appears on the obverses of his bronze coinage (*Ill. 147*).[1] His head is shown facing to the right, with hair combed back from his brow across the crown of his head and long, corkscrew locks hanging down onto his shoulders behind. He has a narrow face and a pointed, jutting beard. He wears no headdress of any kind.

1 Mazard 1955, pp. 53–4, pl. on p. 241, nos. 94–8.

147   Hiarbas: obverse of bronze coin with portrait in typically native style.

Mastenissa (81–46 ? bc)
[No illustration]
Mastenissa, ruler of western Numidia perhaps from
81 to 46 bc, joined Juba I against Rome. He was
put to death by the Romans and his territory
divided up.[1]

Mastenissa's bronze coins depict his head facing
to the left. His hair, which is brushed back from his
brow, falls in long corkscrew ringlets to the base
of his head behind. He has a pointed and very
jutting beard and vertical folds of skin on his
cheeks.[2]

1 Appian, *Bell. Civ.* iv, 54, where he is called Mas-
    anassa; cf. S. Gsell, *Histoire ancienne de l'Afrique du
    Nord*, vii, 1928, p. 291.
2 Mazard 1955, p. 55, pl. on p. 241, nos. 99, 100.

Mastenissa II Arabion
[No illustration]
After the death of his father, Mastenissa II took
refuge in Spain with the Pompeians. But subsequent to Caesar's death he returned to Africa
with a view to recovering his kingdom. This he
partially succeeded in doing by raising partisans
and getting rid, in 43 bc, of the adventurer Sittius
(cf. p. 68), who had acquired a portion of his
lands. In the struggle between the governors Sex-
tius and Cornificius, he espoused the cause first of
the one and then of the other and ended by being
put to death.[1]

Mastenissa's bronze coins portray him facing
left, with the same coiffure as his father's.[2]

1 Appian, *Bell. Civ.* iv, 54ff.
2 Mazard 1955, pp. 55–6, pl. on p. 242, nos. 101,
    102.

Juba I (60–46 bc)
Ill. 148
Juba I, king of eastern Numidia, as a young man in
63 bc had visited Rome, where he had a violent
dispute with Julius Caesar, who pulled his beard.[1]
Naturally he supported the Senate and Pompey in
the Civil War and in 49 bc he defeated the
Caesarian, Caius Scribonius Curio. He enjoyed a

paternum hospitium (inherited patronage) with Pompey;[2] and assisted the exiled Senate, which recognized his kingship.[3] But in Rome he was refused
the title of *socius atque amicus*.[4] After Caesar's victory
at Thapsus, Juba committed suicide and most of his
domain became a Roman province.[5]

Juba's silver coins, some of which are inscribed
REX IVBA, show on the obverses his bust facing to the
right (*Ill. 148*).[6] He wears a cuirass and a cloak and
a sceptre rests against his right shoulder. He has a
powerful nose, a small, determined mouth, and a
thick, long and pointed beard of straight locks.

148 Juba I: obverse of silver coin with portrait bust
showing distinctive hair-style.

Cicero calls him *puer bene capillatus*,[7] and he certainly displays a splendid mop of hair arranged in
serried tiers of short corkscrew curls falling low
across the brow. A diadem encircles the curls. A
diademed marble head found at Cherchel and now
in the Louvre has been identified as Juba I.[8] The
hair and beard are extremely abundant; but the
treatment of the individual locks differs from that
on the coin portraits.

1 Suetonius, *Julius* 71.
2 Caesar, *Bellum Civile* ii, 25, 4.
3 DC, xli, 42, 7.
4 Caesar, *Bellum Civile* i, 6, 3, 4.
5 DC, liii, 26, 2.
6 Mazard 1955, p. 50, pl. on p. 241, nos. 84–6, 88;
    Richter 1965, fig. 2004.
7 *De lege agraria* ii, 22, 59.
8 Richter 1965, figs. 2000–2.

Mauretania

Bocchus II (49–33 BC)
[No illustration]
The first king of a united Mauretania known to history, Bocchus I, and his successors (who divided the country into eastern and western kingdoms) have left no coin portraits. In 49 BC the Caesarian Senate recognized Bocchus II in the east and Bogud in the west as kings.[1] Bocchus II assisted Caesar against the Pompeians in Africa in 46 BC; but after Caesar's murder he joined Octavian, who in 38 BC confirmed him as sole ruler of Mauretania when Bogud (q.v.) went to Spain to fight for Marcus Antonius.[2] Bocchus died in 33 BC without leaving heirs. Rome seems then to have taken over the country's administration, without turning it into a province, until 25 BC, when Augustus gave Bocchus' and Bogud's possessions to Juba II (q.v.).[3]

Bocchus' bronze coins show his head facing generally to the right, occasionally to the left.[4] He wears no diadem and his straight hair is brushed back from his brow to fall in long corkscrew curls down the back of his head. He has a very pointed and projecting beard.

During the period of interregnum that followed Bocchus' death (33–25 BC) bronze coins were struck with obverse portraits labelled REX BOCCHVS, but none of them resembles the likenesses produced on his own coinage. Here he appears either beardless with short straight brushed-back hair or with short curly hair and a short beard.[5]

1 DC, xli, 42, 7.
2 DC, xlviii, 45, 3.
3 DC, liii, 26, 2.
4 Mazard 1955, pp. 62–3, pl. on p. 242, nos. 107–17.
5 Ibid., pp. 68–9, pl. on p. 243, nos. 119–21.

Bogud (49–31 BC)
[No illustration]
Bogud, recognized by Rome as king in western Mauretania, supported Caesar in 49 BC and played an important part in the battle of Munda (45 BC). He joined Marcus Antonius in 43 BC, fighting in 38 BC in Spain (cf. Bocchus II, above), where he was defeated, and then went to Antonius in the East. In 31 BC he was killed on Agrippa's orders at Methone.[1]

On the obverse of a bronze coin issued by Bogud is seen his portrait-head facing to the right.[2] He has short, curly hair, a slight chin-beard and a large nose. On the reverse a prow, a motif borrowed from

the Roman coinage, is accompanied by the legend REX BOCV.

1 DC, l, 11, 3.
2 Mazard 1955, p. 62, pl. on p. 242, no. 106.

Juba II (25 BC–AD 23) and Cleopatra Selene
Ills. 149, 150
Juba II, the son of Juba I of Numidia, was sent to Rome as a child in 46 BC for the occasion of Caesar's triumph. He was brought up under the eye of Octavia in Rome, where he became a Roman citizen. He knew Latin, Greek and Punic, was highly educated in literature and in the arts, and wrote many books in Greek. After being installed as king by Augustus (cf. Bocchus II, above) in 25 BC he called one of his capital cities Iol Caesarea (Cherchel in modern times) and made it a leading centre of Greek and Roman culture. By 20 BC he was married to Cleopatra Selene, the daughter of Marcus Antonius and Cleopatra VII; and she too had received a Roman education under Octavia's tutelage. After her marriage Cleopatra retained her title of queen and seems to have been officially associated with her husband in the royal power. She died in AD 5 or 6.

Juba II ruled for nearly half a century, but throughout his long reign the portrait on the obverses of his silver, bronze and very rare gold coins, with the legend REX IVBA, never changed (*Ill.*

149 Juba II: typical coin portrait showing the king as a young man.

149). He was aged about twenty-five when Augustus placed him on the throne of Mauretania; and the perennial portrait may depict him as he looked at that time, allowing for a certain degree of idealization of his features. But the coins do not give us the slightest notion of him as he was when middle-aged or elderly.

Juba's head faces normally to the right, very rarely to the left. His hair is arranged in neat, chunky clusters of straight, rigid locks encircled by a diadem; occasionally he is laureate. He has a fairly high brow, large eyes, a straight nose, a small, rather thick-lipped mouth, full cheeks and a firm neck. He is completely beardless, after the Roman fashion. Sometimes the portrait is accompanied by a lion's skin or a club, an allusion to Juba's claim to descent from Sophax, son of Hercules.[1]

Six marble heads with diadem, curly hair and clean-shaven cheeks have been claimed to portray Juba II.[2] Some depict him as young, as in his coin portraits, others as older. On all of them the locks of hair are treated in a freer, more naturalistic style than they are on the coins. Richter's suggestion that Juba II is portrayed in the marble head from Cherchel in the Louvre which has been identified as Masinissa (q.v.) is much more convincing.[3] The subject wears a diadem in his loosely curling hair. His cheeks, while still full, are beginning to sag somewhat and he is slightly frowning. The lips are thinner and more tensely set than on the coin portraits. If this is Juba, we have him here as he was when advancing into middle age.

Cleopatra Selene's portrait, facing now left, now right, appears on the reverses of silver and bronze coins with Juba's portrait on the obverses (*Ill. 150*);[4] and on the obverses of silver and bronze coins struck in her own name alone.[5] She is described as ΒΑCΙΛΙCCΑ and wears a broad diadem with *taeniae* fluttering behind. Her hair is combed in neat strands over the crown of her head and gathered into a 'bun' on the nape of her neck, while loose locks escape from it down the sides of the neck

150 Cleopatra Selene: portrait appearing on reverse of coin of Juba II.

and onto the shoulders. Like her husband, she is always shown as young and probably somewhat idealized, with a straight nose, large eyes, a small, full-lipped mouth and full cheeks. A marble head found at Cherchel and now in the museum there

has been held to represent Cleopatra.[6] It is diademed, but its 'melon' coiffure and row of tiny curls framing the brow do not correspond with the coin portraits.

1 Mazard 1955, pp. 76–124, 126, pls. on pp. 243–51, to nos. 391 and 396; Richter 1965, fig. 2005.
2 *Libyca (Archéologie et Épigraphie)*, i, 1953, pp. 23–6, figs. 1, 2 and notes.
3 Richter 1965, figs. 2007–8.
4 Mazard 1955, pp. 117–20, pl. on p. 250, nos. 357–74; Richter 1965, fig. 2006.
5 Mazard 1955, p. 125, pl. on p. 251, nos. 392–5.
6 Richter 1965, figs. 2009, 2010.

PTOLEMY (AD 20–40)
Ills. 151, 152

Ptolemy, the son of Juba II and Cleopatra Selene, was born *c*.6 or 5 BC. He reigned jointly with his father from AD 20 until the latter's death in 23; and from long before, as well as after, 20 his portrait, facing now right, now left, appears on the reverses of silver and bronze coins carrying Juba's portrait on the obverses.[1] In 24, after Juba's death, Ptolemy, in return for his services against the Numidian brigand Tacfarinas, was rewarded by the Senate with the gifts of an ivory sceptre and an embroidered tunic, together with the right to call himself king and ally and friend of Rome.[2] Little is known of the events of his sole rule until his assassination in 40 on Caligula's orders.

Ptolemy's earliest coin likenesses, issued on silver in AD 5/6, in Juba's year XXX, show him as a mere child, with round cheeks, but already diademed.[3] Silver coins of Juba's year XXXVI, that is, AD 11/12, depict Ptolemy with a slight beard.[4] But on a bronze coin of AD 20/1, where Ptolemy's legend reads ANNO PRIMO, namely the first year of his joint rule with his father, he is beardless;[5] and likewise on a fine silver piece in Paris, presumably struck in 20/1 or soon after, with the reverse legend REX PTOLEMAEVS REGIS IVBAE F (*Ill. 151*).[6] Here the young king's hair is arranged in chunks of straight locks, very similar to those of Juba II (q.v.), and his diadem is identical with his father's. He has a large, long and slightly *retroussé* nose, full lips and smooth cheeks.

After the death of Juba, Ptolemy's obverse portraits are both bearded and beardless and are accompanied by the obverse legend REX PTOLEMAEVS.[7] Two unique gold pieces in Paris, one portraying him as bearded (*Ill. 152*),[8] the other as beardless,[9] provide us with more mature likenesses.

Of the sculptural portraits in the round that can with strong probability be identified as Ptolemy the earliest is a very youthful marble head found at Cherchel in 1960.[10] It shows him at about the age of fifteen, with thick, curly, rather chunky hair encircled by a diadem, full, rounded cheeks, small eyes, a heavy chin and tiny side-burns. Another youthful, but somewhat older, marble head in the Louvre, also found at Cherchel, presents him with neat diademed hair arranged in a thick fringe above the brow.[11] Here again the subject has tiny side-burns, small eyes and a long, slightly *retroussé* nose. Yet another Cherchel find, also in the Louvre, is a marble head with diadem, thick hair above the brow, a short beard and side-burns;[12] it closely resembles the bearded portrait of the gold coin referred to above. The face shows no sign of age; but the personage portrayed is no longer quite youthful.

151, 152 Ptolemy: obverse of silver coin showing early beardless portrait, *c.*20/21 AD; and obverse of gold coin showing later, bearded likeness.

1 Mazard 1955, pp. 121–4, pl. on p. 251, nos. 375–88, 390.
2 Tacitus, *Ann.* iv, 26, 4.
3 E.g. Mazard 1955, no. 375.
4 Ibid., no. 383.
5 Ibid., no. 388.
6 Ibid., 379; Richter 1965, fig. 2013.
7 Mazard 1955, nos. 398–514.
8 Ibid., no. 398; Richter 1965, fig. 2014.
9 Mazard 1955, no. 399
10 *Mélanges . . . à André Piganiol*, 1966, i, pp. 395–406, figs. 1–3.
11 *Symbolae Osloenses*, iii, 1925, p. 7, fig. 11; Richter 1965, fig. 2011.
12 *Symbolae Osloenses*, iii, 1925, p. 12, fig. 19; Richter 1965, fig. 2012.

Sicily: Syracuse

HIERO II (269–216 BC) and PHILISTIS
Ills. 153, 154

Hiero II was the first Syracusan king to put his own portrait on his coins. When Rome occupied Messana on the eve of the First Punic War he first joined the Carthaginians against Rome, but in 263 BC made peace with her,[1] entered into clientship with her,[2] and remained her loyal ally until his death. As Rome's client and her friend and ally[3] he sent her – unasked – corn, gold and ships for her wars.[4]

Hiero's portrait appears on rare silver pieces and on much commoner fine bronze coins, with his head facing to the left (*Ill. 153*).[5] He has thick, wavy hair encircled by a diadem; and his face is slightly tilted upwards. His nose is long and straight, his lower lip protrudes somewhat, his jaw is square, and his mouth and prominent chin are firm and determined.

Philistis, Hiero's queen, also faces to the left on the obverses of large sixteen-litra and small five-litra silver pieces (*Ill. 154*).[6] She is diademed and veiled and her hair is worn in a thick roll between her diadem and her brow. She has a slightly aquiline nose, a small mouth, and full cheeks and throat.

1 Polybius i, 16, 9; Diodorus Siculus xxiii, 4.
2 Polybius 1, 16, 10: ὁ δὲ βασιλεὺς Ἱέρων ὑποστείλας ἑαυτὸν ὑπὸ τὴν Ῥωμαίων σκέπην.
3 Appian, *Sic.*, 2: φίλον καὶ σύμμαχον ἔθεντο [sc. the Romans].
4 Diodorus Siculus xxv, 14; Polybius iii, 75, 7; vii, 5, 7; Livy xxii, 37, 3, 4.
5 Newell 1937, p. 95, fig. 5; Richter 1965, fig. 1766.
6 Newell 1937, p. 95, figs. 1, 2; Richter 1965, fig. 1768.

GELON
Ill. 155

Gelon, the son of Hiero II and Philistis, died before his father, whose attitude to Rome he doubtless shared and with whom he reigned jointly.[1] His likeness, facing to the left, is found on eight- and four-litra pieces (*Ill. 155*).[2] He has his mother's aquiline nose, rather more pronounced, her small mouth and her full cheeks and throat, combined with his father's jutting chin. His diademed locks are somewhat wild and wind-blown.

1 Diodorus Siculus xxvi, 15: Γέλωνος καὶ Ἱέρωνος τῶν βασιλέων κατὰ τὴν Σικιλίαν.
2 Newell 1937, p. 95, figs. 3, 4; Richter 1965, fig. 1767.

HIERONYMOS (216–215 BC)
Ill. 156

Hieronymos, the son of Gelon, took a more independent line with Rome, when he succeeded his grandfather Hiero II at the age of fifteen, promising his loyalty to Rome on condition that she

153, 154 Hiero II and his queen, Philistis: obverses of bronze and silver coins.

155 Gelon: coin portrait showing close resemblance to his mother, Philistis (cf. *Ill. 154*).

returned to him the gold, corn and other gifts which she had received from his grandfather.[1] Hoping to gain control of all Sicily, he made an alliance with Carthage, but his arrogance and tyrannical conduct led to his assassination soon after his desertion of Rome.

Hieronymos' leftward-facing portrait is preserved both on bronze coins and on ten- and five-litra silver pieces (*Ill. 156*).[2] His diademed hair resembles his grandfather's, as do also the nose and slightly protruding lower lip. But he has a double chin and a fuller throat and thicker neck than has Hiero, his cheeks are fat, and his mouth is small and impudent. His whole expression is that of a very stupid, self-indulgent and most unpleasant character – amply bearing out Diodorus Siculus' strictures on his luxury (τρυφή), profligacy (ἀκολασία), and despotic cruelty (τυραννικὴ ὠμότης).[3] Unlike Hiero and Gelon, he sports side-burns.

1 Polybius vii, 5, 7.
2 Newell 1937, p. 95, figs. 6, 7; Richter 1965, fig. 1769.
3 xxvii, 15.

156   Hieronymos: coin portrait showing resemblance to Hiero II (cf. *Ill. 153*).

Spain

HAMILCAR BARCA (died 229/8 BC)
Ill. 157

Hamilcar Barca, the Carthaginian general, successfully fought against the Romans in Sicily (247–241 BC) during the closing stages of the First Punic War. In 237 BC he was sent with his young son Hannibal to Spain, where he won the south and east for Carthage and rejected a Roman protest in 231 BC. Among the earliest of the silver coins issued by the Barcids in Spain is one that bears on the obverse a head, facing to the left, with thick laureate hair and curly beard and accompanied by the club of Melkart-Herakles (*Ill. 157*).[1] But the features, in particular the high, sloping brow protruding just above the large, aquiline nose, are realistic; and the head could be a portrait of Hamilcar in the god's guise struck by Hannibal, perhaps at New Carthage, after his father's death.

157 Hamilcar Barca: obverse of silver coin showing laureate head accompanied by club of Melkart-Herakles.

1 Carson and Sutherland 1956, pl. 2, no. 6(a); Richter 1965, fig. 2015; Scullard 1970, pl. 5.

HANNIBAL (247–183/2 BC)
Ills. 158, 159

In 221 BC Hannibal took over the Carthaginian command in Spain, where he campaigned until he left on his march to invade Italy in 218 BC. After fighting there with varying fortunes until 203 BC, he was forced to return to defend Carthage following the invasion of Africa by Scipio Africanus, who finally defeated him at Zama in 202 BC. After a short period at Carthage, Hannibal was forced by political enemies to flee; he found refuge with Antiochus III and, after the latter's defeat by

Rome, with Prusias (q.v.) of Bithynia. He took his own life to avoid falling into Rome's hands (183 or 182 BC).

A laureate head, leftward-facing like that of Hamilcar (q.v.), with the club of Melkart-Herakles which occurs on the obverses of Barcid silver coinage, and probably also from the New Carthage mint, may well be that of Hannibal himself (*Ill. 158*).[1] The brow resembles Hamilcar's, but this is clearly a different personage – clean-shaven, with less exuberant hair, eyes more deeply set, a nose that is straight rather than aquiline, and a somewhat pursed-up mouth. Hannibal may again be identified in the bare, beardless head with almost identical features, but without a club, on another

158, 159 Hannibal: obverses of silver coins probably struck at New Carthage; the portrait on the left also features the club of Melkart-Herakles (cf. *Ill. 157*).

silver issue – doubtless from the same mint (*Ill. 159*).[2]

G. Hafner's arguments for identifying as Hannibal the controversial head in Madrid – a work of imperial times – with un-Roman, almost caricature-like features, are not at all convincing.[3] The man represented could, indeed, be a North African barbarian – and ethnic types were not infrequently the subjects of imperial art – but he has no Semitic features and is wholly different from all the personages portrayed on the Spanish Barcid coinage, which would seem to have a far better claim to depict members of the family.

1 Carson and Sutherland 1956, pl. 3, nos. 6, b–d; Scullard 1970, pl. 7.
2 Carson and Sutherland 1956, pl. 3, nos. 7, b–f, j, k, n; Richter 1965, fig. 2016; Scullard 1970, pl. 9.
3 *Madrider Mitteilungen*, xiv, 1973, pp. 143–50, pl. 17, 18a, 19a, 20b.

recognized by the Romans in an agreement which he negotiated with them in 226 BC.

An alternative attribution has been proposed by Scullard, who argues that the distribution of the finds of these coins points rather to the mint of Gades and to a portrait of Mago, Hannibal's youngest brother.[2] Mago fought in Spain from 215 BC until his defeat at Ilipa in 206 BC; the next year he landed in Liguria, where he tried to raise an army to go to aid Hannibal, but he was defeated by the Romans in 203 BC and died on the return voyage to Carthage. On a fine silver piece in the British Museum the Semitic features of the personage portrayed are especially pronounced (*Ill. 161*).[3]

1 Carson and Sutherland 1956, pp. 38, 49, pl. 2, nos. 4, a–c; Richter 1965, fig. 2017.
2 Scullard 1970, p. 252.
3 Ibid., pl. 13.

HASDRUBAL or MAGO
Ills. 160, 161

A head facing left and thrust well forward from the neck occurs on the obverses of Barcid gold and silver coins. The eyes gaze upwards, the hair is curly and diademed, the sloping brow has a markedly prominent base, the nose is very large and rather *retroussé*, the cheeks are fat and clean-shaven,

HASDRUBAL BARCA
Ill. 162

A laureate head facing left on the obverses of silver coins struck perhaps at Gades, but certainly in Spain (although none has with certainty been found in that country), was at one time erroneously identified as Jugurtha – an identification which is impossible on epigraphic grounds, since the letter

160, 161 Hasdrubal (or Mago): obverses of Carthaginian coins minted in Spain at New Carthage or Gades.

the lips are full and slightly parted and the chin is rounded. Some scholars identify this portrait as that of Hasdrubal, who in 229 BC succeeded his father-in-law, Hamilcar, as Carthaginian commander in Spain and founded New Carthage, to whose mint they attribute these coins (*Ill. 160*).[1] Hasdrubal advanced the Carthaginian frontier in Spain northwards as far as the Ebro; this was

on the reverse must in that case have been in neo-Punic form.[1] The highly individual features make it certain that we have here the portrait, not of a god, but of a human being; and the name of Hasdrubal Barca, Hannibal's younger brother, has been suggested for it (*Ill. 162*).[2] Hasdrubal, if he it is, has a sloping brow, protruding sharply just above the pronouncedly aquiline nose, together

162 Hasdrubal Barca: obverse of silver coin struck in Spain (Gades?).

with large eyes, a small mouth, full cheeks with side-burns, and a jutting chin.

Left by Hannibal in command in Spain in 218 BC, Hasdrubal fought with reasonable success against the Scipios, who were finally defeated in 211 BC, but he failed to break out of Spain to join Hannibal in Italy until after an engagement with Scipio (Africanus) at Baecula in 208 BC. He reached northern Italy in 207, but was defeated and killed at Metaurus before he could reach Hannibal in the south.

1 Mazard 1955, pp. 44–5, pl. on p. 240, nos. 73–5; Carson and Sutherland 1956, p. 43.
2 Carson and Sutherland 1956, pl. 3, nos. 8, a–c; Richter 1965, fig. 2018; Scullard 1970, pp. 252–3, pl. 11.

Britain

The free British kings of the half-century or so before the Roman conquest, while valuing their independence of Rome and being in some cases vehemently antagonistic to her, were far from averse to importing objects of luxury and culture from her world or to imitating her art. The coins that were issued by the British rulers in gold, silver and bronze often carry Latin legends that are sometimes worked in very fine Roman characters, and motifs that are drawn from classical mythology and other Roman subjects in imitation of Roman gems and coin types. Some of these designs are, indeed, so Roman as to suggest that their engravers had been trained at Roman mints. But nowhere is the Romanizing taste that prevailed at the courts of these kings more vividly expressed than in the royal portraits that adorn a number of their obverses, where the features and hair-styles of the persons depicted are not infrequently closely assimilated to those of Roman portraits, including the likenesses of the kings' imperial contemporaries, Augustus and Tiberius. To what extent the British rulers' numismatic iconography really reflects their actual looks we have, of course, no means of checking. But it was for them clearly a way of stating their claim to have attained to the standards of Mediterranean civilization.

TINCOMMIUS (c. 20 BC–AD 5)
Ill. 163
Tincommius, king of the Atrebates (Hampshire, Sussex), was driven from his kingdom by his

brothers Eppillus and Verica (qq.v.) and took refuge with Augustus.[1] A silver coin shows his head facing to the left, beardless and with youthful features and curly hair flowing down the neck behind and crowned by a laurel-wreath (*Ill. 163*).[2]

1 *Res Gestae* xxxii: 'ad me supplices confugerunt reges ... Britannorum ... Tim[commius]'.
2 R. P. Mack, *The Coinage of Ancient Britain*, 2nd ed., 1964, pl. 7, no. 106.

163 Tincommius: obverse of silver coin with laureate head.

VERICA or VIRICA (c. AD 10–40)
Ill. 164
Verica, Tincommius' brother, used the title of REX on his coins, but was, in his turn, expelled from his kingdom, perhaps by the Catuvellaunian king, Epaticcus. He fled to Claudius and is the Bericus recorded by Dio Cassius.[1] On a silver coin his bust,

facing right, with the legend VIRI, is draped and diademed. The king has straight hair, clean-shaven cheeks, a straight nose, and a small mouth (*Ill. 164*).[2]

1 DC, lx, 19: Βέρικος γάρ τις ἐκπεσὼν ἐκ τῆς νήσου κατὰ στάσιν.
2 Mack, op. cit., pl. 8, fig. 130.

164   Verica: obverse of silver coin with diademed head.

TASCIOVANUS (*c.* 20 BC–AD 5)
Ills. 165–7

Tasciovanus, king of the Catuvellauni (Hertfordshire, etc.), of all the Belgic tribes the most hostile to Rome, was perhaps second in succession to Cassivellaunus, Julius Caesar's opponent in 54 BC. He is only known to us from his coins, all in bronze, some of which provide us with his portraits. One obverse shows his head facing to the right with straight hair encircled by a laurel-wreath. He is clean-shaven and has a large nose, a small mouth,

and a jutting chin (*Ill. 165*).[1] Another coin depicts him as bare-headed, beardless, and with similar facial features; he is also rightward-facing (*Ill. 166*).[2] On a third coin he again faces to the right, is bare-headed and has neat hair, while a short beard sheathes his chin (*Ill. 167*).[3] The legends TASC and TASCIO identify his likenesses; and his coins bear the mint-mark VER or VERLAMIO (Verulamium, by St Albans), very occasionally CAMV (Camulodunum, by Colchester), where he seems to have established himself for a brief period.

1 Mack, op. cit., pl. 11, no. 176.
2 Ibid., pl. 11, no. 178.
3 Ibid., pl. 12, no. 192.

CUNOBELINUS (*c.* AD 5–40)
Ills. 168–70

Cunobelinus ('Cymbeline'), the son of Tasciovanus, is the best known of the Catuvellaunian kings and was the most defiant towards Rome, seizing the Trinovantian kingdom (Essex) to the east of his own realm and its capital Camulodunum, in contravention of the settlement made by Caesar with Cassivellaunus.[1] Yet of all the Belgic kings he was perhaps the most Romanized, as finds from pre-Roman Camulodunum indicate; and his bronze coin portraits fully bear this out. One, with the legend CVNO shows his beardless laureate head facing right (*Ill. 168*).[2] On another his laureate

165–7   Tasciovanus: obverses of bronze coins showing various portrait styles.

168–70   Cunobelinus: obverses of bronze coins showing various portrait styles.

head facing left, with clean-shaven cheeks and regular, finely cut features, accompanied by the legend CVNOBELINI, might almost be the portrait of a Roman emperor (*Ill. 169*).[3] On a third piece the king's bust, closely conformed to the Roman shape, faces right again, but is bare-headed, as well as beardless, and is surrounded by the legend CVNOBELINVS REX (*Ill. 170*).[4] The facial features of all three portraits are very similar.

1 *Bellum Gallicum* v, 20, 21.
2 Mack, op. cit., pl. 14, no. 227.
3 Ibid., pl. 15, no. 242.
4 Ibid., pl. 15, no. 246.

DUBNOVELLAUNUS
Ill. 171

Dubnovellaunus, king of the Cantii (Kent), appears to have annexed the Trinovantian kingdom during the closing years of the first century BC. He was, however, driven out, probably by Cunobelinus, and fled the country, taking refuge with Augustus.[1] His portrait head on a silver coin faces to the left, is laureate, beardless, and characterized by a large nose and a small mouth; DVBNO is inscribed beside it (*Ill. 171*).[2]

1 *Res Gestae* xxxii: 'ad me supplices confugerunt reges . . . Britannorum Dumnobellaunus'.
2 Mack, op. cit., pl. 18, no. 288.

EPPILLUS (*c.* AD 5–25)
Ill. 172

Eppillus, brother of Tincommius and Verica (qq.v.), seems to have established himself in Kent when the latter drove him out of his Atrebatan kingdom. A silver coin struck by him with the reverse legend EPIL presents his beardless, laureate head facing left (*Ill. 172*).[1] Other silver coins show Eppillus' head diademed and facing now to the left, now to the right.[2]

1 Mack, op. cit., pl. 19, no. 306; cf. no. 311, which shows a leftward-facing head seemingly laureate.
2 Ibid., pl. 19, nos. 307, 308.

ADMINIUS or AMMINIUS
[No illustration]

Adminius or Amminius would appear to have succeeded Eppillus in Kent. He was the son of Cunobelinus, who, described by Suetonius as *Britannorum rex*, banished him, presumably for pro-Roman leanings, since he deserted to the Romans with a small force at the time of Gaius' abortive invasion of Britain.[1] One bronze coin shows his portrait facing to the right and possibly diademed.[2]

1 *Gaius* 44: 'Adminio Cunobelini Britannorum regis filio, qui pulsus a patre cum exigua manu transfugerat, in deditionem recepto'.
2 Mack, op. cit., pl. 19, no. 315.

171 Dubnovellaunus: obverse of silver coin with laureate head.

172 Eppillus: obverse of silver coin (with reverse legend EPIL) showing laureate head.

Gaul

VERCINGETORIX

Ill. 173

The obverse of a denarius struck by L. Hostilius Saserna in about 48 BC shows the head of a barbarian facing to the right. His wild hair flies out behind, his brow is lofty, his eyes are large, his nose is large and hooked, his cheeks are gaunt, and he has a moustache and a long, pointed beard (*Ill. 173*).[1] The personage portrayed can hardly be

173   Vercingetorix: obverse of denarius struck by L. Hostilius Saserna, *c.*48 BC.

other than a Gaul, for there is an elongated, pointed Gaulish shield behind his head. Furthermore, he has a chain round his neck; and his individual features suggest that he can be almost

certainly identified as Vercingetorix, king of the Averni. Vercingetorix raised a revolt against Caesar in 52 BC, but surrendered to him at Alesia and was taken in captivity to Rome. There he remained until Caesar's triumph in 46 BC, when he was put to death. Meanwhile Roman die-engravers and other artists would have had many opportunities of seeing him paraded in the streets of the capital and of studying his appearance; and there would seem to be a reasonable chance that we have in this head the heroic Gaul's true likeness.

There are gold staters of the Averni which show on their obverses a youthful, beardless head, with regular features, facing to the left. Sometimes this head is helmeted, but more often it is bare and crowned by a cap of thick, crisp, short, curly locks. The legends VERCINGETORIXS or VERCINGETORIXIS accompany these heads, which may well have been intended to represent the king.[2] But the marked contrast between them and the highly realistic head on Saserna's denarius suggests that the Avernian obverses carry strongly idealized 'portraits', of ultimately Greek inspiration, not true likenesses.

1   Vessberg 1941, pl. 14, no. 4; Sydenham 1952, p. 159, no. 952, pl. 26; Crawford 1974, no. 448, 2a, b, pl. 52.
2   *RN*, ser. 4, vi, 1902, pp. 25–9, pl. 2, nos. 1–8; A. Blanchet, *Traité des monnaies gauloises*, 1905, pp. 144, 419, fig. 455, pl. 3, nos. 2, 3; B. Cunliffe, *Rome and the Barbarians*, 1976, pl. opp. p. 49 (in colour and enlarged).

Dacia

DECEBALUS
Ills. 174–6

Decebalus, king of the Dacians, although defeated in a war against Domitian (AD 85–9), received favourable peace terms. However, he was attacked by Trajan in two wars (101–2 and 105–6) and was defeated and killed. It is now generally agreed that the spiral reliefs of Trajan's Column in Rome that depict the course of the two Dacian wars were, to a large extent, at any rate, based on sketches made by artists attached to the Roman army at the front; and that the details depicted there – of dress, armour, weapons and other items of equipment, and works of engineering, on both the Roman and Dacian side can be shown to be extremely accurate and realistic where they can be checked by archaeological material, as though they were ultimately derived from eye-witnesses of the campaigns.[1] It is therefore not impossible that the renderings of the Dacian king Decebalus that can be identified on the reliefs may record something of his actual appearance as seen by such wartime draftsmen when Romans and Dacians met in conflict. Moreover, we know from the Column that the dead king's severed head was displayed to the Roman troops,[2] and from Dio Cassius that the head was sent to Rome,[3] where it would have been exhibited and his features thus made familiar to the Roman people.

Two figures of a Dacian on the Column, wearing the characteristic cap of the native aristocracy, can with a very high degree of probability be equated with Decebalus on account of the prominent position that he occupies. In the famous battle scene of the first war in which Jupiter is hurling his bolt at the Dacian enemy, the king stands isolated among trees, the sorrowful witness of his people's defeat (*Ill. 174*).[4] He has deep-set eyes, a large nose, a protruding mouth, and a long, rather straggly beard. The cheeks are gaunt. The whole expression is one of great determination and dignity. The same figure with the same facial features, but this time

174, 175 Decebalus: details from frieze on Trajan's Column showing an important Dacian, almost certainly Decebalus.

accompanied by two attendants in the background, appears towards the end of the second war,
where he stands on a wooded hill, his right hand
raised to his face as though in great mental distress
as he watches his warriors unsuccessfully attacking
a Roman stronghold (*Ill. 175*).[5] Undoubtedly the
king is the figure sinking to his knees at the centre of
a scene almost at the end of the frieze (*Ill. 176*).[6] He
retains his cap, but his beard is somewhat longer
and more unkempt, and his eyes spell rage as he
turns to gaze at the Roman horseman who is riding
him down. In his right hand he grasps the curved
sword with which he is about to cut his own throat.[7]

1 E.g. *Papers of the British School at Rome*, xiii, 1935, pp.
   1–40.
2 F. B. Florescu, *Die Trajanssäule*, 1969, pl. 118: the
   features of the head are unfortunately worn away.
3 DC, lxviii, 14, 3: ἡ κεφαλὴ αὐτοῦ [sc. Δεκεβάλου]
   ἐς τὴν Ῥώμην ἀπεκομίσθη.
4 Florescu, op. cit., pls. 18, 19, fig. 57 on p. 113.
5 Ibid., pl. 110.
6 Ibid., pl. 116.
7 DC, lxviii, 14, 3: Δεκέβαλος . . . διεχρήσατο ἑαυτόν.

176 Decebalus: detail from frieze on Trajan's Column.

Illyria

GENTHIOS (*c.* 180–168 BC)
Ill. 177
In 169 BC the Illyrian 'regulus' Genthios sided with Perseus of Macedon against Rome. But in the following year the praetor, L. Anicius Gallus, reduced Scodra, Genthios' capital, captured him, and carried him off to Rome. He was kept a prisoner in Italy and died there. Rome divided the country into three areas, but allowed the kingship to continue.[1]

Genthios' portrait bust, facing to the right, appears on his bronze coins. He wears a broad-brimmed Macedonian hat (*kausia*) and is beardless, with a slightly hooked nose, a small mouth, and a jutting chin (*Ill. 177*).[2]

1 J. J. Wilkes, *Dalmatia*, 1969, pp. 23–8.
2 *NC*, n.s. xx, 1880, pl. 13, nos. 6, 7; F. Imhoof-Blumer, *Porträtköpfe auf antiken Münzen hellenischer und hellenisierter Völker*, 1885, pl. 2, no. 18; J. Brunšmid, *Inschriften und Münzen der griechischen Städte Dalmatiens*, 1898, p. 71, nos. 4, 5; Head 1911, pp. 316–17.

BALLAEUS (167–135 BC)
Ill. 178
Ballaeus, Genthios' successor, is known to us only from his coin portraits in silver and bronze. His head faces now left, now right, and his features are remarkably Roman in type. He has a large nose, a small, firm set mouth, and a determined chin. His straight hair forms a thick cap with 'pudding-basin' cut, the individual locks being combed neatly forward on to the brow (*Ill. 178*).[1]

1 *BMCGC Thessaly, etc.*, 1883, pl. 14, nos. 12–14; Imhoof-Blumer, op. cit., pl. 2, no. 19; Richter 1965, fig. 1758.

177 Genthios: obverse of bronze coin.

178 Ballaeus: obverse of silver coin.

Macedon

PHILIP V (238–179 BC)
Ills. 179–81
Clashes between Macedonians and Romans began in 229 BC, when the latter established a bridgehead in Illyria. In 215 BC Philip signed a treaty with Hannibal and in 202 BC reached an agreement with Antiochus III of Syria, with a view to dividing up Egypt. In 200 BC Rome declared war on Philip (Second Macedonian War), landing two legions in Illyria; and in 197 BC the king was defeated by T.

Quinctius Flamininus (q.v.) at Cynoscephalae. Philip was allowed to keep his throne, but had to make peace with Rome on her terms, surrendering all his possessions outside Macedonia and most of his fleet and paying a huge indemnity. He was then advised to seek Rome's friendship.[1] But he never really became Rome's client, maintaining his independence in matters of foreign policy and in his choice of successor. He died at Amphipolis in 179 BC.

Philip's head, facing to the right, appears on the obverses of his silver tetradrachms (*Ill. 179*).[2] He has fairly neat curly hair, encircled by a diadem and growing low on the back of the neck, a low brow, large eyes, a straight nose, a small mouth with slightly parted lips, a moustache and a short, tightly curled beard. Silver tetradrachms of Polyrrhenia in Crete show him facing to the right as Apollo, but with his own portrait-like features (*Ill. 180*).[3] In his curly, agitated hair he wears a fillet; he has side-burns but no beard, and has a bow and quiver projecting from behind his neck.

What may be a third coin portrait of Philip is the head, facing to the left, on the obverses of silver tetradrachms, drachms and hemidrachms. These show a typical circular Macedonian shield, on the boss of which is the leftward-facing head of a man wearing the elaborate helmet of Perseus with wings and a griffin's head surmounting it, while a sword or dagger projects diagonally from behind his neck (*Ill. 181*).[4] He has a short beard, resembling that of Philip V on his rightward-facing coin portrait, but the features, in particular the nose, are somewhat more irregular. The reverse bears a club and the legend ΒΑΣΙΛΕΩΣ ΦΙΛΙΠΠΟΥ. But it could be that the portrait is that of his son Perseus as crown prince struck during his father's lifetime.

1 Livy xxxiii, 35, 5: '[Cn.Cornelius] ei [sc. Philippo] suasit, quoniam pacem impetrasset, ad societatem amicitiamque petendam mitteret Romam legatos'.
2 Newell 1936, pl. 2, nos. 1, 3; F. W. Walbank, *Philip V of Macedon*, 1940, frontispiece (above); Richter 1965, fig. 1746; Scullard 1970, pl. 37; Davis and Kraay 1973, pls. 123, 127.
3 Walbank, op. cit., frontispiece (below).
4 Newell 1937, pl. 2, no. 2; Richter 1965, fig. 1748.

PERSEUS (179–168 BC)
Ills. 182, 183

Perseus, the elder son of Philip V and the last king of Macedon, renewed his father's treaty with Rome and was recognized by her as king.[1] But he proceeded to extend his kingdom, challenging by his eastern policy the predominance of Pergamon and thus bringing on the Third Macedonian War in 171 BC. Defeated decisively at Pydna in 168 BC by L. Aemilius Paullus (q.v.), he was taken to Rome to adorn his conqueror's triumph and died two years later in Italy.

Right
179–81 Philip V: obverses of silver tetradrachms; the example in the centre, minted at Polyrrhenia, shows him in the guise of Apollo, and the lower one as Perseus (although this may be a portrait of his son Perseus as crown prince).

Perseus' coin portraits on his silver tetradrachms, with the reverse legend ΒΑΣΙΛΕΩΣ ΠΕΡΣΕΩΣ show his head facing to the right. He has a rather high, receding brow, a sharp, pointed nose, deep-set eyes, a moustache and a short beard. His diademed hair is sometimes loose and agitated (*Ill. 182*),[2] at other times worn in rather tighter curls (*Ill. 183*).[3]

1 Livy xl, 58, 9: 'Perseus potitus regno . . . legatos Romam ad amicitiam paternam renovandam petendumque, ut rex a senatu appellaretur, misit'.
2 Newell 1937, pl. 2, no. 5; Richter 1965, fig. 1749; Davis and Kraay 1973, pls. 125, 128.
3 Newell 1937, pl. 2, no. 4.

ANDRISCUS (PHILIP VI; 149–148 BC)
Ill. 184

Andriscus was an adventurer from Adramyttium in Mysia, who gave himself out as Philip, the son of Perseus and his queen Laodice, and claimed the Macedonian throne in 150 BC. He managed to establish himself in the country in 149 BC, but was crushed in the next year by Q. Caecilius Metellus. Meanwhile he had struck silver tetradrachms in his own name and with his own portrait. The reverse has a club and the legend ΒΑΣΙΛΕΩΣ ΦΙΛΙΠΠΟΥ, directly copied from the Philip V/Perseus coin (cf. *Ill. 181*). So was the obverse design, showing

Above
182, 183 Perseus: obverses of silver tetradrachms, showing variation in the rendering of the hair.

Left
184 Andriscus (Philip VI): obverse of silver tetradrachm with portrait of the king as Perseus (cf. *Ill. 181*).

Andriscus facing to the left on the boss of a round Macedonian shield. He wears the same winged helmet with griffin's head and has the same sword or dagger projecting from behind his neck. But the locks above his brow are wilder, his jaw is squarer, his mouth more firmly set, and he is beardless (*Ill. 184*).[1]

1 *ZfN*, xxiii, 1902, pp. 153–5; Head 1911, p. 239; Newell 1937, pl. 2, no. 7; Richter 1965, fig. 1750.

Greece

NABIS of Sparta (207–192 BC)
Ill. 185
Nabis of Sparta became an ally of Rome and was recognized by her as king on condition of rendering her assistance.[1] In the Second Macedonian War he had gained Argos, which Philip V betrayed to him, but went over to Flamininus. In 195 BC he was forced to give up Argos and the Laconian ports and two years later was subdued by Flamininus while trying to regain the ports. He was assassinated in a coup d'état in Sparta.

Nabis' portraits on the obverses of his silver tetradrachms show him facing to the right (*Ill. 185*).[2] He has thick, rather untidy hair encircled by a laurel-wreath, a high brow, of which the lower part projects, rather bulging eyes, a straight nose, a small, somewhat weak mouth with parted lips, a short beard and a thick neck. The reverses bear his name in Laconian dialect – ΒΑΙΛΕΟΣ ΝΑΒΙΟΣ.

185 Nabis of Sparta: obverse of silver tetradrachm with laureate head.

1 Livy xxxiv, 30, 31.
2 C. Seltman, *Greek Coins*, 1933, pl. 62, no. 8; Richter 1965, fig. 1760; Scullard 1970, pl. 38.

NIKIAS of Cos (*c*. 50 BC – time of Augustus)
Ill. 186
Nikias, tyrant of Cos, is mentioned by Strabo.[1] His bronze coin portrait shows his head on the obverses facing to the right, with the legend ΝΙΚΙΑΣ (*Ill. 186*).[2] He is remarkably Roman in appearance, with short, neat hair encircled by a diadem, a high brow, large eyes, a huge, hooked nose, a slightly protruding mouth and a clean-shaven chin.

1 xiv, 658: καὶ καθ' ἡμᾶς Νικίας ὁ καὶ τυραννήσας Κῴων.
2 *BMCGC Caria, etc.*, 1897, pl. 32, no. 13; Richter 1965, fig. 1920.

186 Nikias of Cos: obverse of bronze coin with portrait in the Roman style.

Thrace

MOSTIS (*c.* 200–150 BC)
Ills. 187, 188
Tetradrachms carry on their obverses the bust of
Mostis, who was the first Thracian king of Roman
times to place his portrait on his coins (*Ills. 187,
188*).[1] He faces to the right and wears a diadem on
his curly hair and a cloak round his shoulders. He
gazes upwards and has exceptionally fine, well-cut
features – a long nose slightly turned up at the tip,
large eyes, full, clean-shaven cheeks and full lips, a
slightly double chin, and a thick neck.

1 *BMCGC Thrace, etc.*, 1877, p. 206, no. 1; F. Imhoof-
Blumer, *Porträtköpfe*, 1885, pl. 2, no. 15; *CAH*, vol. iii
of plates, p. 19, q.

COTYS III (57–45/44 BC)
[No illustration]
Cotys III sided with Pompey against Caesar. The
obverses of his bronze coins depict his diademed
head facing to the right.[1]

187, 188 Mostis III: obverses of silver coins showing
diademed bust with finely cut features.

1 Head 1911, p. 286.

SADALAS (died childless; 45/44–42 BC)
[No illustration]
Sadalas helped Pompey at the battle of Pharsalus
(48). His head, diademed, faces to the right on his
small bronze coins.[1]

1 *CAH*, vol. iii of plates, p. 19, r.

RHOEMETALCES I (*c.* 11 BC–AD 12)
Ill. 189
Rhoemetalces joined Octavian just before Actium
and was allowed to retain his kingdom. During the
Thracian revolt of 13–11 BC he was chased into the
Chersonese and his ward and nephew, the prince
Rhescuporis I, was slain. Rhoemetalces helped
Rome during the Pannonian revolt of AD 6–7.

Rhoemetalces' bronze coins show on the reverses
his head diademed and facing to the right, both
jugate with his wife (*Ill. 189*) and alone. The
obverses bear the jugate heads of Augustus and
Livia and the head of Augustus alone.[1] The king is
clean-shaven and has long locks of neat, curly hair.

1 *BMCGC Thrace, etc.*, 1877, pp. 208, 209; Imhoof-
Blumer, op. cit., pl. 2, no. 16.

189 Rhoemetalces I: reverse of bronze coin showing
jugate heads of king and queen.

RHESCUPORIS II (AD 12–19)
[No illustration]

Rhescuporis II, the brother of Rhoemetalces I, was given western Thrace by Augustus, while his nephew, Cotys IV, received eastern Thrace, Rhescuporis then tried to extend his dominions and killed Cotys IV (q.v.). Tiberius summoned him to Rome for trial and there he was accused by Cotys' wife, Antonia Tryphaena. He was exiled to Alexandria and killed there. His name, but not his portrait, appears on the reverses of Cotys IV's coins.

RHOEMETALCES III (AD 37/8–46)
Ill. 191

Rhoemetalces III was the last king of eastern Thrace. In, or just before, AD 46 he was murdered by his wife; and Claudius annexed the whole country as a Roman province. His bronze coins bear on the reverses the king's diademed and draped bust facing to the left (*Ill. 191*).[1]

1 *BMCGC Thrace, etc.*, 1877, p. 210, no. 2; Head 1911, p. 286.

COTYS IV (AD 12–19)
Ill. 190

Cotys IV, the nephew of Rhescuporis II, received from Rome as his kingdom the eastern part of Thrace. He married Antonia Tryphaena, the daughter of Polemo I (q.v.) of Pontus and Bosporus, and was murdered by his uncle. His silver and bronze coins show on the obverses his diademed and draped bust facing to the right (*Ill. 190*).[1] He has neat, curly hair, a large, jutting nose, a firm mouth and chin, and no beard.

1 Imhoof-Blumer, op. cit., pl. 2, no. 17.

190 Cotys IV: obverse of bronze coin.

191 Rhoemetalces III: reverse of bronze coin.

RHOEMETALCES II (AD 19–c.40)
[No illustration]

Rhoemetalces II was the son of the disgraced Rhescuporis II, but was allowed by Tiberius to retain his western Thracian kingdom. His bronze coins show on the obverses his beardless head facing to the right and diademed. The reverses carry the head of Tiberius.[1]

1 *RN*, ser. 4, iv, 1900, p. 422, nos. 82, 83; Head 1911, p. 286.

Pergamon

PHILETAIROS (280–263 BC)
Ills. 192, 193
Philetairos is significant in Roman history as the founder of the Attalid dynasty, whose last representative, Attalus III, bequeathed his kingdom to Rome. His highly distinctive coin portrait facing to the right – with its heavy jowl, curly, diademed hair, double chin, low brow, large nose, broad, full, clean-shaven cheeks, small, keen eyes, and protruding lower lip and chin – appears on the silver tetradrachms issued, not by himself, but by his successors, Eumenes I (263–241 BC), Attalus I Soter (241–197 BC), Attalus II Philadelphos (160–138 BC), and Attalus III Philometor (138–133 BC), none of whom struck coin portraits of themselves. Attalus I made an alliance with Rome against Philip V of Macedon, Attalus II

remained faithful to Rome, and Attalus III was well received when he visited Rome as a youth of eighteen and by his bequest to Rome made possible the creation of the Roman province of Asia.

Philetairos' portrait coins are very numerous and, despite some minor variations, all display the same unmistakable, individual likenesses (*Ill. 192*).[1] Almost certainly portraits of the king are a gem in the British Museum (*Ill. 193*)[2] and a marble head at Naples,[3] both of which have his distinctive features and hair, but no diadem.

1 *CAH*, vol. iii of plates, p. 5, d; Newell 1937, figs. on pp. 35, 36; U. Westermark, *Das Bildnis des Philetairos von Pergamon* (a corpus), 1961; Richter 1965, figs. 1913–14; Davis and Kraay, 1973, pls. 180, 184.
2 Richter 1965, fig. 1916.
3 Ibid., figs. 1910–12.

EUMENES II (197–160 BC)
Ill. 194
Eumenes II helped Rome to drive Antiochus the Great's army out of Greece and allowed the Roman army to cross the Hellespont unopposed, while Pergamene forces, particularly naval forces, contributed to Rome's overwhelming defeat of Antiochus at Magnesia (189 BC). In return Rome gave Eumenes the Thracian Chersonese, large slices of Seleucid territory in Asia Minor, and the war-elephants of Antiochus, who had to pay a large cash indemnity to Pergamon. All this enabled Eumenes to transform Pergamon from a city-state into a great kingdom. In 172 BC the king went to

192, 193 Philetairos: obverse of posthumously minted silver tetradrachm, and gem.

194 Eumenes II: obverse of silver tetradrachm.

Rome to complain of the ambitions of Perseus of Macedon and Pergamene troops fought against him at Pydna.

Eumenes II was the only king of Pergamon to issue silver tetradrachms with his own rightward-facing portrait (*Ill. 194*).[1] He has curly, diademed hair and handsome features – a lofty brow, a large, aquiline nose, a small mouth, a lean, tapering, clean-shaven face, and a small chin. His reverse type of the Dioscuri may have been chosen as a compliment to Rome.

1 Richter 1965, fig. 1917; Davis and Kraay, 1973, pls. 182, 185.

Bithynia

PRUSIAS I (228–185 BC)
Ills. 195, 196

It was with Prusias, the first Bithynian king with a coin portrait to figure in Roman history, that Hannibal (q.v.) took refuge in 184 BC. Scipio Africanus had managed to detach him from Antiochus III by means of a letter in which Prusias was assured that Rome did not intend to deprive him of his kingdom.[1]

Prusias' silver tetradrachms show him facing to the right, with fairly neat, diademed hair, a high brow, large eyes, an aquiline nose, a protruding mouth, and a thick, curly beard (*Ills. 195, 196*).[2]

1 Scullard 1970, pp. 204–5.
2 *BMCGC Pontus, etc.*, 1889, pl. 37, nos. 2, 3; *CAH*, vol. iv of plates, p. 7, f; Newell 1937, pl. 3, nos. 2, 3; Richter 1965, fig. 1922; Scullard 1970, pl. 40; Davis and Kraay 1973, pls. 188, 191.

PRUSIAS II (185–149 BC)
Ill. 197

Prusias helped Rome in her war with Perseus of Macedon; and after the defeat of Perseus he went to Rome, according to Polybius' account, as Rome's 'freedman', with his son (later Nicomedes II), to congratulate the Senate;[1] his servility was regarded with contempt. He left Nicomedes to be brought up in Rome.

Prusias' portrait on his silver tetradrachms depicts him facing right, with somewhat agitated hair encircled by a diadem and a receding brow (*Ill. 197*).[2] His gaze is directed upwards. He has a long, pointed nose, a small mouth, full cheeks, on which, on some dies, there are traces of a very slight beard, although he is clean-shaven normally. His mouth is small, his chin prominent, and his neck creased. On both his silver and bronze coins his diadem is winged. Polybius, who had a very low opinion of

Prusias II, describes him as ill-favoured.[3] But his coin portraits hardly support this verdict.

1 Livy xlv, 44.
2 *BMCGC Pontus, etc.*, 1889, pl. 38, nos. 1–3; *CAH*, vol. iv of plates, p. 7, g; Newell 1937, pl. 3, no. 4; Richter 1965, fig. 1923; Davis and Kraay 1973, pls. 192, 196.
3 xxxvii, 2: εἰδεχθὴς κατὰ τὴν ἔμφασιν.

195, 196 Prusias I: obverses of silver tetradrachms (upper example actual size).

NICOMEDES II (149–128? BC)
Ill. 198

Nicomedes II revolted against his father, Prusias II, and ordered his death. He continued his father's friendship with Rome, helping her against Aristonicus, a pretender to the throne of Pergamon in 133 BC.[1]

Nicomedes was certainly no beauty. His silver tetradrachms and gold staters carry his rightward-facing diademed head, with untidy hair, receding brow, upward gazing eyes set very high in his head, a long, pointed nose turned up at the tip, a slightly pouting mouth, fat cheeks, a jutting chin and a full throat (*Ill. 198*).[2]

1 Strabo xiv, 646; Eutropius iv, 20.
2 *BMCGC Pontus, etc.*, 1889, pl. 38, no. 10, pl. 39, nos. 1–3; *CAH*, vol. iv of plates, p. 7, h; Newell 1937, pl. 3, no. 5; Richter 1965, fig. 1924; Davis and Kraay 1973, pls. 194, 197.

197 Prusias II: obverse of silver tetradrachm.

198 Nicomedes II: obverse of silver tetradrachm.

MUSA and ORADALTIS of Prusias-ad-Mare (Cius)
Ills. 199, 200

After Nicomedes III (or IV?) bequeathed the kingdom of Bithynia to Rome in 74 BC,[1] the city of Prusias-ad-Mare, on the Propontis, the one-time Cius, seems to have been ruled at some period by two independent queens, Musa and Oradaltis (or Orodaltis), whose portraits and names appear on their bronze coinage. Musa's diademed head faces to the left. Her face is slightly tilted up and she has full cheeks and lips and a rounded chin (*Ill. 199*).[2] Oradaltis' draped bust faces right and she too is diademed, with facial features closely resembling those of Musa (*Ill. 200*).[3]

1 Livy, *Epit.*, 93.
2 T. Reinach, *Trois royaumes de l'Asie Mineure*, 1888, p. 135, no. 22, pl. 8, fig. 7; W. H. Waddington, *Recueil général des monnaies d'Asie Mineure*, i, 1904, p. 316, no. 26, pl. 50, fig. 7.
3 Reinach, op. cit., p. 136, no. 23, pl. 8, fig. 8; Waddington, op. cit., p. 163, no. 27, pl. 50, figures 8 and 9.

199, 200 Musa and Oradaltis of Prusias ad Mare: obverses of bronze coins.

Pontus and Bosporus

MITHRADATES II or III of Pontus (*c.*250–*c.*185
BC)
Ill. 201

Mithradates II or III, although married to Laodice, the sister of Seleucus II of Syria, supported
Antiochus Hierax against the latter's brother Seleucus (*c.*239). His expansionist policy in Asia Minor
was significant for Rome's future contacts with the
Pontic kingdom.

Mithradates' silver tetradrachms present his
draped bust facing to the right. His short, neat hair
is encircled by a diadem and his facial features are
highly individual. He has a high, receding and
furrowed brow, large eyes, a long, projecting nose,
curved at the bridge and slightly turned up at the
tip, broad cheeks, a small beard that leaves his
rounded chin exposed, a moustache and full, parted lips. There are creases of flesh on his neck (*Ill.
201*).[1]

1 *BMCGC Pontus, etc.*, 1889, pl. 8, no. 2; Head 1911, p.
500, fig. 261; *CAH*, vol. iv of plates, p. 3, l; Newell
1937, p. 42, fig. 1; Richter 1965, fig. 1925; Davis and
Kraay 1973, pls. 198, 202.

PHARNACES I (*c.*185–170 BC)
Ill. 202

Pharnaces I, the son of Mithradates III, tried
(despite Roman disapproval) to continue his
father's expansionist policy at the expense of the
Pergamene and Bithynian kingdoms. In this he
largely failed, and had to surrender most of his
conquests in 179 BC, but he retained Sinope which
now became the chief residence of the kings of
Pontus. His treaty with Chersonesus suggests that
he had his eye on the Crimea – a project which,
however, proved abortive.

Pharnaces' portrait head on his silver tetradrachms is even more individual than his
predecessor's. He has a skull that projects markedly
behind, and short, neat, diademed hair, a very
furrowed brow, very large, deep-set eyes, a long
pointed nose with heavy nostrils, a thick and jutting
lower lip, a lean, tapering face, a slight moustache
and a slight beard (*Ill. 202*).[1]

1 *BMCGC Pontus, etc.*, 1889, pl. 8, no. 3; Head 1911, p.
500, fig. 262; *CAH*, vol. iv of plates, p. 3, m; Newell
1937, p. 42, fig. 2; Richter 1965, fig. 1926; Davis and
Kraay 1973, pls. 200, 203.

MITHRADATES IV PHILOPATOR PHILADELPHOS
(*c.*170–150 BC) and LAODICE
Ill. 203

Mithradates IV was the brother of Pharnaces I and
the husband of his own sister Laodice. In 168/7 BC
he made a dedication in Rome, whose friend and
ally he became.[1] He supported Attalus II of Pergamon against Prusias II of Bithynia.

On his silver tetradrachms Mithradates' portrait
appears either alone, with his head poked forward
and facing to the right, or as a draped bust jugate
with that of Laodice and again facing right (*Ill.
203*).[2] He has neat, short, diademed hair, a furrowed brow, a slightly hooked nose, a small mouth

201   Mithradates II (or III) of Pontus: obverse of silver
tetradrachm.

202   Pharnaces I: obverse of silver tetradrachm.

with thick and parted lips, a slight moustache and beard, a small, round chin and a thick, creased neck. Laodice, who is also diademed, bears a close resemblance to her brother/husband, particularly as regards her eyes, nose, mouth and chin.

Mithradates V Euergetes, who was probably the son of Pharnaces I, has left us no coin portraits. He combined a philo-Roman[3] with an expansionist policy, aiding Rome against Carthage in 149–146 BC and against Aristonicus in 132–129 BC. He received Phrygia from Rome as a reward, gained control of Galatia, and brought Cappadocia under his influence. He was murdered in 120 BC at Sinope.

1 H. Dessau, *Inscriptiones Latinae Selectae*, no. 30.
2 *CAH*, vol. iv of plates, p. 3, n, o; Richter 1965, fig. 1927; Davis and Kraay 1973, pls. 204, 206.
3 Appian, *Mithradates* 10.

203 Mithradates IV: obverse of silver tetradrachm.

MITHRADATES VI EUPATOR DIONYSOS ('the Great'; 120–63 BC)

Ills. 204, 205

The life of Mithradates VI, the son of Euergetes, his achievements and his confrontations with Rome in the three Mithradatic Wars, are very well known and need not be repeated in detail here. An ardent expansionist, he first acquired the northern shore of the Black Sea (the Bosporan region), then most of Asia Minor and a large part of Greece, but after his armies had been defeated in Greece by Sulla he had to relinquish most of these conquests when concluding peace with Sulla in 85 BC. In 74 BC he occupied Bithynia, but was expelled from Pontus by Lucullus in 72 BC. Recovering his kingdom in 67 BC, he was defeated the next year at Nicopolis by Pompey and fled to Colchis and then to the Crimea. In 63 BC his son Pharnaces II revolted against him and was recognized as king of Bosporus by Pompey; whereupon Mithradates died a voluntary death.

The contrast between the limited attempts at expansion of his predecessors and Mithradates' own determined, sustained and uninhibited bids for empire on an unprecedented scale is vividly reflected in his coin portraits. In place of the earlier short, neat hair, short moustaches and beards and realistic features, Mithradates' likenesses consciously imitate the idealized Alexander iconography (*Ill. 204*).[1] The locks of his hair are wild and sinuous and almost conceal his diadem. He has side-burns on some dies, but never a beard. His eyes gaze upwards, his brow is unfurrowed, his nose is regular, his parted lips are slightly smiling, his head is thrust eagerly forward on his long neck, on which a small 'Adam's apple' can be discerned below his firm, rounded chin.

204, 205 Mithradates VI: idealized coin portrait, and marble head with lion's-scalp head-dress in imitation of Alexander the Great.

Mithradates' most authentic sculptural portrait is the splendid marble head in the Louvre, where he has side-burns and wears a lion's-scalp head-dress, in imitation of Alexander (*Ill. 205*).[2] Another marble sculpture that very probably depicts him is the draped and diademed bust of Helios in Venice, which has his characteristic hair and features.[3]

1 *CAH*, vol. iv of plates, p. 5, a, b, c; Newell 1937, p. 42, fig. 3, 4; Richter 1965, figs. 1928–9; Davis and Kraay 1973, pls. 207, 209. For a detailed discussion of the coin portraits, see *JDAI*, lxviii, 1953, pp. 73–95.
2 *CAH*, vol. iv of plates, p. 44, c, d; Richter 1965, figs. 1930, 1933.
3 *AA*, 1969, pp. 189–95, figs. 1–3, 5.

PHARNACES II (63–47 BC)
Ill. 206

Pharnaces II was the son of Mithradates VI of Pontus. In 63 BC he plotted against his father, informed Pompey of the latter's death, and sought Rome's recognition of his claim to the Bosporan kingdom, holding it as her client.[1] Rome regarded him as a *rex externus*, which gave him considerable independence.[2] When Rome was distracted by the civil war between Pompey and Caesar he expanded his kingdom and overran part of Pontus, defeating Caesar's lieutenant, Calvinus, in 68 BC. However, in 47 BC he was defeated by Caesar at Zela in Pontus and fled to Sinope and then to Panticapaeum, where he was besieged by his subordinate, Asander, and killed.[3]

Pharnaces' gold coin portraits depict him on the obverses facing to the right, diademed and with sinuous locks of hair, a large nose, a wide, smiling mouth, a jutting, clean-shaven chin and a full throat (*Ill. 206*).[4]

1 Plutarch, *Pompey* 41, 5; Appian, *Mithradates* 113.
2 Caesar, *Bellum Alexandrinum* 34, 2.
3 DC, xlii, 47.
4 F. Imhoof-Blumer, *Porträtköpfe*, 1885, pl. 5, no. 5.

ASANDER (47–17/16 BC)
Ill. 207

After Pharnaces II's death and the defeat of Mithradates of Pergamon, whom Rome had made king of Bosporus as a *rex amicissimus*,[1] Asander took command of Bosporus, ruling it first as archon and then as king, a title that first appears on his coins in 41 BC. He may have bribed Marcus Antonius to recognize his kingship; and Octavian enrolled him as an *amicus populi Romani*.[2] He married Dynamis, daughter of Pharnaces II (q.v.). An adventurer, Scribonius, revolted against him in 17 BC and he committed suicide at the age of ninety-two.

Asander's gold coin portrait faces to the right.[3] He is beardless and diademed, and has thick curly hair, a large nose, and a prominent chin (*Ill. 207*).

1 Caesar, *Bellum Alexandrinum*, 78.
2 Asander is φιλορώμαιος in R. Cagnat, *Inscriptiones Graecae ad Res Romanas Pertinentes*, i, 1911, no. 874.
3 *BMCGC Pontus, etc.*, 1889, pl. 10, nos. 9–11.

206   Pharnaces II: obverse of gold coin.

207   Asander: obverse of gold coin.

208   Dynamis: obverse of gold stater with draped bust and diademed hair.

DYNAMIS
Ill. 208

After Asander's death Dynamis married Scribonius, but kept the Bosporan power in her own hands, since gold coins struck by her in 17/16 BC carry her own portrait and name alone (*Ill. 208*).[1] Her draped bust faces to the right and she wears her diademed hair in a thick roll round her brow. She is later described as φιλορώμαιος.[2]

1 *CAH*, vol. iv of plates, p. 209, j.
2 Cagnat, op. cit., no. 905.

POLEMO I (*c.*37/6–8 BC) and PYTHODORIS
Ills. 209, 210

Polemo I had held Laodicea-on-the-Lycus against the Parthians and was granted a kingdom by Marcus Antonius, with his headquarters at Iconium in Cilicia Tracheia. But he lost it when Antonius gave Cilicia to Cleopatra, receiving in exchange, in 37/6 BC, the old kingdom of Pontus, plus Armenia Minor. After Actium, Polemo made peace with Octavian, who deprived him of Armenia Minor, but had him recognized, probably by a senatorial decree, as 'friend of the Roman people'.[1] In 14 BC Agrippa sent Polemo to attack Scribonius (see above) in Bosporus;[2] and after a struggle the Bosporans submitted, Scribonius being now dead, and were forced to accept Polemo, who married Dynamis (q.v.), as their king.[2] The marriage only lasted, however, for a year and Polemo then married Pythodoris, a granddaughter of Marcus Antonius, a remarkable woman who, after Polemo's death, ruled the Pontic kingdom till *c.*AD

8 BC. Dynamis was now recognized by Augustus as queen of Bosporus and φιλορώμαιος. But her coins now bear the heads of Augustus and Agrippa and her monogram but not her portrait. She died in AD 7/8.

The silver coins of Polemo and Pythodoris, struck in Pontus, show their portraits, both facing to the right (*Ills. 209, 210*).[3] Polemo is curly-haired, diademed and beardless; Pythodoris' hair forms a chignon on the nape of her neck.

1 DC, liii, 25, 1.
2 Ibid., liv, 24.
3 W. H. Waddington, *Recueil général des monnaies d'Asie Mineure*, i, 1904, p. 20, fig. 3.

ASPURGUS (*c.*AD 10/11–37/8) and GEPAEPYRIS
Ills. 211–13

Aspurgus (see above) was not officially associated with his wife Dynamis (q.v.) during her lifetime; and he does not appear to have become ruler of Bosporus until AD 10/11 or to have borne the royal title until AD 14/15, when Tiberius granted him Roman citizenship and recognized him as a friend of Rome.[1] He died in AD 37/8, leaving two sons, Mithradates by Dynamis, and Cotys by his second wife, Gepaepyris, a Thracian princess, who ruled conjointly with her step-son for a short while after Aspurgus' death.

Aspurgus' coin portraits are something of a mystery. The British Museum Catalogue (where he is given wrong dates) ascribes to him gold coins which carry an undiademed and beardless head with straight hair and a turned-up tip to the nose

209, 210　Polemo I and Pythodoris: silver coin portraits (actual size; after Waddington).

211　Aspurgus(?): obverse of gold coin attributed to Aspurgus.

23. Meanwhile Dynamis had taken refuge with Aspurgus (q.v.), the ruler of a Sarmatian tribe, married him, and organized a revolt in Bosporus against Polemo. This revolt lasted for several years; Polemo failed to crush it, and he was put to death in

(*Ill. 211*).[2] On the other hand it is possible that we have his portrait on bronze coins which have on the obverses portraits of Tiberius and Caligula and on the reverses a diademed, rightward-facing head, beardless and with thick hair growing low on

the neck (*Ill. 212*).[3] These coins bear the monogram BAR, which is interpreted in the Catalogue as
BA(*sileus*) R(*hescuporis*), a name that is not known as
that of kings of Bosporus until the late first century
AD; and the monogram could be explained,
perhaps, as B(*asileus*) A(*spu*) R(*gus*). Possibly the
undiademed head on the reverses of the gold coins
cited above, which have portraits of Augustus on
the obverses, may portray Aspurgus before he
obtained the royal title. But the features of the two
portraits do not show much resemblance.

The bronze coin portrait of Gepaepyris presents
her draped bust facing to the right. She is diademed
and has corkscrew curls hanging down the sides of
her neck. Her later coins, with the same portrait of
herself (*Ill. 213*), bear on the reverses the diademed
and draped bust of her step-son Mithradates.[4]

1 Cagnat, op. cit., no. 906.
2 *BMCGC Pontus, etc.*, 1889, pl. 10, nos. 12, 13.
3 Ibid., pl. 11, nos. 5, 6.
4 Ibid., pl. 11, no. 8; *CAH*, vol. iv of plates, p. 209, h, i.

MITHRADATES (AD 37/8–44/5)
Ill. 214

Mithradates, the son of Aspurgus, was recognized
as king of Bosporus by Claudius in AD 41. But,
despite the protests of Gepaepyris, he sought to
assert his independence of Rome by placing his
name and royal title on his bronze coins (*Ill. 214*).[1]
On the obverses of these his head faces to the right
and is diademed and he has long, lank locks, fairly
short on the neck, and a short beard. Mithradates
sent his half-brother Cotys to Rome to report to
Claudius; but instead Cotys betrayed to the emperor Mithradates' rebellious designs.[2] Cotys was
rewarded with the throne of Mithradates, who was
defeated when trying to recover it, carried off to
Rome and eventually put to death by Galba.

1 *BMCGC Pontus, etc.*, 1889, pl. 11, no. 7.
2 Tacitus, *Ann.* xii, 15–21.

COTYS I (AD 44/5–?)
Ill. 215

Cotys I, the betrayer of his half-brother Mithradates, was installed as king of Bosporus in AD 44/5
by a Roman armed force. The date of his death is
unknown. His bronze coin portraits show his diademed head facing to the right on the obverse (*Ill.
215*).[1] He is beardless and his hair grows low on the
nape of his neck. A portrait of Britannicus occupies
the reverse.

1 *BMCGC Pontus, etc.*, pl. 11, no. 13.

212 Aspurgus(?): reverse of bronze coin with portrait
accompanied by monogram BAR.

213 Gepaepyris: obverse of bronze coin with draped bust.

214 Mithradates of Bosporus: obverse of bronze coin
inscribed with the king's name and title.

ANTONIA TRYPHAENA
Ill. 216

Antonia Tryphaena, the daughter of Polemo I of
Pontus and Bosporus and of Pythodoris (qq.v.) was
the wife of Cotys IV of Thrace and the accuser of

215 Cotys I: obverse of bronze coin (Cotys was installed by Rome as king of Bosporus).

216 Antonia Tryphaena: reverse of silver coin with diademed and draped bust.

217 Polemo II: obverse of silver coin with youthful portrait.

218 Rhescuporis I of Bosporus: obverse of gold coin with diademed bust.

her husband's murderer, his uncle Rhescuporis II (q.v.) of Thrace. Her portrait, a diademed and draped bust facing to the right, appears on the reverses of silver coins (*Ill. 216*), with that of her son, Polemo II, on the obverses.[1]

> 1 *BMCGC Pontus, etc.*, 1889, pl. 10, no. 6; Waddington, op. cit., pl. 3, no. 11.

POLEMO II (AD 38–64/5)
Ill. 217

In AD 38 Polemo II, the son of Cotys of Thrace and Antonia Tryphaena (q.v.), was given the kingdom of Pontus-with-Bosporus by Caligula. Since Pythodoris' death in AD 23 (cf. p. 117), Pontus had been under Roman wardship, but the kingdom was now restored. As for Bosporus, Polemo never ruled it, since Gepaepyris and her step-son Mithradates (q.v.) remained in possession of that kingdom till 44/5. In 41, when Claudius revoked Caligula's grant of Bosporus to Polemo, the latter was compensated with the Cilician principality of Olbia, etc. In 63/4 Nero annexed the Pontic realm by adding it to the province of Galatia and Polemo returned to his Cilician territory.

The king's coin portrait, on silver, depicts him on the obverses as facing to the right, youthful and beardless, and with a diadem encircling his neat, straight hair. Portraits of Agrippina II, Claudius, Nero, Britannicus and Antonia Tryphaena feature on the reverses (*Ill. 217*).[1]

> 1 *BMCGC Pontus, etc.*, 1889, pl. 10, nos. 1–7; Waddington, op. cit., pp. 22–5, pl. 3, nos. 11–24.

RHESCUPORIS I of Bosporus (*c.*AD 68/69–*c.*90)
Ill. 218

Cotys' son Rhescuporis was granted the kingdom in AD 68/69. On the gold and bronze coins of Rhescuporis I (not II) the obverse portraits show his bust facing to the right, with a diadem in his very thick hair, which sometimes falls low on the neck. He is occasionally slightly bearded. In one type there is a queen(?) confronting him; and his bust is sometimes accompanied by a trident and a club. One reverse has the portrait of Domitian (*Ill. 218*).[1]

> 1 *BMCGC Pontus, etc.*, 1889, pl. 12, nos. 3–8.

SAUROMATES I of Bosporus (*c.*AD 90–124)
Ill. 219

The bust of Sauromates I on the obverses of his gold and bronze coins is diademed and faces right. He has straggly hair, very thick on the neck, a straight nose, a small mouth and a moustache. He is beardless (*Ill. 219*). Occasionally there are a club

and a trident in the field. On the reverses are
portraits of Nerva, Trajan and Hadrian.[1]

1 *BMCGC Pontus, etc.*, 1889, pl. 13, nos. 1–4, 6–12.

219 Sauromates I of Bosporus: portrait on obverse of
gold coin.

Cotys II of Bosporus (AD 124–32/3)
Ill. 220
This king's electrum and bronze coins carry his
obverse bust facing to the right, sometimes with a
trident in front. He is diademed and his hair grows
thick and long on the nape of his neck. He is
beardless (*Ill. 220*). Portraits of Hadrian appear on
the reverses.[1]

1 *BMCGC Pontus, etc.*, 1889, pl. 14, nos. 4–8.

220 Cotys II of Bosporus: portrait on obverse of electrum
coin.

Rhoemetalces of Bosporus (AD 132–54)
Ill. 221
Rhoemetalces' electrum and bronze coins display
on the obverses his bust facing right. His hair is long
and flowing on the neck. He is diademed and
bearded and his nose is aquiline (*Ill. 221*). A
trident and a club are occasionally seen in the
field. On the reverses are portraits of Hadrian and
Antoninus Pius.[1]

1 *BMCGC Pontus, etc.*, 1889, pl. 14, nos. 10, 11, pl. 15,
nos. 1–3.

221 Rhoemetalces of Bosporus: portrait on obverse of
electrum coin.

Eupator of Bosporus (AD 155–71/4)
Ill. 222
The bust of Eupator on his electrum and bronze
coins faces to the right and is diademed. His long,
lanky locks fall low on his neck. His beard is now
long and pointed, now thick and rounded at the
bottom (*Ill. 222*). The reverse portraits are those
of Antoninus Pius, Marcus Aurelius and Lucius
Verus.[1]

1 *BMCGC Pontus, etc.*, 1889, pl. 15, nos. 4–9.

222 Eupator of Bosporus: portrait on obverse of electrum
coin.

Sauromates II of Bosporus (AD 172/5–211)
Ill. 223
Electrum and bronze coins show on their obverses
Sauromates' bust turned to the right and dia-
demed. He has straight hair, large eyes and a
fairly full beard (*Ill. 223*). The reverse types are
portraits of Commodus, Septimius Severus and
Caracalla.[1]

1 *BMCGC Pontus, etc.*, 1889, pl. 15, nos. 11–15, pl. 16,
nos. 1–6, 9.

223 Sauromates II of Bosporus: portrait on obverse of electrum coin.

224 Rhescuporis II of Bosporus: portrait on obverse of electrum coin.

225 Cotys III of Bosporus: portrait on obverse of electrum coin.

226 Sauromates III of Bosporus: portrait on obverse of electrum coin.

227 Rhescuporis III of Bosporus: portrait on obverse of billon coin.

RHESCUPORIS II of Bosporus (AD 212–29)
Ill. 224
The obverse bust of Rhescuporis II (not III) is rightward-facing and diademed on his electrum and bronze coins. He has long, zigzag locks of hair, an aquiline nose and no beard (*Ill. 224*). Caracalla, Elagabalus and Alexander Severus are portrayed on the reverses.[1]

1   *BMCGC Pontus, etc.*, 1889, pl. 16, nos. 11–14, pl. 17, nos. 1–5.

COTYS III of Bosporus (AD 228–35)
Ill. 225
On the obverses of his electrum and bronze coins is a bust of Cotys III facing to the right and diademed. He is beardless, but has long, thick hair and an aquiline nose (*Ill. 225*). On the reverses are portraits of Alexander Severus.[1]

1   *BMCGC Pontus, etc.*, 1889, pl. 17, nos. 6, 7.

SAUROMATES III of Bosporus (AD 230–3)
Ill. 226
The rightward-facing bust of Sauromates on the obverses of his electrum and bronze coins is diademed and beardless. His hair grows long on his neck and his nose is aquiline (*Ill. 226*). The reverse portraits are those of Alexander Severus.[1]

1   *BMCGC Pontus, etc.*, 1889, pl. 17, no. 8.

RHESCUPORIS III of Bosporus (AD 234–5)
Ill. 227
Rhescuporis III's (not IV's) billon coins show his obverse portrait bust diademed, beardless, and facing right. He has a long, aquiline nose and a

weak chin and mouth (*Ill. 227*). Alexander Severus is portrayed on the reverses.[1]

> 1 *BMCGC Pontus, etc.*, 1889, pl. 17, no. 9.

229). On the reverses are portraits of Gordian III, Valerian I and Gallienus.[1]

> 1 *BMCGC Pontus, etc.*, 1889, pl. 18, nos. 1–6.

ININTHIMEUS of Bosporus (AD 235–9)
Ill. 228

This king's billon and bronze coins have his bust, facing to the right, on the obverses. He has a fairly heavy beard (*Ill. 228*). The reverse portraits are those of Maximinus and Gordian III.[1]

> 1 *BMCGC Pontus, etc.*, 1889, pl. 17, nos. 10–12.

SAUROMATES IV of Bosporus (276)
Ill. 230

The king's bust faces to the right on the obverses of his billon coins. He is diademed and is portrayed with long straight hair and a pointed beard (*Ill. 230*).[1]

> 1 *BMCGC Pontus, etc.*, 1889, pl. 18, no. 7.

RHESCUPORIS IV of Bosporus (AD 240–76)
Ill. 229

The billon coins of Rhescuporis IV (not V) carry obverse busts of the king rightward-facing and diademed, sometimes with a club or trident in front, One type shows him with curly hair, the other types with straight hair. He is beardless (*Ill.*

THOTHORSES of Bosporus (279–309)
Ill. 231

The bronze coins of this king have on their obverses his bust turned to the right and diademed. He has straight hair, a long nose, and no beard (*Ill. 231*).[1]

> 1 *BMCGC Pontus, etc.*, 1889, pl. 18, no. 8.

228   Ininthemeus of Bosporus: portrait on obverse of billon coin.

229   Rhescuporis IV of Bosporus: portrait on obverse of billon coin.

230   Sauromates IV of Bosporus: portrait on obverse of billon coin.

231   Thothorses of Bosporus: portrait on obverse of bronze coin.

RHADAMSADES of Bosporus (309–23)
Ill. 232
On the obverses of Rhadamsades' bronze coins is his rightward-facing diademed bust. He is beardless and has a long nose and a small, slightly open mouth (*Ill. 232*).[1]

1 *BMCGC Pontus, etc.*, 1889, pl. 18, no. 9.

RHESCUPORIS V of Bosporus (*c.*323–42)
Ill. 233
Rhescuporis V (not VI or VII) has on the obverses of his bronze coins his bust facing to the right and diademed. He is beardless, his nose is bulbous and his neck is long (*Ill. 233*).[1]

1 *BMCGC Pontus, etc.*, 1889, pl. 18, nos. 10–15.

232 Rhadamsades of Bosporus: portrait on obverse of bronze coin.

233 Rhescuporis V of Bosporus: obverse of bronze coin.

Cilicia

TARCONDIMOTUS I PHILANTONIUS (64–31 BC)
Ill. 234
Tarcondimotus I was made dynast by Pompey in 64 BC, and king by Marcus Antonius in 63 BC,[1] with his capital at Hieropolis-Castabala. Cicero describes him as 'the most faithful ally beyond the

Taurus and the staunchest friend of the Roman people'.[2] He was killed at Actium in 31 BC fighting on Antonius' side.[3] His sons, Philopator I and Tarcondimotus II, then went over to Octavian[4] who, however, deposed Philopator I, but in 20 BC restored the kingdom of Cilicia to Tarcondimotus II, except for a few places on the coast.[5] Tarcondimotus' dynasty lasted until the death of his grandson, Philopator II, in AD 17. Tarcondimotus I's bronze coins show his head diademed and facing to the right (*Ill. 234*).[6] He has thick, neat hair, deep-set eyes, an aquiline nose, a small, firmly set mouth, full cheeks, a protruding, determined chin and a thick neck with a slight 'Adam's apple.'

1 *BMCGC Lycaonia, etc.*, 1900, pp. xxix, ci, cxxx; *CAH*, ix, p. 393.
2 *Ad Fam.*, xv, i, 2: 'Tarcondimoto, qui fidelissimus socius trans Taurum amicissimusque p. R. existimatur'.
3 DC, i, 14, 2.
4 DC, li, 7, 4.
5 DC, liv, 9, 2.
6 *BMCGC Lycaonia, etc.*, 1900, pl. 39, no. 8. Cf. Head 1911, p. 735.

234 Tarcondimotus I Philantonius: portrait on obverse of bronze coin.

AJAX, High-priest and King of Olba in Cilicia
(AD 10–17)
Ill. 235
Ajax, called 'son of Teucer', was High-priest of the
famous temple of Zeus at Olba (Outa) in Cilicia
Tracheia, which the hero Ajax was said to have
founded. By appointment of Augustus he ruled
over Olba, together with Cennatis and Lalassis.[1]
His bronze coins display his bust facing to the right,
in the guise of Hermes (*Ill. 235*).[2] He wears a close-
fitting round cap or *petasos*, and in front of his bust is
a *caduceus*. His hair forms a neat, thick fringe above
his brow and he has a short beard outlining his
chin. His eyes are large, his nose is long and hooked,
and his mouth and chin are firm and determined.

1 *BMCGC Lycaonia, etc.*, 1900, p. lii; Head 1911, pp.
726–7.
2 *BMCGC Lycaonia, etc.*, pl. 21, nos. 8, 10, 12; *CAH*, vol.
iv of plates, p. 209, e.

nape of the neck (*Ill. 236*).[1] He has fat cheeks, an
open mouth and a generally rather stupid look.

1 *BMCGC Lycaonia, etc.*, 1900, pl. 22, nos. 6, 7; *CAH*,
vol. iv of plates, p. 209, f.

235 Ajax (high-priest and king of Olba): obverse of
bronze coin with portrait in the guise of Hermes.

MARCUS ANTONIUS POLEMO, Priest-king of Olba
in Cilicia (*c.*AD 17–36)
Ill. 236
Marcus Antonius Polemo was the son of Polemo I
(q.v.) of Pontus and Bosporus and his queen
Pythodoris, and the brother of Antonia Tryphaena
(q.v.), the wife of Cotys IV of Thrace. He was, like
his sister, called after Marcus Antonius because the
latter had installed his father as king of Pontus and
Bosporus. His bronze coins show his bust facing
right, bare-headed and affecting the Roman Julio-
Claudian coiffure, with a thick mat of hair on the

236 M. Antonius Polemo (priest-king of Olba): obverse
of bronze coin.

Cappadocia

Ariarathes IV Eusebes (*c.* 220–163 BC)
Ill. 237

Ariarathes IV was the son of Ariarathes III (*c.* 230–220 BC), the first Cappadocian ruler to style himself king on his coinage; and to the latter has been attributed (*Ill. 237*)[1] a unique silver tetradrachm in Paris which carries on the obverse a diademed bust facing to the right (as do all the subsequent coin-portraits of the Cappadocian kings). O. Mørkholm, however, has produced cogent arguments for attributing this coin to Ariarathes IV.[2] The fillet border surrounding the obverse portrait was first introduced in Syria at the accession of Antiochus III in 223 BC; and on the reverse of the Cappadocian coin, in the field, is a most unusual miniature motif, an owl perched upon a bunch of grapes, which also appears on a tetradrachm of Antiochus IV of Syria, whose accession was in 175 BC. Since the Cappadocian mint is much more likely to have imitated the Syrian than vice versa, the Paris tetradrachm would seem to have been struck after 175 BC, that is to say, during the latter years of Ariarathes IV. It could even have been the work of a Syrian die-engraver employed at the Cappadocian mint. The king has thick hair, large, deep-set eyes, a large nose, a slightly protruding lower lip, and heavy, sagging cheeks: he is definitely growing elderly. On the other hand, the youthful head, facing to the left and wearing a leather helmet with ear- and cheek-flaps, might well be Ariarathes III, as Simonetta holds.[3]

Ariarathes IV was the first king of Cappadocia to enter Rome's orbit. He sided with Antiochus III of Syria against Rome at the battle of Magnesia in 190 BC;[4] but after her victory he turned philo-Roman and in 188 BC was formally admitted to the friendship of the Roman people.[5] Furthermore, he supported the pro-Roman policy of Eumenes II of Pergamon who, however, changed his attitude to Syria at the time of Antiochus IV's accession, and throughout the latter's reign Syria and Pergamon remained on friendly terms. This 'triple alliance' of Syria, Pergamon and Cappadocia aroused the suspicions of Rome, who sent two embassies to the East in 165 and 164 BC to investigate what it portended. One of these embassies visited Ariarathes, who continued his friendship with Rome[6] and sent his son to Rome to be educated in Roman ways.[7]

1 By T. Reinach, *Trois royaumes de l'Asie Mineure*, 1888, pp. 34–5, no. 7; *BMCGC Galatia, etc.*, 1899, p. xxvi; B. Simonetta, *NC*, 1961, p. 28, pl. 2, no. 5; *Numismatica e Antichità Classiche*, 1973, p. 39, fig. 2, and p. 40; Richter 1965, fig. 1935.
2 *NC*, 1962, pp. 409–11, pl. 20, no. 1.
3 *NC*, 1961, p. 28, pl. 2, nos. 6, 7; *Numismatica, etc.*, 1973, pp. 38, 39, fig. 1, and p. 40.
4 Livy xxxvii, 31, 4.
5 Polybius xxi, 45, 1; Livy xxxviii, 37, 5, and 39, 6; Strabo xii, 2, 11.
6 Polybius xxxi, 2, 13; Livy xlii, 29, 4.
7 Livy xlii, 19, 3, 4.

Ariarathes V Eusebes Philopator
(163–130 BC)
Ill. 238

Ariarathes V was recognized as king by Rome, who renewed her friendship and alliance with him.[1] As her client, he was restored by Rome after being driven from his kingdom by Demetrius of Syria,[2] but allowed Orophernes, his usurping half-brother, to retain half of it in 158 BC. In the next years Ariarathes went to Rome to ask for help against Orophernes.[3] Orophernes was soon expelled by his subjects[4] and Ariarathes resumed control over the whole of Cappadocia. He sent one of his sons, Demetrius, to Rome to be presented to the Senate;[5] in 130 BC he died fighting on Rome's behalf against Aristonicus, the illegitimate son of Eumenes II of Pergamon.[6]

In view of the very close stylistic resemblance of the obverse portrait on the tetradrachm formerly attributed to Ariarathes IV to that of the tetradrachm that bears the name and portrait of Orophernes (q.v.), Mørkholm convincingly ascribes the former to Ariarathes V (*Ill. 238*).[7] Its reverse also shares with that of Orophernes the arrangement of the legend in three straight lines so as to form a three-sided frame around the type. Ariarathes wears a diadem on his neatly curling

237 Ariarathes IV: obverse of silver tetradrachm.

hair, which grows low on the neck behind. He has a high brow, a long, straight nose, full cheeks, a slightly scornful mouth and a small 'Adam's apple'. A series of silver drachms carries the same obverse portrait.[8] The very youthful and shock-headed portrait on tetradrachms assigned by Newell,[9] Simonetta[10] and Richter[11] to Ariarathes V must be attributed elsewhere (cf. Ariarathes IX).

1   Polybius xxxi, 14; Livy, *Epit.*, 46.
2   Polybius xxxii, 20; Livy, *Epit.* 47; Appian, *Syr.* 47.
3   Polybius xxxii, 20, dates his visit by the names of the consuls for 157 BC.
4   Polybius xxxii, 20.
5   Polybius xxxiii, 10.
6   Strabo xiv, 1, 38; Eutropius iv, 20.
7   *NC*, 1961, p. 29, pl. 2, no. 8; 1962, pp. 409–10, pl. 20, no. 2; Richter 1965, fig. 1936.
8   *BMCGC Galatia, etc.*, 1899, pl. 6, no. 2; Newell 1937, pl. 4, fig. 3; *NC*, 1961, pp. 29–31, pl. 2, nos. 9–11, pl. 3, nos. 18, 19.
9   Newell 1937, p. 44, pl. 4, fig. 4.
10   *NC*, 1961, p. 32, pl. 2, no. 12, pl. 3, nos. 13–17, 20.
11   Richter 1965, fig. 1937.

OROPHERNES NIKEPHOROS (158–157 BC)
Ill. 239

Orophernes, the half-brother of Ariarathes V, marked his brief rule of one year by striking a silver tetradrachm which bears his particularly fine portrait-head on the obverse and his name on the reverse (*Ill. 239*).[1] His diademed hair is arranged in neat tiers of curls, he has a large nose and fairly lean cheeks, while a somewhat self-satisfied expression plays about his mouth. This appears to be the handsomest and most exquisitely modelled of all the Cappadocian royal likenesses – perhaps the work of an immigrant Syrian artist.

1   *BMCGC Galatia, etc.*, 1899, pl. 6, no. 5; *NC*, 1961, pl. 3, no. 21, 1962, pl. 20, no. 3; Richter 1965, fig. 1939; Davis and Kraay 1973, pls. 210–12.

ARIARATHES VI EPIPHANES PHILOPATOR (130–116 BC)
Ills. 240–2

Ariarathes VI succeeded to the throne of Cappadocia when he was still a child, under the regency of his mother, Queen Nysa, who had liquidated her elder sons with a view to enjoying a longer term of control. A silver drachm shows on the obverse the jugate heads, facing right, of Nysa and Ariarathes, the former in the foreground, veiled and diademed, the latter in the background, wearing a tall tiara, to which is attached a kind of 'wimple' muffling the chin (*Ill. 240*).[1] The names of the queen and her son are inscribed on the reverse. The king's features can best be studied on the obverses of the drachms on which he appears alone, wearing not a tiara, but the Hellenistic diadem binding his sinuous locks of hair (*Ill. 241*).[2] He has a low brow, large eyes, a large nose, a somewhat cynically smiling mouth with parted lips, and a prominent chin. A tiny silver obol, with ΑΡΙΑΡΑΘ inscribed on the reverse, shows what must be a portrait of this king with the same type of tall tiara equipped with a 'wimple'.[3] Again, the same type of tall tiara with 'wimple' and features closely resembling those of the obverse portraits of Ari-

238   Ariarathes V: obverse of tetradrachm (= Richter, fig. 1936).

239   Orophernes Nikephoros: obverse of silver tetradrachm.

240–2 Ariarathes VI: obverses of silver drachm (jugate with Nysa); silver drachm (alone, with Hellenistic diadem); and bronze coin (showing tiara).

243 Ariarathes VII: obverse of drachm with diademed head.

arathes VI's drachms are found on small bronze coins almost certainly issued by him (*Ill. 242*).[4]

1 *NC*, 1961, p. 35, pl. 3, no. 22; *Numismatica, etc.*, 1973, p. 39, fig. 3.
2 *BMCGC Galatia, etc.*, 1899, pl. 6, nos. 6, 7; Newell 1937, pp. 44–5, pl. 4, fig. 5; *NC*, 1961, pp. 36–7, pl. 3, nos. 23–5; Richter 1965, fig. 1940.
3 *Numismatica, etc.*, 1973, p. 39, fig. 7.
4 Ibid., figs. 4–6; *BMCGC Galatia, etc.*, 1899, pl. 7, no. 12.

ARIARATHES VII PHILOMETOR (116–*c.*100 BC)
Ill. 243

Ariarathes VII, son of Ariarathes VI, also came to the throne while still a child, with his mother Laodice, daughter of Mithradates of Pontus, as regent. Nicomedes III of Bithynia seized Cappadocia and married Laodice, but Mithradates VI of Pontus drove out Nicomedes and Laodice and reinstated Ariarathes. Later, however, Mithradates turned against Ariarathes and made his own eight-year-old son king of Cappadocia.

Ariarathes' drachms carry the king's diademed head on their obverses (*Ill. 243*).[1] He has short, tightly curled hair, a high brow, full cheeks, a long, straight nose, a small, weak mouth, and sometimes a small 'Adam's Apple' on his full throat.

1 *BMCGC Galatia, etc.*, 1899, pl. 6, nos. 8, 9; Newell 1937, p. 45, pl. 4, fig. 6; *NC*, 1961, pp. 38–9, pl. 3, nos. 26, 27; Richter 1965, fig. 1941.

ARIARATHES IX EUSEBES PHILOPATOR (*c.*99–86 BC)
Ills. 244, 245

At the age of eight Ariarathes IX, son of Mithradates VI of Pontus, was made king of Cappadocia by his father, in place of Ariarathes VII (q.v.), but was not recognized by Rome. His diademed coin portraits are distinguished from those of all the other kings of Cappadocia by the extreme unruliness of his very abundant snaky locks. To the first years of his reign must be assigned the very youthful portraits on the tetradrachms and drachms (*Ill. 244*) that have been erroneously attributed to Ariarathes V (q.v.).[1] In these the nose is long, the mouth small and button-like, the cheeks are full and round, and there is generally a great mass of tangled locks on the nape of the neck. His later tetradrachms and drachms all show a plump and youthful, if slightly more mature, face, with the hair on the crown of the head forming an even more agitated whirl of curls, while the strings of his diadem flutter wildly behind; his head is thrust well forward (*Ill. 245*).[2] The coiffure is obviously that of

244, 245 Ariarathes IX: obverses of tetradrachm and drachm showing youthful and mature portraits and characteristic hair-style.

Ariarathes' father, Mithradates VI (q.v.) of Pontus, who might, indeed, have sent engravers from his own royal mint to Cappadocia.

Ariarathes had to yield to the Cappadocians' own choice of Ariobarzanes I (q.v.), who was installed as their king by Sulla in 96 BC when proconsul of Cilicia; his father reinstated him

several times, however. He died in Thessaly in 86 BC.[3]

1 *BMCGC Galatia, etc.* 1899, pl. 6, nos. 3, 4; Newell 1937, p. 45, pl. 4, fig. 7; *NC*, 1961, pl. 2, no. 12, pl. 3, nos. 13–17; 1962, pl. 20, nos. 5, 6; Richter 1965, fig. 1937.
2 *BMCGC Galatia, etc.*, 1899, pl. 7, nos. 1–4; Newell 1937, p. 45, pl. 4, fig. 8; *NC*, 1961, pp. 39–40, pl. 4, nos. 28–30; 1962, pl. 20, no. 7; Richter 1965, fig. 1944. A diademed marble head in Athens (Richter 1965, figs. 1942–3) certainly resembles Ariarathes' coin portraits both in features and in the head's forward thrust.
3 Plutarch, *Sulla* 11; Appian, *Mithr.* 35.

ARIOBARZANES I PHILOROMAIOS (96–63 BC)
Ill. 246

On the death of Ariarathes VIII (of whom we have no coin portraits) Rome refused to recognize Ariarathes IX as king and declared Cappadocia a republic. But the Cappadocians, 'refusing liberty', demanded a king and Ariobarzanes was chosen, receiving Rome's approval, being installed by Sulla, and inaugurating a new dynasty.[1] He had a chequered career, being six times driven from his throne and six times restored by Rome as her client. In 93 BC he was overthrown by Tigranes and Gordios, supported by Mithradates, and restored by Sulla; driven out again, but reinstated by Aquillius in 90 BC; expelled by Mithradates in 89 BC, but put back on his throne by Curio, acting for Sulla, in 85/84 BC; thrown out again in 82 BC, but restored next year by Murena; driven away again by Mithradates in 74 BC, but put back by Lucullus; expelled yet again by Mithradates and Tigranes in 67 BC, he was finally reinstated by Pompey in 66 BC.[2] It is not surprising that he styled himself 'Philoromaios'[3] or that, after all this, he joyfully abdicated in favour of his son.

Ariobarzanes' portraits on his drachms reflect his position as the protégé of Rome (*Ill. 246*).[4] His diademed hair is short and neat, his brow is

246, 247 Ariobarzanes I and his son Ariobarzanes II: obverses of drachms showing the first two kings of the new dynasty founded with Rome's approval.

furrowed, his nose is aquiline, his mouth is set, his cheeks are full and fleshy and sometimes sag in vertical folds, and he has a double chin. His is almost the veristic likeness of a Roman of his day.

1 Strabo xii, 2, 11.
2 Plutarch, *Sulla* 5, 22, 24; Livy, *Epit.*, 70, 74, 76; Appian, *Mithr.*, 10, 15, 56, 57, 64, 66, 67, 105, 114.
3 *CIG*, 357.
4 *BMCGC Galatia, etc.*, 1899, pl. 7, nos. 5–7 (no. 5 shows Ariobarzanes with somewhat different and decidedly younger features); Newell 1937, pp. 45 and 47, pl. 4, figs. 9, 10; *NC*, 1961, pl. 4, nos. 31, 32; Richter 1965, fig. 1945.

ARIOBARZANES II PHILOPATOR (63–52 BC)
Ill. 247

Ariobarzanes II was the son of Ariobarzanes I (q.v.); he married a daughter of Mithradates VI of Pontus. According to Valerius Maximus, at the time of his father's abdication the latter's face showed joy, and the new king's sadness.[1] His unsettled reign, during which he needed (in 57 BC) the intervention of Gabinius, ended with his murder.[2] On his drachms, Ariobarzanes' head is diademed and shows short, rather woolly, hair; he has a receding brow, large eyes, a very large aquiline nose with pronounced bridge, very large ears, full cheeks and thick lips (*Ill. 247*).[3] He looks sensuous and stupid.

1 V, 7, 2.
2 Cicero, *Ad Fam.*, xv, 2, 6.
3 *BMCGC Galatia, etc.*, 1899, pl. 7, no. 8; Newell 1937, p. 47, pl. 4, fig. 11; *NC*, 1961, pl. 4, no. 33; Richter 1965, fig. 1946.

ARIOBARZANES III EUSEBES PHILOROMAIOS
(52–42 BC)
Ill. 248

Recognized by Rome as king and client, Ariobarzanes III was patronized by Cicero;[1] he assumed

the title of 'Philoromaios'.[2] He sided with Pompey against Caesar,[3] but Caesar forgave him and his lieutenant protected him against Pharnaces II of Bosporus (q.v.).[4] He was put to death by order of Cassius.[5]

Ariobarzanes' diademed portrait on his drachms shows hair somewhat untidier than that of his predecessor, and his cheeks are leaner (*Ill. 248*).[6] He has a low brow, large eyes, a large, long nose ending in a kind of knob, an open mouth, a very lightly bearded, pointed chin and a small 'Adam's apple'. His head is thrust well forward from the neck. This is a weak and rather foolish face.

1 Cicero, *Ad Fam.*, ii, 17, 7; xv, 2, 4; 2, 8; 4, 6; *Ad Att.* v, 20, 6; vi, 1, 3; 3, 5; xiii, 2, 2; Plutarch, *Cicero* 36.
2 *CIG*, 358.
3 Lucan ii, 592; iii, 244.
4 *Bellum Alexandrinum* 34, 1; DC, xlii, 48.
5 DC, xlvii, 33, 4; Appian, *Bell. Civ.* iv, 63.
6 *BMCGC Galatia, etc.*, 1899, pl. 7, nos. 9, 10; Newell 1937, p. 47, pl. 4, fig. 12; *NC*, 1961, pl. 4, fig. 34; Richter 1965, fig. 1947.

ARIARATHES X EUSEBES PHILADELPHOS
(42–36 BC)
Ill. 249

Ariarathes X was the brother of Ariobarzanes III. Caesar had placed him under his brother's authority,[1] but gave him little land, with the result that he came to Rome to try to secure some territory for himself.[2] Ascending the throne in 42 BC, he was opposed by a rival, Sisenes, in whose favour Marcus Antonius decided in 41 BC.[3] Ariarathes was eventually driven out by Antonius in 36 BC.[4]

Ariarathes' portrait on his drachms shows him diademed, with thick, curly hair closely resembling his brother's, a low brow, large eyes, a very large aquiline nose, a small, tight mouth set close to the nostrils, and a pointed chin sheathed in a beard that is rather heavier than Ariobarzanes' (*Ill. 249*).[5]

1 *Bellum Alexandrinum* 66, 5.
2 Cicero, *Ad Att.*, xiii, 2, 2.

248, 249 Ariobarzanes III and his brother Ariarathes X: obverses of drachms showing the third and last of the family succession, Ariarathes being ousted in favour of his rival Sisenes.

3 Appian, *Bell. Civ.*, v, 7.
4 DC, xlix, 32, 3.
5 *BMCGC Galatia, etc.*, 1899, pl. 7, no. 11; Newell 1937,
   p. 47, pl. 4, fig. 13; *NC*, 1961, pl. 4, nos. 35, 36;
   Richter 1965, fig. 1948. The portraits with a tall tiara
   on the small bronze coins attributed to Ariarathes X
   in the *BMCGC*, pl. 7, no. 12 cannot be he, since they
   are actually beardless. For their attribution to Ariarathes VI, see p. 126.

Archelaus Philopatris Ktistes (36 BC–AD 17)
Ill. 250

Sisenes, now named Archelaus, son of the priest of
Comana, was placed on the throne of Cappadocia
by Marcus Antonius[1] and confirmed on it by
Octavian,[2] who, as Augustus, transferred to him
Cilicia Tracheia, eastern Lycaonia and Lesser
Armenia.[3] In AD 17, when of advanced age, he was
summoned to Rome by Tiberius, whom he had
offended, on a treason charge, but his life was
spared and he died soon afterwards; in the same
year Cappadocia became a Roman province.[4]

Archelaus seems to have been a scholar of the
type of Juba II of Mauretania (q.v.) and Artavasdes I of Armenia (q.v.), since he wrote a book on
stones, including observations on amber, and a
geographical treatise.[5] His portraits on his drachms
and hemidrachms certainly suggest a man of culture, with youthful, idealizing features. He wears a
diadem on his neat, curly hair and is beardless, with
rounded cheeks, a straight nose, and a 'rose-bud'

mouth – a typical Hellenistic 'pretty boy', certainly
not like the real man as he was in the twentieth to
the forty-ninth year of his reign, the period during
which these coins were issued (*Ill. 250*).[6]

1 Appian, *Bell. Civ.*, v, 7; DC, xlix, 32, 3.
2 DC, li, 2, 1.
3 Strabo xii, 1, 4; xiv, 5, 6; DC, liv, 9, 2.
4 Strabo xii, 1, 4; Tacitus, *Ann.*, ii, 42; Suetonius,
   Tiberius, 37, 4; DC, lvii, 17. Cf. M. Pani, *Roma e i re
   d'oriente da Augusto a Tiberio*, 1972, pp. 93–145, 192–3
   and *passim*.
5 Pliny, *NH*, xxxvii, 11 (46).
6 *BMCGC Galatia, etc.*, 1899, pl. 7, no. 14; Newell 1937,
   p. 47, pl. 4, figs. 14, 15; *NC*, 1961, p. 48, pl. 4, nos. 37,
   38; Richter 1965, fig. 1949. For recent controversy
   concerning the attribution of the coins of the Cappadocian kings, see *Numismatica e Antichitá Classiche*,
   1974, pp. 49–62 and p. 50, n. 2.

250 Archelaus (formerly Sisenes): obverse of drachm
showing the last king of Cappadocia before the territory
became a Roman province.

Armenia

TIGRANES I ('the Great'; *c*.94–56 BC)
Ills. 251–3

Tigranes I had lived for a long time as a hostage in Parthia, which, in return for a substantial sum, placed him on the Armenian throne.[1] No sooner had he gained his kingdom than he began to expand it, making an alliance with Mithradates VI (q.v.) of Pontus, whose daughter he married. With Mithradates he drove Ariobarzanes I from the throne of Cappadocia, but was forced to withdraw his troops from that country by Sulla,[2] who made an agreement with Parthia with a view to curbing him.[3] But Tigranes continued his expansionist policy, founding a new capital, Tigranocerta, in southern Armenia and becoming the most powerful ruler in Nearer Asia, with a realm that included Syria. In 71 BC, when Lucullus drove Mithradates VI from Pontus, it was with Tigranes that the latter took refuge. Lucullus sent his legate, Appius, to demand the surrender of Mithradates – a demand that Tigranes refused; and he now assumed the title of 'King of Kings'.[4] In 69 BC Lucullus made war on Tigranes and captured Tigranocerta, from which the king fled with Mithradates.[5] Lucullus then marched against Artaxata, where Tigranes' wives and children were, and defeated the king in battle; but he failed to take the city.[6] He did, however, capture Nisibis, which Tigranes had taken from Parthia.[7] In 66 BC Pompey, now in command in the East, with the aid of Tigranes' son, who had rebelled against his father, entered Armenia. Tigranes lost his nerve and surrendered himself and Artaxata to the Romans. Pompey restored to Tigranes Armenia proper, while stripping him of all his external acquisitions, and enrolled him as a friend and ally of the Roman people.[8] After that Tigranes kept peace with Rome.

Tigranes' portrait, facing right, appears on tetradrachms and bronze coins minted at Antioch-on-the-Orontes, when he ruled Syria, but undated. He has distinctively Semitic features – arched eyebrows, large and rather puffy eyes, a large aquiline nose, a wide and somewhat sardonic mouth, lean cheeks, a heavy, jutting and clean-shaven chin, sometimes with an 'Adam's apple' below it (*Ill. 251*).[9] He wears a tall tiara, encircled by a diadem, the strings of which hang down behind. The head-dress has divided ear-flaps and its upper portion is richly adorned and edged with pearls. At the top are five triangular projections, possibly intended to represent the sun's rays, and on the side is generally embroidered a star between two eagles. The re-

verses show the famous seated statue of the Tyche of Antioch and a Nike. Another series of tetradrachms, struck at Damascus in the years 71–69 BC, depicts Tigranes with similar facial features, but with a row of corkscrew curls along his brow and a slightly less elaborate version of the same tiara type (*Ill. 252*).[10] The Tyche of Damascus forms the reverse type. During the years 77–73 BC, at an uncertain mint, Tigranes struck tetradrachms and

251–3 Tigranes I: coin obverses showing characteristic tall tiara and head-dress, struck respectively at Antioch-on-the-Orontes, at Damascus, and at an uncertain mint.

drachms, and bronze coins on the obverses of which his features and tiara are the same as those on his earlier Antiochene issues (*Ill. 253*).[11] The reverse types are the Tyche of Antioch and Herakles and the title 'King of Kings' accompanies them. Coins probably struck at Nisibis show Tigranes facing, unusually, to the left; and his tiara is undecorated on the sides and has undivided ear-flaps.[12] A seated Zeus forms the reverse type.

1 Strabo xi, 15.
2 Plutarch, *Sulla* 3.
3 Ibid., 4; Livy, *Epit.*, 70.
4 Plutarch, *Lucullus* 19, 21.
5 Ibid., 29.
6 Ibid., 31, 32.
7 DC, xxxvi, 6, 7, 8.
8 Cicero, *Pro Sestio* 27, 58, 59; Livy, *Epit.*, 101; Plutarch, *Pompeius* 33; DC, xxxvi, 51–3.
9 *BMCGC Seleucid Kings of Syria*, 1878, pl. 27, nos. 6, 9; Head 1911, p. 772, fig. 342; Newell 1937, p. 48, fig. 1; Richter 1965, fig. 1950; *NC*, 1973, pl. 14, nos. 1, 4, 7.
10 *BMCGC Seleucid Kings of Syria*, 1878, pl. 27, nos. 5, 7; Head 1911, p. 773; Newell 1937, p. 48, fig. 2; *NC*, 1973, pl. 14, nos. 5, 6.
11 *BMCGC Seleucid Kings of Syria*, 1878, pl. 27, nos. 8–11; Newell 1937, p. 48, fig. 3.
12 *NC*, 1973, pp. 24, 25, fig. 4; pl. 14, no. 3.

ARTAVASDES I (56–30 BC)
Ill. 254

Artavasdes I (or II?: see *NC*, 1973, p. 37) was the son of Tigranes I and began as a friend of Rome.[1] He helped Crassus when the latter invaded Mesopotamia in 54 BC,[2] but he soon went over to the Parthians. However, in 36 BC he joined Marcus Antonius in his Parthian campaign, persuading him to invade Media,[3] but then deserted him[4] and refused to obey his summons to Egypt.[5] In 34 BC Antonius invaded Armenia and captured Artavasdes, carrying him off to Alexandria, where he was imprisoned and eventually put to death.[6]

Artavasdes' portraits on his silver coins show him facing to the right. He is beardless and wears the tiara with diadem and triangular projections (*Ill. 254*) already noted on the coins of Tigranes I (q.v.).[7] On the reverses, which depict the king riding in a chariot, he styles himself 'King of Kings'. Like Juba II (q.v.) of Mauretania and Archelaus (q.v.) of Cappadocia, Artavasdes was a cultivated man and wrote tragedies, orations and histories.[8]

1 Strabo xi, 15 (here called Artabazus).
2 Plutarch, *Crassus* 19.
3 DC, xlix, 25, 1.
4 Plutarch, *Antonius* 37–9.
5 DC, xlix, 33, 1.
6 Livy, *Epit.*, 131; Tacitus, *Ann.* ii, 3, 2; Plutarch *Antonius* 50; DC, xlix, 39, 6.
7 *BMCGC Galatia, etc.*, 1899, pl. 14, no. 2.
8 Plutarch, *Crassus* 33.

TIGRANES II (20–*c*.6 BC)
Ill. 255

Tigranes II, the son of Artavasdes I (or II) and the grandson of Tigranes I, was living in Rome with his eldest brother Artavasdes II (or III?) when his other older brother, Araxias, who had secured the throne of Armenia, was killed. The romanizing party in Armenia then invited Roman intervention and asked for Tigranes II to be sent from Rome to be their king. Tiberius was despatched to install and crown him in 20 BC.[1]

Tigranes' portrait appears on the obverses of his silver drachms, facing to the right (*Ill. 255*).[2] He wears a tiara of the same type as that of Tigranes I (q.v.) and has extremely realistic features, with a very hooked nose, a moustache, and a beard sheathing his chin. On the reverses is the standing figure of the king wearing his tiara and grasping a long sceptre.

1 *Res Gestae* 27; Tacitus, *Ann.*, ii, 3, 4; Suetonius, *Tiberius* 9, 1; DC, liv, 9, 4 and 5. Cf. M. Pani, *Roma e il re d'oriente da Augusto a Tiberio*, 1972, *passim*.
2 Newell 1937, p. 48, fig. 4.

254, 255   Artavasdes I and Tigranes II: obverses of silver coins showing the son and grandson respectively of Tigranes I, both with the same tall tiara.

TIGRANES III (*c*.6 and *c*.2 BC) and ERATO
Ills. 256, 257
Tigranes III was crowned by the pro-Parthian
party in Armenia on the death of his father,
Tigranes II. He was to rule jointly with his sister-
queen Erato; but Rome expelled him, nominating
Artavasdes II (q.v.) as king. However, in *c*.2 BC he
was restored after the murder of the Roman
nominee. He then sent envoys to Rome with gifts
and a petition for Roman recognition as king.[1] He
was attacked by Augustus' grandson, C. Caesar,
and died in battle; Erato abdicated, and the
Armenian royal house became extinct.[2]

Tigranes' bronze coins show his bust facing to
the right. He is beardless and wears the tiara. The
reverse types include a portrait of Erato (*Ills. 256,
257*).[3]

1 DC, lv, 10, 20.
2 Ibid., 10a, 5. Cf. Pani, op. cit., *passim*.
3 Head 1911, pp. 754–5.

ARTAVASDES II (*c*.6–2 BC)
Ill. 258
Artavasdes II (or III? – see *NC*, 1973, p. 37),
probably the eldest brother of Tigranes II (q.v.),

258 Artavasdes II (or III): reverse of silver coin with
portrait in the Roman style.

256, 257 Tigranes III and Erato: obverse and reverse of
bronze coin with portraits of brother and sister.

with whom he had been living in Rome, was
installed by Rome as king of Armenia in place of
Tigranes III (q.v.), but was driven out with
Parthian aid.[1] His silver coins show on their re-
verses his portrait with typical Roman features and
Roman hair-style, as befits a protégé of Rome
(*Ill. 258*).[2]

1 Tacitus, *Ann*. ii, 4, 1. Cf. Pani, op. cit., *passim*.
2 *BMCGC Galatia, etc.*, pl. 14, no. 3.

Commagene

ANTIOCHUS I THEOS (69–*c*.31 BC)
Ills. 259–62

Antiochus I made friends with Lucullus in 68 BC, after the latter's defeat of Tigranes I (q.v.) of Armenia in 69 BC and Lucullus recognized Antiochus as king.[1] In 64 BC Pompey acknowledged him as a friend of Rome and gave him Seleucia on the Euphrates, while describing him in his triumph as a 'conquered king': Antiochus received the *toga praetexta* and assumed the title of 'philoromaios'.[2] He now kept an eye on the Parthians for Rome, informing Cicero in Cilicia in 51 BC when they were advancing westwards.[3] In the Civil War he helped Pompey.[4] But in 38 BC he received Parthian refugees – a breach of his clientship – and Publius Ventidius beseiged him in Samosata; Marcus Antonius superseded Ventidius (who was charged with having taken bribes from Antiochus), but failed to take the city himself, according to Plutarch and Dio Cassius.[5] Josephus, however, states that Antiochus surrendered Samosata to him.[6] The precise date of Antiochus' death is not known, but it must have been by 31 BC, since at that date a Mithradates was king of Commagene.[7]

Antiochus' bronze coins show his head facing right. He has a receding brow, large eyes, a straight nose, a small, straight mouth set close below the nostrils, full cheeks, and a weak, clean-shaven chin (*Ill. 259*).[8] The king wears the Armenian tiara, with divided ear-flaps, encircled by a diadem, topped by five triangular projections and decorated on the sides with a star between two eagles (cf. p. 131). On the reverse of these coins is a lion walking to the right.

260　Antiochus I : colossal head at Nemrud Dagh, *in situ*; from the king's monumental tomb.

259　Antiochus I : obverse of bronze coin showing the king wearing the characteristic Armenian tall tiara.

Among the stone sculptures that adorned Antiochus' monumental tomb at Nemrud Dagh are several portraits of him, two in the round and others in relief.[9] One head, of colossal size, depicts his characteristic facial features somewhat idealized: he wears a plain, conical tiara with neck-flaps (*Ill. 260*). Of the second portrait in the round the face is badly mutilated: only the low brow, the rounded cheeks and the ears survive. The top of the tiara is also lost, but its lower portion is seen to consist of two horizontal decorated bands, a frieze of animals and a mixed vine and pomegranate scroll above, while there is a lion on each side above the bands. Of the various reliefs, the best preserved portrays the king's full-length figure facing to the right and clasping the right hand of Herakles-Verethragna, who stands opposite him,

261, 262   Antiochus I : stone reliefs from the monumental tomb at Nemrud Dagh, showing the king with Herakles-Verethragna (*top*) and with Apollo-Mithras.

facing left. Antiochus, readily recognizable in features, wears elaborate oriental dress – a girded tunic caught up between the knees and cloak fastened on the right shoulder. He grasps a long sceptre in his left hand. His tiara has neck-flaps; the figure of a lion is embroidered on the side; and the five triangular projections at the top take the form of veined leaves (*Ill. 261*). Another relief, on which Antiochus again stands facing to the right, this time opposite Apollo-Mithras, displays the king's slightly damaged, but characteristic, facial features. He has the same type of oriental dress and again grasps a long sceptre. His tiara appears to have neck-flaps and it is embroidered on the side with the figure of a lion; and each of the five triangular projections that top it terminates above in a round knob (*Ill. 262*). On yet another relief, where Antiochus stands opposite the seated figure of Zeus, the king's face is completely destroyed, but his oriental dress and tiara are well preserved, the latter having neck-flaps, five triangular projections at the top, and a foliate design on the side.

1   DC, xxxvi, 2.
2   Cicero, *Ad Quint. Frat.* ii, 10, 2; Appian, *Mithr.* 106, 114, 117; Le Bas-Waddington, *Inscript.* iii, 2, no. 136d.
3   Cicero, *Ad Fam.* xv, 1, 2; 3, 1; 4, 3.
4   Caesar, *Bell Civ.* iii, 4; Appian, *Bell Civ.* ii, 49.
5   Plutarch, *Antonius* 34; DC, xlix, 20–22.
6   *Ant. Iud.* xiv, 447; *Bell. Iud.* i, 222.
7   Plutarch, *Antonius* 61.
8   *BMCGC Galatia, etc.*, 1899, pl. 14, no. 8; Head 1911, p. 775; *NC*, 1970, p. 19, fig. 1; 1973, pl. 14, no. 2.
9   K. Humann and O. Puchstein, *Reisen in Kleinasien und Nordsyrien*, 1890, pl. 38, fig. 2, pl. 39, figs. 1, 2; cf. also the relief from Selik showing Antiochus and Herakles: ibid., p. 368, fig. 52; Ghirshman 1962, figs. 75, 78a, 79, 80; *AJA*, lxviii, 1964, pp. 29–34; M. Pani, *Roma e i re d'oriente da Augusto a Tiberio*, 1972, pp. 253–4.

ANTIOCHUS IV EPIPHANES (AD 38–72)
Ill. 263

In AD 17/18, after the death of Antiochus III (of whom we have no portraits), Tiberius had made Commagene a Roman province.[1] But in 37 Gaius restored the kingdom, giving it to Antiochus IV, the son of Antiochus III, together with a gift of a hundred million sesterces, since he had ties of friendship with him.[2] In 40, however, Gaius removed Antiochus from Commagene, which Claudius gave back to him in 41;[3] and under Claudius, in 52, the king suppressed the Cilician Clitae.[4] Under Nero he supported the Romans in Corbulo's

263 Antiochus IV: obverse of bronze coin showing the king with typically Roman hair-style.

264 Iotape Philadelphus: obverse of bronze coin with portrait executed in the Roman manner.

Armenian war in 54[5] and again in 58;[6] and in 60 he was rewarded with a portion of Armenia.[7] In 69 he espoused the cause of Vespasian and is described by Tacitus as 'the richest of all the client kings with his vast ancestral wealth'.[8] In 70 he sent *auxilia* to Titus for the siege of Jerusalem.[9] But in 72 he earned the displeasure of the governor of Syria, Caesennius Paetus, and fled to Cilicia with his sister-wife Iotape and his sons Epiphanes and Callinicus (qq.v.). He was captured at Tarsus and imprisoned first at Sparta and then in Rome, where he eventually died; and Commagene was united as a Roman province with Syria.[10]

Antiochus' bronze coins show his bust facing to the right. He is beardless and wears a diadem in his thick hair, which is dressed in the Roman Julio-Claudian style. He has a large, aquiline nose, deep-set eyes, a small mouth and full cheeks (*Ill. 263*).[11]

1 Tacitus, *Ann.* ii, 56, 5; Strabo xvi, 2, 3.
2 Suetonius, *Gaius* 16, 3; DC, lix, 8, 2; 24, 1.
3 DC, lx, 8, 1.
4 Tacitus, *Ann.*, xii, 55, 1.
5 Ibid., xiii, 7, 1.
6 Ibid., 37, 2.
7 Ibid., xiv, 26, 3.
8 *Hist.*, ii, 81: 'Antiochus vetustis opibus ingens et serventium ditissimus'. Cf. Josephus, *Bell. Iud.*, v, 461.
9 Tacitus, *Hist.*, v, 1; Josephus, *Bell. Iud.*, iii, 68.
10 Josephus, *Bell. Iud.*, vii, 219–43; Suetonius, *Vespasianus* 8, 4.
11 *BMCGC Galatia, etc.*, 1899, pl. 14, nos. 9, 10, pl. 15, nos. 1–3; Head 1911, p. 775; *CAH*, vol. iv of plates, p. 209, n. d.

265, 266 Epiphanes and Callinicus: obverse and reverse of bronze coin, struck at Selinus, showing the two sons of Iotape.

IOTAPE PHILADELPHUS and her sons EPIPHANES and CALLINICUS

Ills. 264–6

The likeness of Iotape, Antiochus IV's sister-queen, is known from her bronze coinage. Her bust faces to the right, she wears a diadem, and she has classical features and coiffure, with a small 'bun' on the nape of the neck, resembling those of a Roman princess (*Ill. 264*).[1] A rare bronze coin in Paris, struck at Selinus, bears the portrait-busts of her sons by Antiochus, Epiphanes and Callinicus, on the obverse and reverse respectively (*Ills. 265, 266*).[2] They are diademed and have facial features resembling those of their father; and their hair is dressed in the Roman style, as befits men 'who could not contemplate living outside the Roman Empire'.[3] Epiphanes made a foolhardy assault on the walls of Jerusalem at the time of Titus' siege of the city.[4] After the capture of their father both brothers tried to resist Rome, but were forced to yield and took up their abode in the capital.[5]

1 *BMCGC Galatia, etc.*, 1899, pl. 15, no. 4; Head 1911, pp. 775–6.
2 E. Babelon, *Les monnaies des rois de Syrie, etc.*, 1890, p. 222, no. 38, pl. 30, no. 16; *BMCGC Galatia, etc.*, 1899, p. xlvii; Head 1911, p. 776.
3 Cf. note 5.
4 Josephus, *Bell. Iud.*, v, 460–5.
5 Ibid., vii, 232–43.

Osrhoene: Edessa[1]

Edessa, the capital of Osrhoene, first contacted Rome in 69 BC when her phylarch, Abgar I (94–68 BC), was defeated in alliance with Tigranes of Armenia by Sextilius.[2] But his successor, Abgar II bar Abgar (68–53 BC) was in 66 BC confirmed as ruler of Edessa by Pompey in his settlement of the East and became an ally of Rome.[3] In 53 BC, however, this same king is alleged by Plutarch to have contributed in no small degree by his treacherous acts to Crassus' disaster.[4] The next Edessan king to appear on the Roman scene is Abgar V (4 BC–AD 7 and 13–57), Tacitus' Acbarus 'king of the Arabs', who was accused of treachery to Mihrdad (Meherdates), the Roman nominee to the throne of Parthia, in AD 49.[5]

The next important contact was under Agbar VII bar Ezdad (100–16) who, when Trajan was at Antioch for his Parthian war in the winter of 113–14, sent the emperor presents and a message of friendship, but did not come to see him in person, wishing to adopt a neutral attitude for fear of Parthia.[6] But Trajan himself visited Edessa and Abgar, at the persuasion of his son Arbandus, a handsome youth who had won the emperor's favour, met Trajan on the road, apologized for not having put in an appearance earlier, and entertained his imperial guest at a banquet, at which the young prince performed a 'barbaric dance'.[7] But in 116 Abgar joined in the general revolt of Mesopotamia against Rome and Lusius Quietus was sent to sack and destroy Edessa.[8] Abgar presumably perished on this occasion.

Of the Edessan kings mentioned so far no portraits have survived.

1 For the dates and succession of the Edessan kings, see *BMCGC Arabia, etc.*, 1922, pp. xciv–cvii; *Yale Classical Studies*, v, 1935, pp. 142–54; J. B. Segal, *Edessa: 'the Blessed City'*, 1970, pp. 9–15. The basis for the chronology is the Syriac *Chronicle* of Dionysius of Tell-Mahrê.
2 Plutarch, *Lucullus* 25.
3 DC, xl, 20.
4 *Crassus* 21, 22 (called here Ariamnes).
5 *Ann.*, xii, 12, 14.
6 DC, lxviii, 18.
7 Ibid., 21.
8 Ibid., 30, 2.

MA'NU VIII bar MA'NU PHILOROMAIOS (AD 139–63 and 165–77)

Ill. 267

Ma'nu (Mannus) VIII, the first king of Edessa whose portrait we possess, reigned from 139 to 163, when he was driven from his throne by Waël bar Sahru (Vologeses; q.v.), a Parthian nominee. In 163 the Roman army, fighting in Lucius Verus' Parthian campaign, took Edessa from Waël, and Ma'nu – who had sought Rome's protection – was restored and ruled for another twelve years. He became Rome's client and took the title of 'Philo-romaios'.[1]

Ma'nu's bronze coins present on their obverses his bust facing to the right. He has a long, straight nose, is bearded, and wears a diademed conical tiara with a crest of 'hooks' (*Ill. 267*).[2]

1 Silver denarii struck at Edessa with portraits of Marcus Aurelius, Faustina II and Lucius Verus on their obverses bear the reverse legend ΒΑCΙΛΕΥC ΜΑΝΝΟC ΦΙΛΟΡΩΜΑΙΟC : *BMCGC Arabia, etc.*, 1922, pl. 13, nos. 9–13, pl. 50, no. 8.
2 *Ibid.*, pl. 13, no. 9.

267 Ma'nu VIII: obverse of bronze coin showing diademed conical tiara.

a large force of archers.[2] Septimius now recognized him as a client king. Later, presumably soon after Septimius' return to Italy from the East, Abgar visited him in Rome, accompanied by an immense escort.[3]

All the coins struck by Abgar at Edessa are of bronze. Most of them bear the obverse portraits of Septimius Severus and the king's own rightward-facing portrait on the reverse (*Ill. 270*).[4] Abgar has a very large, pointed nose, a moustache and an abundant, curly beard, obviously dressed in a manner imitative of the emperors. His tiara is domed and diademed and equipped with short ear-flaps. On pieces with Commodus' bust on the obverse, the tiara has no crest of 'hooks' and shows a cross on the side. But on the coins with Septimius' obverse portrait the tiara has the crest of 'hooks' along the top and a crescent with two or three stars on the side; and on these a sceptre is included in front of the king's face. There is also a coin with Abgar's portrait on the reverse and a portrait of Caracalla on the obverse (*Ill. 271*).[5] Still further coins show the same portrait of Abgar on the obverses and those of his son Ma'nu on the reverses.[6] Ma'nu's portrait is either beardless, with the legend ΜΑΝΝΟC or bearded with the legend

WAËL (Vologeses) bar SAHRU (AD 163–5)
Ills. 268, 269
Waël, the Parthian nominee who usurped for two years the throne of Ma'nu VIII (q.v.), struck at Edessa bronze coins with the bust of Vologeses III of Parthia (q.v.) on the obverse and his own bust on the reverse (*Ill. 268*).[1] The Parthian king faces left and wears a domed tiara with a crest of 'hooks' and ear-flaps and has a long beard. Waël also faces to the left and is bare-headed, with a thick mop of hair growing low on the nape of the neck, a large nose, a moustache, a thin face and a short, pointed beard. Other bronze coins issued by Waël carry the same portrait of him on the obverses (*Ill. 269*).[2]

1 *BMCGC Arabia, etc.*, 1922, pl. 13, no. 6.
2 *Ibid.*, pl. 13, nos. 7, 8; J. B. Segal, *Edessa, etc.*, 1970, pl. 28, b, ii.

ABGAR VIII bar MA'NU ('the Great';
AD 177–212) and his son MA'NU
Ills. 270–2
Abgar VIII, who took the Roman names of Lucius Aelius Aurelius Septimius, as a compliment to Marcus Aurelius, Commodus, and Septimius Severus, was the son of Ma'nu VIII. In 195 he was defeated by Septimius Severus.[1] But in 197/8 he took refuge with the emperor, to whom he entrusted his sons as hostages, and presented him with

268, 269 Waël bar Sahru: reverse of bronze coin struck at Edessa, and distinctive obverse portrait.

270, 271 Abgar VIII bar Ma'nu: reverses of bronze coins showing different treatment of tiara.

272 Ma'nu: reverse of bronze coin of Abgar VIII with his son depicted beardless, and the tiara without diadem.

273 Abgar IX bar Abgar: reverse of bronze coin showing the domed and diademed tiara.

MANNOC ΠAIC, the second word indicating Ma'nu's continuing juniority after he had grown a beard; he wears the domed and crested tiara, but without a diadem (*Ill. 272*).

1 SHA, *Severus* 18, 1; Aurelius Victor, *De Caes.*, xx, 14.
2 Herodian iii, 9, 2.
3 DC, lxxx, 16, 2.
4 *BMCGC Arabia, etc.*, 1922, pl. 13, nos. 14–16, pl. 14, nos. 1–7, pl. 50, nos. 10, 11; J. B. Segal, *Edessa, etc.*, 1970, pl. 28, b, i.
5 *BMCGC Arabia, etc.*, 1922, pl. 50, no. 12.
6 Ibid., p. ci and pls. 14, nos. 8, 9, and 50, nos. 13, 14.

ABGAR IX bar ABGAR (AD 212–14)

Ill. 273

Abgar IX, who took the name of Severus, was the son of Abgar VIII. According to Dio Cassius,[1] Caracalla tricked him, inducing him to visit him as a friend and then arresting and imprisoning him. Probably in 213/4 Edessa became Colonia Aurelia Antoniniana. The Abgar who died in Rome at the age of twenty-six and his brother Antoninus, who erected his funerary inscription, were probably the sons of Abgar IX.[2]

Abgar's portrait-bust appears on the reverses of bronze coins with Caracalla's head on the obverses. The king is beardless, has a long, aquiline nose, and wears the domed and diademed tiara with a crest of 'hooks' (*Ill. 273*).[3]

Abgar's son, Ma'nu IX, reigned *de iure* from 214 to 240, during which period the kingdom of Edessa was in abeyance, the country being occupied by the Persians. He has left no portraits of himself.

1 lxxviii, 12, 1.
2 *CIG*, 6196.
3 *BMCGC Arabia, etc.*, 1922, pl. 14, no. 10.

ABGAR X bar MA'NU, PHRAHATES

(Frahad; AD 240–2)

Ills. 274–6

In 240 Gordian III re-occupied Mesopotamia and restored the kingdom of Edessa under Abgar X, who was probably the son of Ma'nu IX.

Large bronze coins with Gordian's bust on the obverses show on the reverses the emperor seated on the left and facing Abgar, who stands before him, holding a figure of Nike on his extended right hand. He wears a very tall, conical, diademed tiara, a long-sleeved tunic and trousers; his left hand rests on the hilt of his sword (*Ill. 274*).[1] Other large bronze pieces with Gordian III on the obverses bear on the reverses the figure of Abgar riding towards the right on a pacing horse. He wears similar dress, but his diademed tiara is

domed and has the crest of 'hooks' (*Ill. 275*).[2] Series of smaller bronze coins, with the imperial obverse portrait, have Abgar's rightward-facing, deep bust on the reverses (*Ill. 276*).[3] He wears the domed, diademed, and 'hook'-crested tiara with short ear-flaps, a necklace, a mantle, and an under-robe with buttons down the front. In the field behind the king's head there is a star.

A funerary inscription erected to this Abgar by his wife Hodda came to light in Rome.[4] He would seem to have withdrawn to Rome from Edessa and to have died there. With him the Edessan monarchy ended.

1   *BMCGC Arabia, etc.*, 1922, pl. 16, no. 7.
2   Ibid., pl. 16, no. 8.
3   Ibid., pl. 16, nos. 9–11, pl. 17, nos. 1–4. Cf. a lead seal with his portrait: *Syria*, xviii, 1937, pl. 6, fig. 3.
4   *CIL*, vi, 1797: 'D M/Abgar/Phrahates/filius rex/ principis/Orrhenoru(m)   Hodda/coniugi   bene/ merenti fec(it)'.

274, 275   Abgar X: reverses of bronze coins showing (*left*) Abgar facing the seated Gordian III and (*right*) on horseback.

276   Abgar X: reverse of bronze coin featuring a deep bust occupying the full height of the flan.

Syria[1]

ANTIOCHUS III ('the Great'; 223–187 BC)
and his son Antiochus
Ills. 277–80

Antiochus III, born in 241 BC, was the second son
of Seleucus II. No sooner did he come to the throne
than he began to plan attempts to regain the
Seleucid possessions that his predecessors had lost.
His first aim was to snatch Coele-Syria and Pales-
tine from Egypt, but he was defeated at the battle of
Raphia in Palestine in 217 BC by Ptolemy IV. He
then turned north and recovered most of the
Seleucid possessions in Asia Minor; after which his
expansionist policy led him to acquire Armenia,
Parthia and Bactria as dependent kingdoms, and
even to penetrate to India. His agreement with
Philip of Macedon in 202 BC to partition the
various possessions of Ptolemy alarmed the Roman
Senate. By 198 BC he had gained possession of
Coele-Syria down to the Egyptian frontier. His
next move was to attempt to secure the whole of
Asia Minor and Thrace, which he overran in 196.
This was a challenge to Rome, who declared war
on Antiochus, after protracted negotiations with
him had failed and he had invaded Greece. Rome
routed him at Thermopylae. The king then with-
drew from Greece to Asia Minor, where he was
utterly defeated, probably in January 189 BC, by
the Romans. Antiochus now came to terms of peace
and friendship with Rome;[2] and by the treaty of
Apamea he had to cede the whole of Asia Minor
west of the Taurus, pay a huge indemnity, and
deliver up his elephants and fleet. His outlying
possessions now rebelled and he was left with Syria,
Mesopotamia and Media. He met his death in 187
BC while trying to seize the temple treasure of
Elymais.

Antiochus III's coin portraits appear on the
obverses of his gold staters, silver tetradrachms and
drachms, and bronze pieces (*Ills. 277–9*).[3] They
vary somewhat, as indeed one would expect, given
the length of his reign, but his main features remain
constant. His diademed hair is generally fairly
neat, except at the top of the head, and grows low
on the nape of the neck. He has a receding brow, a
very long and pointed nose, a small, rather weak
and sometimes slightly supercilious mouth, and a

277–9 Antiochus III: obverses of gold stater, silver
tetradrachm and bronze coin, showing slight variations in
treatment of details.

neck that is sometimes creased. On his most youthful portraits he has side-burns. His cheeks grew thinner as he aged; and the diademed marble head in the Louvre, which has sunken cheeks and a mouth, brow and nose that resemble those on his coin portraits, is reasonably to be regarded as his likeness.[4]

The portrait on the obverse of a tetradrachm struck at Tyre after 202–200 BC, when the city passed from Ptolemaic to Seleucid hands, may depict Antiochus, the eldest son of Antiochus III and his co-regent from 210/9 to 193/2, the year in which he died. His boyish features, in particular his very projecting nose, and the style of his diademed hair closely resemble those of Antiochus' youthful portraits: he has a receding brow and side-burns (*Ill. 280*).[5]

280 Antiochus (son of Antiochus III)(?): obverse of tetradrachm, possibly depicting the king's co-regent.

small mouth with parted lips, and chubby cheeks (*Ills. 282*).[4]

1 Polybius xxxi, 12, 1.
2 Ibid., xxiv, 5, 1.
3 *BMCGC Seleucid Kings of Syria*, 1878, pl. 10, nos. 5–7; Newell 1937, pl. 5, no. 9; Richter 1965, fig. 1880; Davis and Kraay 1973, pls. 78, 79, 84.
4 *BMCGC Seleucid Kings of Syria*, 1878, pl. 8, nos. 1, 2; *CAH*, vol. iii of plates, 1930, p. 13, f; Newell 1937, pl. 5, no. 10; Richter 1965, fig. 1881.

1 The coin portraits of the Seleucid kings of Syria form a more or less continuous series from the late fourth to the first half of the first century BC; and they are among the most superbly modelled and the most realistic of all the royal likenesses that Hellenistic artists produced. But here only the portraits of those kings who had contacts with Rome are included, since only they can claim to rank as characters in Roman history. All Seleucid royal coin portraits are rightward facing.
2 Polybius xxi, 14; Livy xxxviii, 38; Appian, *Syr.*, 38.
3 *BMCGC Seleucid Kings of Syria*, 1878, pl. 8, nos. 3–8, pl. 9, nos. 1–10; Newell 1937, pl. 5, fig. 8; Richter 1965, figs. 1875–7; Scullard 1970, pl. 39; Davis and Kraay 1973, pls. 72–7.
4 Richter 1965, figs. 1878–9.
5 *NC*, 1973, pp. 220–1, with fig.

SELEUCUS IV PHILOPATOR (187–175 BC)
and his son (the 'Boy-King')
Ills. 281, 282

Seleucus IV, the second son of Antiochus III, sent his son Demetrius to Rome as a hostage.[1] In 183 BC Titus Flamininus visited him,[2] no doubt in order to investigate his attitude to Rome; and indeed he seems to have been on friendly terms with Rome throughout his reign. The indemnity incurred by his father, which he still had to work off, severely curbed his activities. He died by assassination.

Seleucus' coin portraits show him with neat curly hair, a diadem, a receding brow, large eyes, a long, pointed and hooked nose, and a rather grim mouth, which is turned down at the corners (*Ill. 281*).[3]

Some tetradrachms bear on the obverse the features of a very young boy, quite distinct from those probably of the Antiochus who was Antiochus III's eldest son. They are likely to be those of the 'Boy-King' Antiochus, the younger son of Seleucus IV who, since he is diademed, must have reigned for a very brief period in 175 BC, before he was apparently done away with by his uncle, Antiochus IV. He has a straight nose, large eyes, a

281, 282 Seleucus IV and his son, the 'Boy-King' Antiochus: obverses of silver tetradrachms.

ANTIOCHUS IV THEOS EPIPHANES NIKEPHOROS
(175–164 BC)
Ills. 283, 284

Antiochus IV Epiphanes was the third son of
Antiochus III and the younger brother of Seleucus
IV. He had been sent as a hostage to Rome by his
father and there he had enjoyed Roman society
and learnt to admire Roman ways.[1] Seleucus IV
(q.v.) sent his eldest son, Demetrius, to replace
Antiochus, who now travelled east to Syria via
Greece and, on learning of his brother's death,
seized the throne with the aid of Eumenes of
Pergamon;[2] it was doubtless then that the 'Boy-
King' Antiochus disappeared. In 173 BC he sent an
embassy to Rome to seek friendship and recognition of his kingship and to pay up the last
instalment of Antiochus III's indemnity.[3] He did,
however, in defiance of the treaty of Apamea,
maintain a large herd of elephants.[4] In 171 BC,
quarrelling with Egypt, he first appealed to Rome.[5]
But when Rome would not listen to him he invaded
the country and captured Memphis. In 168 BC he
again invaded Egypt and was on the point of
reducing it when a Roman mission, headed by
Caius Popillius Laenas, appeared at Alexandria
and Antiochus was faced with an ultimatum demanding his evacuation of Egypt, which he uncon-
ditionally carried out.[6] His exploits in Jerusalem
after his return to Syria have been rendered famous
by the story of the Maccabees' revolt against him.[7]

In 165 BC, in imitation of the Roman games held
by Lucius Aemilius Paullus at Amphipolis to mark
his victory over Perseus of Macedon, Antiochus
staged at Daphne near Antioch a magnificent
display, including a great triumphal procession, in
which many elephants took part, and athletic
games.[8] He died on an expedition into Persia in 164
BC.

Antiochus IV's coin portraits on his silver and
bronze depict him with thick, tightly curled, diademed hair, a straight nose, continuing the line of
his brow, a somewhat sensuous mouth with full lips,
and full cheeks (*Ill. 283*).[9] Of all the Seleucid kings
he has, perhaps, the most regular and handsome
features. One silver obverse portrays him as Zeus,
with laurel-wreath, moustache, and flowing hair
and beard that do not disguise his unmistakable
facial traits (*Ill. 284*).[10] A diademed bronze head
from Herculaneum, now in the Naples Museum,
may well be his likeness.[11]

7 Tacitus, *Hist.*, v, 8.
8 Polybius xxxi, 3; Athenaeus 194c–195.
9 *BMCGC Seleucid Kings of Syria*, 1878, pl. 11, nos, 1–8,
pl. 12, nos. 1–10, 13–16, pl. 13, nos. 1–5, pl. 28, no. 5;
CAH, vol. iii of plates, 1930, p. 13, g, h; Newell 1937,
pl. 6, nos. 12, 13; Richter 1965, fig. 1884; Davis and
Kraay 1973, pls. 80, 81, 85.
10 *BMCGC Seleucid Kings of Syria*, 1878, pl. 11, no. 9;
CAH, vol. iii of plates, 1930, p. 13, i; Newell 1937, pl.
6, no. 14. The reverse legend reads 'Basileos Anti-
ochou Theou Epiphanous Nikephorou'.
11 Richter 1965, figs. 1882–3.

283, 284 Antiochus IV: obverses of silver coins showing
the king diademed and (below) bearded and laureate as
Zeus.

ANTIOCHUS V EUPATOR (164–162 BC)
Ill. 285

Antiochus V, the son of Antiochus IV, was born in
173 BC and ascended the throne at the age of nine.
Ambassadors were sent from Rome under Cnaeus
Octavius (who was assassinated on this occasion) to

1 Livy xlii, 6.
2 Appian, *Syr.*, 45.
3 Livy xlii, 6. Cf. xlii, 26, 7 and xlv, 13, 2 for Antiochus'
attitude of subservience to Roman commissions sent
to visit him.
4 Polybius xxxi, 3.
5 Ibid., xxvii, 17.
6 Ibid., xxix, 11.

help to establish the boy as king:[1] a weak government in Syria suited Rome's book. But the child met his death at Antioch when Demetrius I (q.v.) arrived in Syria.

Antiochus V's coin portraits show a boyish face, with neatly curling diademed hair, a rather *retroussé* nose, a small mouth and a weak chin. He has rounded cheeks and a small 'Adam's apple' (*Ill. 285*).[2]

1 Polybius xxxi, 12; Cicero, *Phil.*, ix, 2, 4.
2 *BMCGC Seleucid Kings of Syria*, 1878, pl. 13, nos. 11–14; Newell 1937, pl. 6, no. 16; Richter 1965, fig. 1885.

285   Antiochus V: obverse of silver coin.

DEMETRIUS I SOTER (162–150 BC)
Ills. 286–8

Demetrius I, the eldest son of Seleucus IV, had been a hostage in Rome since round about the time of his father's death. He was now heir to the throne of Syria, Antiochus V being only a child, but the Senate refused his request to leave Rome and claim it. He therefore, at the instigation of his friend Polybius and with the connivance of certain influential Romans, planned and carried through a daring escape from Italy by sea, landed in Phoenicia, and was enthusiastically received by the Syrians.[1] Rome did nothing beyond at first refusing him recognition.

One of Demetrius' first achievements as king was the liquidation of the Milesian Timarchus, who had once been a favourite of Antiochus Epiphanes, probably in Rome. He had set himself up as 'Great King' in Babylonia and Media, had issued tetradrachms, drachms, and bronze coins with his own portraits – a helmeted head, with forceful features and a double chin (copied from the portraits of Eucratides of Bactria – 165–150 BC: Richter 1965,

fig. 1986)[2] and a diademed bust[3] – and had received verbal recognition from Rome. For his removal of Timarchus, Demetrius was acclaimed as 'Soter' by Seleucia on the Tigris (Appian, *Syr.*, 67); and in 160 BC, envoys from Demetrius met in Rhodes a Roman commission under Tiberius Sempronius Gracchus, who had known him in Rome and recognized him as king. In the same year an embassy to Rome from Syria, bringing a golden crown and Cnaeus Octavius' assassin (cf. p. 143), secured from the Senate Demetrius' formal recognition.[4] Another of Demetrius' services to Rome was the capture and dispatch to the capital of the Macedonian pretender Andriscus.[5] Beset throughout his reign by troubles with the Jews, with the kings of Pergamon, Cappadocia and Egypt, and with his own Syrian people, Demetrius died in 150 BC while fighting the pretender Alexander I Balas (q.v.).

Demetrius' coin portraits in silver and bronze present him with rather straggling locks of diademed hair growing low on the nape of the neck and forming a thick crest above the brow. He has a long, aquiline nose, a slightly smiling mouth and a firm chin. He sometimes has an 'Adam's apple' and a creased neck (*Ills. 286, 287*).[6] There are two distinct versions of his likeness, one with a face much broader and heavier than the other, which is more idealized. Demetrius married Laodice, the widow of Perseus, and struck bronze coins with their jugate heads on the obverse, the king diademed in the foreground and the queen, wearing a *stephane* (upstanding coronet), in the background (*Ill. 288*).[7] A bronze statue in the Museo Nazionale Romano displays a nose, a mouth, a chin and a crest of hair very similar to those on Demetrius' coin portraits. The head is not diademed, but must represent a divinized Hellenistic ruler, since the body is nude and there is a sceptre in the raised left hand.[8]

1 Polybius xxxi, 12, 19–23.
2 *CAH*, vol. iii of plates, 1930, p. 15, a: on the reverse is Timarchus' name with the title 'Basileus Megalos'.
3 *BMCGC Seleucid Kings of Syria*, 1878, pl. 15, no. 3, pl. 28, no. 6 – same reverse legend.
4 Polybius xxxii, 4.
5 Livy, *Epit.*, 49.
6 *BMCGC Seleucid Kings of Syria*, 1878, pl. 14, nos. 1–11; Newell 1937, pl. 6, nos. 17, 18; Richter 1965, figs. 1887, 1888; Davis and Kraay 1973, pls. 87, 88, 91.
7 *BMCGC Seleucid Kings of Syria*, 1878, pl. 15, nos. 1, 2.
8 Richter 1965, figs. 1886, 1889.

ALEXANDER I BALAS THEOPATOR EUERGETES EPIPHANES NIKEPHOROS (150–145 BC)
Ills. 289, 290

Alexander I, a young man of low birth from Smyrna, was said to bear a remarkable likeness to

Antiochus V Eupator (q.v.), son of Antiochus IV, and gave himself out as the latter's son. He was put forward by Attalus III of Pergamon as claimant to the Syrian throne against Demetrius I (q.v.), was tricked out with a diadem and given the name of Alexander.[1] Herakleides the former finance minister of Antiochus IV, brought him to Rome with his alleged sister, Laodice, daughter of Antiochus IV; and in 153/2 BC the Senate gave him recognition as king and friend and ally of Rome.[2] By 152 BC he had secured Ptolemais, from which position he could, with the king of Egypt's support, threaten Demetrius; and he succeeded in winning the allegiance of the Maccabaean Jonathan.[3] In 150 BC Demetrius I was slain in battle against him.[4]

Alexander was now undisputed king of Syria and in 150/49 BC he married Cleopatra Thea, daughter of Ptolemy VI, at Ptolemais with immense pomp.[5] After this his rule endured for five years.[6] In 147 BC Demetrius II, the young son of Demetrius I, arrived in northern Syria and Alexander went north to defend Antioch against him. Ptolemy, turning against his son-in-law, now occupied the coastal towns of Coele-Syria and offered Cleopatra Thea to Demetrius II, with whose aid he inflicted a crushing defeat on Alexander in Cilicia in 145 BC. In this battle both Ptolemy and Alexander perished.[7]

Alexander's coin portraits occur on his silver and bronze issues.[8] He has loosely curling hair, a rather low brow, a large nose, a small, full-lipped mouth, a heavy jaw and a prominent chin. Some portraits show him as Zeus, with laurel-wreath and flowing hair and beard (*Ill. 289*; cf. *Ill. 284*);[9] others show him wearing a lion-skin on his head;[10] others again as equipped with a crested helmet.[11] Bronze coins depict him jugate with Cleopatra

286–8 Demetrius I: coin obverses with variant portraits and (below) jugate with Laodice.

289 Alexander I: obverse of silver coin showing the king in the guise of Zeus (cf. *Ill. 284*).

Thea, the latter in the foreground, veiled and wearing a *stephane* (upstanding coronet).[12] She has a rather turned-up nose, a large mouth and a prominent chin. Silver coins also show the pair jugate, with Cleopatra again in the foreground, but wearing a *polos* (tall head-dress) on her veiled and diademed hair and with two corkscrew curls hanging down in front of each ear (*Ill. 290*).[13] Alexander's high-flown titles appear on his coins in the legends of his reverse types.

1 Livy, *Epit.*, 52; Diodorus Siculus xxxi, 32a.
2 Polybius xxxiii, 14, 16.
3 Appian, *Syr.*, 67; Josephus, *Ant. Iud.*, xiii, 35–45.
4 Appian, *Syr.*, 67; Josephus, *Ant. Iud.*, xiii, 58–61.
5 Ibid., 80–3.
6 Ibid., 119.
7 Livy, *Epit.*, 52; Appian, *Syr.*, 67; Josephus, *Ant Iud.*, xiii, 109–19.
8 *BMCGC Seleucid Kings of Syria*, 1878, pl. 15, nos. 4–6, pl. 16, nos. 1–11, 14–15, pl. 17, nos. 1–5; Newell 1937, pl. 6, nos. 19, 20; Richter 1965, fig. 1892; Davis and Kraay 1973, pls. 89, 90, 92.
9 *BMCGC Seleucid Kings of Syria*, 1878, pl. 16, no. 1.
10 Ibid., pl. 16, no. 10.
11 Ibid., pl. 16, no. 11.
12 Ibid., pl. 17, no. 6.
13 Richter 1965, fig. 1893.

290   Alexander I and Cleopatra Thea: obverse of silver coin showing the queen wearing a *polos*.

ANTIOCHUS VI EPIPHANES DIONYSOS (145–142 BC)
Ill. 291

Antiochus VI was the son of Alexander I Balas and Cleopatra Thea. Since Demetrius II Nikator was greatly disliked by his subjects, a former general of Alexander, Diodotus Tryphon (q.v.), put Antiochus forward as Syrian king.[1] It would appear that Rome recognized him as king, for when Tryphon, after murdering Antiochus, tried to win Rome's recognition for himself by sending the Senate a golden statue of Victory, the Senate ignored him and accepted the gift in the dead child's name.[2]

Antiochus' silver and bronze coins, which bear his titles on their reverses, depict on their obverses the young king's portrait. He has thick, tightly curled hair encircled by a diadem and by a radiate crown, a straight nose, a small mouth, a weak chin and full cheeks (*Ill. 291*).[3]

1 Diodorus Siculus xxxiii, 4a and 20; Josephus, *Ant. Iud.*, xiii, 145 (ὁ παῖς Ἀντίοχος); Livy, *Epit.*, 52.
2 Diodorus Siculus xxxiii, 28a.
3 *BMCGC Seleucid Kings of Syria*, 1878, pl. 19, nos. 1–9, 11–14; Newell 1937, pl. 7, nos. 23, 24; Richter 1965, fig. 1896; Davis and Kraay 1973, pls. 99, 100, 105.

DIODOTUS TRYPHON (140–139 BC)
Ill. 292

Diodotus Tryphon, the former general of Alexander Balas and the murderer of Antiochus VI (q.v.), succeeded in driving out Demetrius II, usurped the Syrian throne, and sought in vain to gain Rome's recognition. Failing to hold the Syrian kingdom, he committed suicide.[1]

Tryphon's silver and bronze coins carry on their obverses his diademed head. He has rather wild, untidy hair, a straight nose, a small mouth, full cheeks and a heavy jowl. There is sometimes an 'Adam's apple' (*Ill. 292*).[2] The reverses display his titles – 'Basileos Tryphonos Autokratoros'.

Rome now left Syria to her own devices until the reign of her last king, Antiochus XIII (q.v.).

1 Strabo xiv, 5, 2.
2 *BMCGC Seleucid Kings of Syria*, 1878, pl. 20, nos. 1–3, pl. 28, nos. 9, 10; Newell 1937, pl. 7, no. 25; Richter 1965, fig. 1897; Davis and Kraay 1973, pls. 101, 102, 106.

291   Antiochus VI: obverse of silver coin showing the king wearing a radiate crown.

292 Diodotus Tryphon: obverse of silver coin struck by the usurper of the Syrian throne who held power briefly, 140–139 BC.

293 Antiochus XIII: obverse of silver coin depicting the last king of Syria before the territory became a Roman province.

ANTIOCHUS XIII ASIATICUS (69–64 BC)
Ill. 293

Antiochus XIII got his title from the fact that he had spent his youth in Asia Minor.[1] In about 75 BC, while still a boy, he went to Rome with his brother to claim Egypt for himself and for his mother, Cleopatra Selene; but the Senate very naturally refused his request. He remained in Rome for two years, living in regal state, as the friend and ally of the Roman people, and then returned to the East via Sicily.[2] When Tigranes of Armenia's rule in Syria ended, Antiochus was welcomed by the Syrians as their king and was recognized as such by Lucullus in 69 BC. But in 65 BC, when Pompey took command in the East, Antiochus' kingship was doomed[3] and he was captured by Sampsiceramus of Emesa.[4] In 64 BC he is said to have asked Pompey, now in Syria, to confirm him on his throne. But Sampsiceramus had Antiochus put to death; and Pompey brought the Syrian dynasty to an end by turning the country into a Roman province.

The coins attributed to Antiochus XIII display on their obverses the portrait of a young man, diademed and with rather wild, untidy hair (*Ill. 293*).[5] He has large eyes, a hooked nose, a rather foolish expression on his lips, a pointed chin and an 'Adam's apple.'

1 Appian, *Syr.*, 70.
2 Cicero, *Verr.*, iv, 27, 28, 30.
3 Appian, *Syr.*, 49.
4 Diodorus Siculus xl, 1b.
5 Newell 1937, pl. 8, no. 39; Richter 1965, fig. 1909.

Palmyra

SEPTIMIA ZENOBIA (AD 267–271/2) and her sons
HERODIANUS and VABALATHUS
ATHENODORUS PERSICUS MAXIMUS[1]
Ills. 294–6

Zenobia, queen of Palmyra, took her name Septimia from her husband Septimius Odenathus
(Odaenath), who was murdered in 267. Odenathus
had received from Gallienus the title 'totius orientis
imperator'[2] for his services against the Persians and
also the title of 'Augustus', together with the right
of coinage.[3] At the time of his death his dominions
extended from the Taurus on the north to the
Arabian Gulf on the south.

Nothing of this Empire was Zenobia, now regent
for her young sons Herodianus and Vabalathus,
disposed to forgo. But it was not until the death of
Claudius II in 170 that she resolved to defy Rome
in her expansionist policy, which included the
occupation by Palmyrene troops first of large
portions of Asia Minor and then of Arabia and
Egypt. Her aim at first seems to have been an
eastern Roman Empire centred at Palmyra, but still
on good terms with Rome; and in 270 there were
struck at Alexandria billon coins with Aurelian's
bust on the obverses and on the reverses Vabalathus' bust facing to the right, laureate, diademed, and wearing the Roman *paludamentum* and
cuirass,[4] and bronze coins on the obverses of which
are the confronted busts of Aurelian and Vabalathus, the latter facing left and again with laurel-
wreath, diadem, *paludamentum* and cuirass.[5] But by
270/1 it became clear that Zenobia's ultimate aim
was a Palmyrene Roman Empire independent of
the West. First, antoniniani were issued at Antioch
with Aurelian's portrait on the *reverse* and on the
*ob*verse Vabalathus' draped, laureate and slightly
bearded bust, facing to the right and accompanied
by the legend VABALATHUS V(*ir*) C(*larissimus*) R(*ex*)
I(*mperator*) D(*ux*) R(*omanorum*).[6] Then, also at Antioch, were minted antoniniani with Vabalathus'
draped and rightward-facing bust on the obverse
and no reference whatsoever to Aurelian: the
young king wears a diadem and a radiate crown
and the accompanying legend reads IM(*p*)
C(*aesar*) VHABALATHVS AVG(*ustus*) (*Ill. 294*).[7]
Similarly at Alexandria we get bronze coins with
the obverse bust of Vabalathus facing to the right,
diademed and laureate, with *paludamentum* and
cuirass and CEB(αστός) in his legend, again without
mention of Aurelian.[8] Probably contemporary
with the last coins are the bronze pieces struck at
Alexandria with Zenobia's own rightward-facing

obverse portrait – a draped bust with the legend
CEΠTIM(ἰα) ZENOBIA CEB(αστή).[9] A lead seal with
the portrait of Zenobia's son Herodianus on one
side presents her own likeness on the other: she
faces to the right and wears a laurel-wreath in her
hair, which is gathered in a 'bun' on the nape of her
neck (*Ill. 295*).[10] Herodianus, also facing right,
wears the tall, conical oriental tiara with a crest of
'hooks'. He seems to be bearded (*Ill. 296*).

294 Vabalathus: obverse of *antoninianus* minted at
Antioch, showing the king diademed and wearing a radiate
crown.

295, 296 Septimia Zenobia and her son Herodianus:
portraits on either side of a lead seal.

In 271 Aurelian's campaign against Zenobia's empire began. He recovered Asia Minor and captured Antioch and Palmyra, from which Zenobia escaped, only to be caught and brought back a prisoner. After settling Egypt and the West, the emperor held a splendid triumph in Rome in 274, in which Zenobia walked, adorned with jewels and golden chains.[11] Her life was spared and she spent the remainder of her days on a country estate at Tibur (Tivoli) not far from Hadrian's villa.[12]

Zenobia was certainly one of the most remarkable and intellectually gifted women in history. She had literary tastes and must have spoken at least four languages – Palmyrene, Greek, Egyptian and Latin.

1   For the most recent full-dress account of Zenobia, see Pauly-Wissowa, *Real-Encyclopädie der classischen Altertumswissenschaft* Xa, 1972, cols. 1–8. For Vabalathus as 'Persicus Maximus', see *Année Épigr.*, 1904, no. 60.
2   SHA, *Gallienus* 3 and 10.
3   Ibid., 12.
4   *BMCGC Alexandria*, 1892, pp. 309–10, nos. 2384–93.
5   Ibid., p. 310, nos. 2394–6.
6   *RIC*, V, i, 1927, p. 308, no. 381, pl. 9, nos. 130–1; *CAH*, vol. v of plates, 1939, p. 239, b.
7   *RIC*, V, i, pl. 9, no. 132; ibid., V, ii, 1933, p. 585, nos. 1–8, pl. 20, no. 13.
8   *BMCGC Alexandria*, 1892, p. 311, no. 2397.
9   Ibid., p. 311, nos. 2398–401.
10 *Syria* xviii, 1937, pl. 6, figs. 1, 2; *CAH*, xii, 1939, p. 724 (2).
11 SHA, *Aurelianus* 34; *Tyranni Triginta* 30.
12 Ibid.

Chalcis

Lysanias (40–36 BC)
Ill. 297

Lysanias was the son of the Ptolemaeus who had been confirmed on the throne of Chalcis by Marcus Antonius and of whom no portraits are known. He joined Pacorus of Parthia when he invaded Syria in 40 BC,[1] in return for which Antonius had him executed in 36 BC and gave his kingdom to Cleopatra.[2]

Lysanias' bronze coins show on their obverses his head diademed and facing to the right. He has neat hair, a very large hooked nose, a prominent chin and a small 'Adam's apple' beneath it (*Ill. 297*).[3] His reverse legends describe him as tetrarch and high priest.

1   Josephus, *Bell. Iud.*, i, 248; ii, 215; *Ant. Iud.*, xiv, 330, 332.
2   Josephus, *Bell. Iud.*, i, 440; *Ant. Iud.*, xv, 92; DC, xlix, 32, 5.
3   *BMCGC Galatia, etc.*, 1899, p. 280, no. 6, pl. 34, no. 1.

297   Lysanias: obverse of bronze coin showing the diademed head of the tetrarch and high-priest.

298   Zenodorus: reverse of bronze coin with bare-headed portrait.

Zenodorus (*c.* 30–20 BC)
Ill. 298

By Octavian's settlement with the eastern client kings after Actium, the city of Chalcis was declared free, but Zenodorus, the son of Lysanias (q.v.), was permitted to rule in Abila and to lease his father's possessions. He governed very badly, however, and despite an appeal by him to Rome his territory was taken from him and given to Herod 'the Great'.

Zenodorus conveniently died of a ruptured intestine.[1]

Bronze coins show Octavian's head on their obverses and on their reverses Zenodorus' bare head facing to the left. He has a thick 'cap' of short hair, an aquiline nose, a small mouth and a long neck (*Ill. 298*).[2] Like Lysanias, he describes himself as tetrarch and high priest.

1 Josephus, *Bell. Iud.*, i, 398, 400; *Ant. Iud.*, xv, 344–59, 363; xvi, 271.
2 *BMCGC Galatia, etc.*, 1899, p. 281, no. 7, pl. 34, no. 2.

HEROD II of Chalcis (AD 41–8)
Ill. 299

Herod II of Chalcis was the brother of Marcus Julius Agrippa I (q.v.) of Judaea and received the kingdom of Chalcis from Claudius in AD 41,[1] together with the right of supervising the Temple of Jerusalem.[2] He was twice married, first to Mariamne, granddaughter of Herod 'the Great', and second to Berenice, his niece, the daughter of Agrippa I.[3] He died in 48/9[4] and was succeeded by his nephew, the son of Agrippa I, Agrippa II (q.v.), who ruled Chalcis until 53.

transferred by Claudius to a larger kingdom consisting of Philip's tetrarchy, namely Trachonitis, Batanaea and Gaulanitis, and some other territories.[2] In 61 Nero added to his dominions parts of Peraea and Galilee.[3] He was present, with his sister, Berenice, at Festus' trial of St Paul at Caesarea (*Acts* xxv, xxvi). He was unswervingly loyal to Rome and was the first of his line to use officially his full Roman name – Marcus Julius Agrippa. In a long speech he did his best to dissuade the Jews from war in 66;[4] and joined the governor of Syria, Cestius Gallus, in his attempt to quell the Jewish rebels and in his unsuccessful attack on Jerusalem.[5] In 67 he sent a contingent to assist Vespasian.[6] He then went to Rome; but hearing a report that the eastern provinces were intending to proclaim Vespasian as emperor, he hurried back to Palestine to offer Vespasian his support. In 70 he assisted Titus at the siege and destruction of Jerusalem. In 75 he visited Rome again, this time in the company of his sister Berenice and was made titular praetor. It was

299 Herod II: obverse of bronze coin showing diademed head.

300 Agrippa II: obverse of bronze coin (3:2) with bare-headed portrait bust.

Herod II's bronze coins portray him facing to the right and wearing a diadem in his closely fitting 'cap' of short hair. He has hollow cheeks, a large, projecting nose and a set mouth (*Ill. 299*).[5]

1 Josephus, *Bell. Iud.*, ii, 217.
2 Josephus, *Ant. Iud.*, xx, 13, 15, 16.
3 Ibid., xviii, 134; xix, 277, 354.
4 Ibid., xx, 104.
5 F. Imhoof-Blumer, *Porträtköpfe auf antiken Münzen hellenischer und hellenisierter Völker*, 1885, pl. 6, no. 20'

AGRIPPA II (MARCUS JULIUS)
of Chalcis (AD 50–3) and a Mixed Kingdom (53–*c*.93)
Ill. 300

Agrippa II was the son of Agrippa I (q.v.) of Judaea. He was made king of Chalcis in AD 49/50[1] and ruled the kingdom until 53, when he was

on this occasion that Titus succumbed to Berenice's charms. Agrippa ruled his kingdom until the closing decade of the first century. He was well versed in Greek culture and offended the Jews of Berytus by his buildings and spectacles in the city.[7]

Agrippa's small bronze coins show on the obverses his bust facing to the left. He is bare-headed, with no diadem, and has curly hair and youthful features (*Ill. 300*).[8]

1 Josephus, *Bell. Iud.*, ii, 223; *Ant. Iud.*, xx, 104.
2 Josephus, *Bell Iud.*, ii, 247; *Ant. Iud.*, xx, 138.
3 Josephus, *Bell. Iud.*, ii, 252.
4 Ibid., ii, 344–407.
5 Ibid., ii, 523–40.
6 Ibid., iii, 68, 443, 445, 454–61.
7 Josephus, *Vita*, 359; *Ant. Iud.*, xx, 211–12.
8 *ZfN*, xiii, 1885, pl. 4, no. 17; *BMCGC Palestine*, 1914, p. xlvi, pl. 42, no. 12. Agrippa styles himself 'Philokaisar' on the reverses.

For a full account of Agrippa II, see A. H. M. Jones, *The Herods of Judaea*, 1967, pp. 217–61.

ARISTOBULUS (the Younger; AD 54–*c.*92)
Ill. 301

Aristobulus was the son of Herod of Chalcis and Mariamne.[1] He married Salome, the widow of Philip, tetrarch of Trachonitis.[2] Claudius expressed a high opinion of him.[3] In AD 54 Nero gave him Armenia Minor[4] and in 60 part of Armenia Maior.[5] He seems to have received his father's kingdom of Chalcis at a later date, since he is very probably the Aristobulus of Chalcidice who assisted the Roman general Caesennius Paetus against Antiochus of Commagene.[6]

Aristobulus' bronze coins depict on their obverses his bust facing to the left and wearing a diadem. He has a hooked nose and a firm mouth and chin (*Ill. 301*).[7]

1 Josephus, *Bell. Iud.*, ii, 221.
2 Josephus, *Ant. Iud.*, xviii, 137.
3 Ibid., xx, 13.
4 Ibid., xx, 158; *Bell. Iud.*, ii, 252; Tacitus, *Ann.*, xiii, 7.
5 Ibid., xiv, 26.
6 Josephus, *Bell. Iud.*, vii, 226.
7 *RN*, 1883, pl. 4, no. 9 (Paris): cf. *RN*, 1900, pp. 484–5; Imhoof-Blumer, op. cit., pl. 6, no. 21.

SALOME, wife of ARISTOBULUS, and her mother HERODIAS
Ills. 302–3

Salome was the daughter of Herodias, who was married to Herod Antipas, the son of Herod 'the Great' by Mariamne, daughter of Simon the High Priest. After the birth of Salome, Herodias married Herod, tetrarch of Galilee, the brother of her husband, who was still alive.[1] Salome was first married to Philip, son of Herod 'the Great' and tetrarch of Trachonitis, and then to Aristobulus (q.v.).[2]

Bronze coins display Salome's bust facing to the left and wearing a diadem. She has her hair gathered into a 'door-knocker' on the nape of the neck, after the Roman fashion. Her nose is very long and straight (*Ill. 302*).[3]

A marble panel, probably of second century AD date and carved in high relief, found (with some other panels similar in form) in a debris-filled ditch near the paved Roman street of Petra, displays

301 Aristobulus the Younger: obverse of bronze coin with diademed bust.

302 Salome: reverse of bronze coin showing bust with diadem and Roman-style coiffure.

303 Herodias(?): marble panel showing the mother of Salome holding the severed head of John the Baptist, found at Petra.

what may well be the matronly portrait-bust of Salome's mother, Herodias, holding up in triumph by the hair the severed head of St John the Baptist. She has a straight nose, a cruel mouth, and heavy cheeks and jaw. Her hair is parted in the centre and waved laterally, in Roman style, and she wears a laurel-wreath as queen. The Baptist's chin and the lower portion of his beard are broken off (*Ill. 303*).[4]

1 Josephus, *Ant. Iud.*, xviii, 136; Mark vi, 17.
2 Josephus, *Ant. Iud.*, xviii, 137.
3 Imhoof-Blumer, op. cit., pl. 6, no. 22.
4 *Illustrated London News*, 9 December 1967.

Judaea

AGRIPPA I (MARCUS JULIUS; 'the Great'; AD 37–44)
[No illustration]
Marcus Julius Agrippa I (wrongly called Herod in the Acts of the Apostles, ch. xii) was the grandson of Herod 'the Great'. He was sent to Rome at the age of three by his mother, Berenice.[1] While living there, he came to be on friendly terms with Tiberius' son, Drusus, and with Antonia, the wife of the Elder Drusus, who was a friend of his mother. Tiberius dismissed him from Rome, but he returned in AD 36, after spending some time in the East. He now struck up a friendship with the future emperor Gaius and was eventually imprisoned by Tiberius.[2] After Tiberius' death Gaius placed a diadem on his head and made him king of the tetrarchies of Philip and Lysanias, with the titular rank of praetor.[3] In the autumn of 38 he set out to take possession of his kingdom, travelling via Alexandria, where his presence provoked a most unpleasant anti-Jewish pogrom, and proceeding to Palestine. Returning to Rome he interceded with Gaius on behalf of the Jews, deflecting him from his project of having a statue of himself set up in the Temple of Jerusalem.[4]

In 41 Claudius, whose accession had been made easier by Agrippa's help, added to Agrippa's realm Judaea, Samaria and the tetrarchy of Abilene, giving him the titular rank of consul.[5] His dominions were now virtually co-extensive with those of Herod 'the Great'. His open friendship with Rome was expressed in the titles 'Philokaisar' and 'Philoromaios' which he used on his coinage. There is no evidence that his attempt to refortify Jerusalem[6] and his convening of a conference of client kings[7] implied any disloyalty to Rome, although the governor of Syria, Vibius Marsus, put a summary end to both of those enterprises. Agrippa died in 44 and Judaea became once again a Roman province.

Agrippa I was the first of his line to place his own portrait on his bronze coins. They show his head facing right and diademed. He is depicted as having an aquiline nose, a firm mouth and chin, and a heavy jaw.[8]

1 Josephus, *Ant. Iud.*, xviii, 143.
2 Ibid., 142–236.
3 Ibid., 237.
4 Ibid., 289–301.
5 Ibid., xix, 274, 275.
6 Ibid., 326–7.
7 Ibid., 338–42.
8 G. Macdonald, *Catalogue of Greek coins in the Hunterian Collection*, iii, 1905, p. 290, pl. 78, no. 8.
For a full account of Agrippa I, see A. H. M. Jones, *The Herods of Judaea*, 1967, pp. 184–216.

Arabia: the Nabataean Kings

ARETAS III (*c*.87–62 BC)
Ill. 304

In *c*.85 BC Aretas III, with his capital at Petra, gained possession of Damascus, having been invited to take charge of the city by its inhabitants out of hatred for their ruler Ptolemaeus, son of Mennaeus.[1] At Damascus, Aretas proceeded to issue bronze coins with his portrait on the obverse and the legend 'Basileos Aretou Philhellenou' on the reverse. But later the citizens threw him out and in 66 BC the Romans under Lollius and Metellus captured Damascus.[2] According to Dio Cassius, who describes him as king of the Arabs subject to Rome, with dominions stretching as far as the Red Sea, Aretas devastated Syria and so found himself in conflict with the Romans, who were defending Syria. Aretas was defeated, but continued the war, until he was again defeated, this time by Pompey.[3] In 65 BC Aretas came to the aid of the high priest Hyrcanus II and besieged Aristobulus II, the rival high priest, in Jerusalem.[4] But when told that if he did not withdraw he would be declared an enemy of Rome, Aretas immediately raised the siege and went home.[5]

In 63 BC Pompey was preparing an expedition to Petra, the Nabataean capital, the Nabataeans supposedly being ready to obey Rome, but he abandoned the project before reaching the city.[6] In 62 BC, however, he sent Scaurus against Aretas, who bought him off with a substantial bribe.[7] Nevertheless, in 58 BC Scaurus did not scruple as curule aedile to strike coins on which REX ARETAS is depicted as kneeling suppliant-wise beside his camel.[8]

Aretas' rightward-facing coin portraits show him beardless (as are all the Nabataean kings) and diademed, with hair growing low on the nape of the neck. He has a thick neck, a very hooked nose, a cynical mouth and a prominent chin (*Ill. 304*).[9]

1 Josephus, *Ant. Iud.*, xiii, 392; *Bell. Iud.*, i, 103. For a recent list and chronology of the Nabataean kings, see *JRS*, lxi, 1971, pp. 222–3.
2 Josephus, *Ant. Iud.*, xiv, 29.
3 DC, xxxvii, 15.
4 Josephus, *Ant. Iud.*, xiv, 19–21.
5 Ibid., 32.
6 Plutarch, *Pompeius* 41, 42; Appian, *Mithr.*, 106.
7 Josephus, *Ant. Iud.*, xiv, 80, 81; *Bell. Iud.*, i, 159.
8 Sydenham 1952, pp. 151–2, nos. 912–14, pl. 25.
9 *BMCGC Arabia, etc.*, 1922, pp. 1, 2, nos. 1–6, pl. 1, nos. 2, 3. Cf. pl. 49, no. 1. For the very plausible suggestion that the rock-cut Khasne tomb at Petra dates from the reign of Aretas III, see M. Lyttelton, *Baroque Architecture in Classical Antiquity*, 1974, p. 75.

MALCHUS I (*c*.62–30 BC)
Ill. 305

In 47 BC Julius Caesar called upon Malchus I to supply him with cavalry for his Alexandrine war.[1] In 39 BC Publius Ventidius Bassus exacted a large sum from Malchus as a punishment for the help that he had given to Pacorus of Parthia.[2] In 36 BC Marcus Antonius presented large portions of his territory to Cleopatra[3] and he had to pay tribute via Herod 'the Great'.[4] For the Actium campaign of 31 BC Malchus sent Antonius contingents.[5] According to Josephus, it was Cleopatra who contrived his death in *c*.30 BC.[6]

304 Aretas III: obverse of bronze coin with diademed, beardless head.

305 Malchus I: obverse of silver coin showing diademed head with hair arranged in long curls.

Malchus' silver coins depict him diademed, facing to the right, with his hair worn in long curls (*Ill. 305*).[7] He has large eyes, a straight nose and a pronounced chin.

1 *Bell. Alex.*, i, 1: 'equites ab rege Nabataeorum Malache evocat'.
2 DC, xlviii, 41, 5.
3 Ibid., xlix, 32.
4 Josephus, *Bell. Iud.*, i, 276; *Ant. Iud.*, xiv, 372; ibid., xv, 107.
5 Plutarch, *Antoninus* 61, 2.
6 Josephus, *Bell. Iud.*, i, 440.
7 *BMCGC Arabia, etc.*, 1922, p. 3, no. 1, pl. 1, no. 5. Cf. pl. 49, no. 4. Coins with the obverse portrait of an unnamed king, with short, diademed hair and an elderly face with a double chin, are said to be not far removed in fabric and style from the didrachms of Malchus I; however, they do not display his features (see ibid., p. xii, pl. 49, nos. 2, 3).

306 Obodas II: obverse of silver coin showing the king jugate with his queen.

Obodas II[1] (or III?; *c.*30–9 BC)
Ill. 306

Obodas is stated by Josephus to have been an inactive and sluggish king, who left the management of his kingdom to his minister Syllaeus. Herod 'the Great' had loaned to the king sixty talents via Syllaeus and the governor of Syria, Lucius Volusius Saturninus, and the military tribune (or procurator) Voluminius agreed that the debt should be paid. When this was not done Herod invaded Arabia in 12 BC and defeated the Arabs. Syllaeus then appealed to Rome and Augustus refused to receive a counter-embassy from Herod. At this point Obodas died and Syllaeus was accused of having poisoned him.[2]

Obodas' silver coins show his bust jugate with that of his queen, who wears a *stephane* (upstanding coronet) and a necklace. Both face towards the right. Obodas' hair hangs down in long ringlets. He is draped and diademed and has a straight nose, a small mouth and a weak chin (*Ill. 306*).[3]

1 So numbered in Pauly-Wissowa, *Real-Encyclopädie der classischen Altertumswissenschaft*, XVII, 1937, cols. 1736–8. Numbered III in *BMCGC Arabia, etc.*, 1922, p. 4.
2 Josephus, *Ant. Iud.*, xvi, 220, 279–80, 286–8, 294, 296.
3 *BMCGC Arabia, etc.*, p. 4, nos. 1–3, pl. 1, nos. 6–8. Cf. pl. 49, no. 5.

Aretas IV Philopatris (9 BC–*c.* AD 40 or later)
Ills. 307, 308

Aretas IV claimed his throne without securing Augustus' consent, with the result that the embassy and gifts, including a golden crown, that he sent to Rome were not accepted and the king remained unrecognized.[1] In 4 BC his hatred of Herod 'the Great' led him to seek again Rome's

friendship and he sent a considerable force of infantry and cavalry to assist Publius Quinctilius Varus, the legate of Syria.[2] He quarrelled with Herod Antipas, who had divorced Aretas' daughter in order to marry Herodias (cf. p. 151), made war on him, and defeated him. Lucius Vitellius, now governor of Syria, was on the point of making war on Aretas, but desisted on receiving the news of Tiberius' death.[3]

Towards the end of his reign Aretas seems to have regained Damascus for the Nabataean kingdom, since the imperial coins of the city come to an end in AD 34. Moreover, it was in order to elude the guards of Aretas that St Paul was lowered in a hamper through a window in the city-walls.[4]

The title 'Philopatris' was doubtless adopted by Aretas as a mark of independence and a counter-blast to the 'Philoromaios' and 'Philokaisar' used by the more subservient client kings.

Aretas IV's silver and bronze coins depict on the obverses his bust facing to the right, either laureate or with a head ornament, and with hair growing low on the nape of the neck (*Ills. 307, 308*). Other obverses have the rightward-facing jugate busts of the king and his second queen, Shaqilath I. On some reverses there is the rightward-facing bust of Aretas' first queen, Hulda, with veil and head ornament; on others that of Shaqilath I, similarly equipped.[5] Aretas has a long, pointed nose, a small mouth and a square jaw.

1 Josephus, *Ant. Iud.*, xvi, 295–6, 353.
2 Ibid., xvii, 287.
3 Ibid., xviii, 109–24.
4 II Corinthians xi, 32.
5 *BMCGC Arabia, etc.*, 1922, pp. 5–10, nos, 1–35, pl. 1, nos. 9–21, pl. 2, nos. 1–12, pl. 49, nos. 7–9. For the very plausible suggestion that the rock-cut Deir tomb at Petra dates from the reign of Aretas IV, see p. 153 (footnote 9).

307,308   Aretas IV Philopatris: obverses of coins showing distinctive portrait types, with the king depicted laureate in each.

MALCHUS II (*c.*AD 48–71)
Ill. 309
All that we know of Malchus II's dealings with Rome is that he sent a thousand cavalry and five thousand infantry to assist Vespasian in his Jewish war in AD 67.[1]

Malchus' silver coins bear on their obverses his bust facing right. He has long hair and is laureate; his brow and nose form a continuous line, and he has a small mouth and projecting chin (*Ill. 309*). On the reverses is the rightward-facing bust of his queen, Shaqilath (II?), who is veiled and laureate and has a somewhat hooked nose. The obverses of his bronze pieces show Malchus and Shaqilath jugate, and facing to the right. The king, again, is laureate.[2]

1 Josephus, *Bell. Iud.*, iii, 68.
2 *BMCGC Arabia, etc.*, 1922, p. 11, nos. 1–5, pl. 2, nos. 13–17.

RABEL II (AD 71–106) and GAMILATH
Ills. 310, 311
Rabel II was the last Nabataean king before the country became the Roman province of Arabia in AD 106. He was the son of Malchus II and began his reign as a minor under the regency of his mother, Shaqilath (II?). Bronze coins show on the obverses his bust jugate with that of his mother, facing to the right.[1] Later coins present his bust alone on the obverses of his silver, facing right, laureate, with long hair, a straight nose and a rounded chin; on the reverses is the rightward-facing veiled bust of his queen Gamilath (*Ill. 310*).[2] Bronze pieces depict Rabel and Gamilath jugate, the king laureate and wearing a head ornament on his long hair: here his nose is very large and prominent (*Ill. 311*).[3]

1 *BMCGC Arabia, etc.*, 1922, pl. 49, no. 10.
2 Ibid., p. 12, nos. 1, 2, pl. 2, nos. 18, 19.
3 Ibid., p. 13, nos. 3–7, pl. 2, nos. 20–3.

309–11   Malchus II (left), Rabel II (centre), and Rabel II and his queen, Gamilath, jugate: obverses of silver and (right) bronze coins.

Parthia: the Arsacid Kings[1]

ARSACES (c.250–248 BC)
Ill. 312

Arsaces, regarded as the founder of the Arsacid dynasty of Parthia – which was destined to become Rome's rival in the East – probably ruled briefly about the middle of the third century BC. His portrait appears on the obverses of the silver and bronze coins struck by his immediate successors down to 171 BC. His bust faces to the left, he is beardless and he wears a diadem round his conical helmet and a torc round his neck. His nose is extremely large, hooked and prominent. He has a small mouth, a projecting chin and full cheeks. The features are very definitely portrait-like and could well be true to life (*Ill. 312*).[2]

1   For a detailed study of relations between Rome and Parthia from the point of view of international law, see K.-H. Ziegler, *Die Beziehungen zwischen Rom und dem Partherreich*, 1964. See also N. C. Debevoise, *A Political History of Parthia*, 1938; *Historia*, viii, 1959, pp. 222–38; xi, 1962, pp. 138–45. The precise dates of some of the kings are uncertain. For a selection of coin portraits of Parthian kings, see M. A. R. Colledge, *The Parthians*, 1967, pl. 6.
2   *BMCGC Parthia*, 1903, pp. 1–5, nos. 1–30, pl. 1, nos. 1–15; Newell 1937, pl. 12, no. 1; Ghirshman 1962, p. 114, fig. 136 (*not* Mithradates I); Richter 1965, fig. 1951.

MITHRADATES I ('the Great'?; 171–138 BC)
Ill. 313

Mithradates I, sometimes called 'the Great', was the first Parthian king to place his own portrait on his coinage. On the reverses of his obols and of some of his bronze pieces there is the rightward-facing bust, helmeted and with a long beard, who may be an ancestor or predecessor of Mithradates, whose bust, facing generally to the right, occasionally to the left, appears on the obverses of all his coins. It was Mithradates, recognized as king in Mesopotamian Seleucia in 141 BC, who began to build up Parthia as the great power, extending from Syria possibly to India, that was later to confront Rome; and his portraits are correspondingly imposing (*Ill. 313*).[1] On some of the obverses on which he faces to the right he is diademed and has neat hair that forms a thick fringe above the brow. His nose is long and aquiline and his thick beard is trimmed square. On other rightward-facing likenesses and on those that face left his heavy, silky beard is much longer and pointed and the locks on the nape of the neck are more luxuriant. The reverses bear, as do those

of Mithradates' successors, Arsaces' title of 'Great King' and that of 'Philhellene'.

1   *BMCGC Parthia*, 1903, pp. 6–15, nos. 1–61, pl. 2, nos. 1–13, pl. 3, nos. 1–13; Newell 1937, pl. 12, nos. 2–4; Ghirshman 1962, p. 114, fig. 135; Richter 1965, fig. 1952.

312   Arsaces: obverse of posthumously minted coin; probably a true-to-life likeness.

313   Mithradates I: obverse of bronze coin showing this king's characteristic thick hair and beard.

PHRAATES II (138–128/7 BC)
Ill. 314

Phraates II, the son of Mithradates I, is noted for practically bringing to an end the Seleucid power on his western boundaries. But the barbarians from the Steppes irrupted from the north, plundering and destroying his kingdom; and he died in battle against them.

Phraates' coin portraits, in silver and bronze, present his head or bust facing now to the right, now to the left. He has very straight and extremely neat diademed hair, sometimes growing low on the neck, broad cheeks, small side-burns, and a slight beard sheathing the chin. His long nose sometimes juts out in a way that gives him a somewhat plebeian look. On likenesses that show his bust he wears an elaborate spiral necklace (*Ill. 314*).[1]

The coins attributed in the *British Museum Catalogue* to an unknown Himerus have obverse portraits resembling those of Phraates II, but with fatter cheeks.[2]

1 *BMCGC Parthia*, 1903, pp. 16–19 (Berlin piece) and nos. 1–32, pl. 4, nos. 1–11; Newell 1937, pl. 12, nos. 5, 6; Richter 1965, fig. 1953.
2 *BMCGC Parthia*, 1903, p. 23, nos. 1, 2, pl. 5, nos. 9, 10.

ARTABANUS I (128/7–123 BC)
Ill. 315

Artabanus I, the uncle of Phraates II, spent most of his short reign fighting the northern barbarians. His obverse coin portraits on silver and bronze depict his bust facing now to the right, now to the left. His diademed hair is arranged in very neat tiers or ridges of locks. He has a straight nose, lean cheeks and a long, pointed beard. He wears earrings, a heavy spiral necklace, and an ornamented cuirass (or embroidered robe?) (*Ill. 315*).[1]

1 *BMCGC Parthia*, 1903, pp. 20–2, nos. 1–12, pl. 5, nos. 1–8; Newell 1937, pl. 12, no. 7: Richter 1965, fig. 1954.

MITHRADATES II ('the Great'?; 123–*c*.88 BC)
Ill. 316

Mithradates II, also known, like Mithradates I (q.v.), as 'the Great', was the son of Artabanus I. He was the first Parthian monarch to use the title 'King of Kings' on his coinage, to which he added the epithets 'Dikaios', 'Euergetes' and 'Philhellen'. He restored the power of Parthia, which his predecessors had allowed to weaken, fighting with his neighbours, in particular with Armenia. It was now for the first time that Rome and Parthia made contact, when in 92 BC Sulla as propraetor in Cilicia received on the Euphrates an embassy from Mithradates who, according to Plutarch, was seeking alliance and friendship with Rome.[1] The story goes that Mithradates emphasized his equality with Rome by putting his envoy, Orobazus, to death for allowing Sulla to take the seat of honour between Orobazus and Ariobarzanes of Cappadocia.

Mithradates' long reign produced a large series of coin portraits on his silver and bronze (*Ill. 316*).[2]

His bust always faces to the left; and he generally wears a diadem on his short-clipped, cap-like hair. He has a low brow and an enormous curved, vulture-like nose. His curly beard is sometimes square-cut and short, at others long and pointed. He wears an ornamented cuirass (or embroidered robe?). In the latter part of his reign he adopted the 'tea-cosy'-shaped oriental tiara, equipped with

314 Phraates II: obverse of silver coin with portrait bust featuring an elaborate spiral necklace.

315 Artabanus I: obverse of silver coin showing a heavy necklace similar to that of Phraates II, and carefully arranged diademed hair.

316 Mithradates II: obverse of bronze coin showing the typical diademed bust of the earlier issues of his reign.

ear-flaps and stitched with pearls and precious stones.

1 *Sulla* 5, 4 (here called Arsaces).
2 *BMCGC Parthia*, 1903, pp. 24–37, nos. 1–139, pl. 6, nos. 1–11, pl. 7, nos. 1–13, pl. 8, nos. 1–9; Newell 1937, pl. 12, nos. 8, 9, 10; Ghirshman 1962, p. 110, fig. 130, p. 114, fig. 137; Richter 1965, fig. 1955; Debevoise, op. cit., frontispiece.

ARTABANUS II (*c*.88–77 BC)
Ill. 317

Artabanus II, Mithradates II's successor, was mainly occupied in fighting, both on his eastern borders and against Armenian attacks from the north-west. While Parthia was also torn with internal strife, the title of 'King of Kings' was usurped by the Armenian king. It is possible that Artabanus II should be identified with either Gotarzes (I) or the Orodes (I) mentioned on Babylonian clay tablets.[1]

This king's portraits on his silver and bronze coins presents him facing left and wearing an enormous spiral necklace and a heavy ornamented cuirass (or embroidered robe?). He inaugurated a new, and much more oriental-looking coiffure, with the hair hanging down the back and sides of the neck in long, regular, wig-like ringlets. He is diademed and has a spreading moustache, a short, curly beard, and the great hooked nose that characterizes Mithradates II (q.v.) (*Ill. 317*).[2] His titles are 'Euergetes', 'Theopator', 'Eusebes', 'Epiphanes' and 'Philhellen'.

1 Newell 1937, p. 77; Richter 1965, fig. 1956. Cf. *CAH*, ix, 1932, p. 587.
2 *BMCGC Parthia*, 1903, pp. 38–41, nos. 1–33, pl. 8, nos. 10–12, pl. 9, nos. 1–12; Newell 1937, pl. 13, fig. 11.

SINATRUCES (77–70 BC)
Ill. 318

Sinatruces was the uncle and opponent of Artabanus II. According to Lucian, he lived to the age of eighty.[1] He took the same titles as his nephew, apart from 'Theopator', and added 'Autokrator'. Under his rule Parthian power began gradually to re-assert itself vis-à-vis Armenia.

Sinatruces' silver and bronze coins show his bust facing to the left, wearing the 'tea-cosy' type of tiara embroidered with pearls and a star on each side, and equipped with ear-flaps. He has a thin, pinched face, a great hooked nose, and a pointed beard (*Ill. 318*).[2] He certainly looks his age.

1 *Macrob.*, 15.
2 *BMCGC Parthia*, 1903, pp. 42–4, nos. 1–32, pl. 10, nos. 1–7; Newell 1937, pl. 13, no. 12.

PHRAATES III (70–57 BC)
Ill. 319

Phraates III was the son of Sinatruces. According to Plutarch,[1] Lucullus received in 69 BC an embassy from Phraates inviting the Romans to make a pact of friendship and alliance with him. Lucullus, being agreeable to this, sent ambassadors to Parthia. But finding that Phraates was secretly asking for Mesopotamia as a reward for alliance with Tigranes of Armenia, he decided to attack Parthia, yet in the end did not do so. In Appian's account,[2] Tigranes and Mithradates of Pontus asked Phraates for reinforcements. Meanwhile, Lucullus

317 Artabanus II: obverse of silver coin showing new hair-style introduced by this king.

318 Sinatruces: obverse of silver coin showing the characteristic Parthian 'tea-cosy' tiara with embroidered decoration.

requested Phraates either to help him or neither of the others; and Phraates made secret promises to both sides, but helped neither. When Pompey succeeded Lucullus in 66 BC he renewed the alliance with Phraates;[3] but in 65 BC, although Phraates expressed his wish to confirm the treaty, Pompey snubbed him, refusing him the title 'King of Kings' and addressing him merely as 'King'; he did not, however, take any hostile measures against him.[4] In c. 55 BC Phraates was murdered by his sons.[5]

Phraates III's silver and bronze coin portraits, all facing to the left, show him sometimes diademed and wearing garments that are similar to those of Artabanus II, with the same hair-style as that of the latter, but with a longer and more pointed beard. On other obverses he wears a helmet or tiara that is edged at the top with horn-like features. He has the family nose, large and hooked (*Ill. 319*).[6] He uses 'Theos' as one of his titles.

1 *Lucullus* 30, 31.
2 *Mithr.*, 87.
3 DC, xxxvi, 45.
4 Ibid., xxxvii, 5, 6; Plutarch, *Pompeius* 38.
5 DC, xxxix, 56, 2.
6 *BMCGC Parthia*, 1903, pp. 45–55, nos. 1–96, pl. 10, nos. 9–14, pl. 11, nos. 1–15; Newell 1937, pl. 13, nos. 13, 14; Ghirshman 1962, p. 114, fig. 139; Richter 1965, fig. 1958.

MITHRADATES III (57–55 BC)
Ill. 320

Mithradates III, the son of Phraates III, was expelled from his throne by the Parthian nobility in 55 BC on account of his cruelty. He fled to Lucius

Gabinius, the proconsul of Syria, who promised to restore him, but failed to do so. However, Mithradates managed to raise some troops and secured Babylon, where he surrendered, after a prolonged siege, to his brother Orodes II, who immediately had him put to death.[1]

Mithradates' silver and bronze coins have on their obverses the king's bust facing to the left. He is diademed and has the same hair and beard style as Artabanus II (q.v.) and wears a similar cuirass (or embroidered robe?). He has large eyes and a very straight nose (*Ill. 320*).[2] The profile busts facing left that have been ascribed to an 'unknown king' have features very much like those of Mithradates and may well be he, although the titles on the reverses

320 Mithradates III: obverse of silver coin showing diademed bust in the same style as that of Artabanus II (cf. *Ill. 317*).

do not fully correspond to his.[3] Similarly, the full-face portraits of this 'unknown king',[4] with a diadem, a short beard, and the wig-like hair bunched on either side of the face, are ascribed by Newell[5] and Ghirshman[6] to Mithradates III.

1 DC, xxxix, 56: Appian, *Syr.*, 51; Josephus, *Bell Iud.*, i, 175, 178; *Ant. Iud.*, xiv, 103.
2 *BMCGC Parthia*, 1903, pp. 61–7, nos. 1–53, pl. 13, nos. 1–15; Newell 1937, pl. 13, no. 15; Richter 1965, fig. 1959.
3 *BMCGC Parthia*, 1903, pp. 58–60, pl. 12, nos. 7–12.
4 Ibid., pp. 56–8, nos. 1–25, pl. 12, nos. 1–6.
5 Newell 1937, pl. 13, no. 16.
6 Ghirshman 1962, p. 114, fig. 140.

ORODES II (57–37 BC) and
PACORUS I (c. 38 BC)
Ills. 321–3

Orodes II, the brother of Mithradates III (q.v.), is famous for his crushing defeat, via his general Surenas, of Marcus Licinius Crassus at Carrhae in 53 BC.[1] Crassus had invaded Mesopotamia and Orodes had sent envoys to him in Syria to censure him for this and to enquire what the causes of this invasion were. Crassus had given him an insulting

319 Phraates III: obverse of silver coin showing the king's helmet or tiara with horn-like features.

answer and war between Rome and Parthia was openly declared.[2]

In 52 and 51 BC the Parthians crossed the Euphrates and invaded Syria,[3] but were driven out by Cassius, while Bibulus, his successor, managed to get Orodes' son, Pacorus, set up as a rival king.[4] Father and son came to terms; but by the middle of 50 BC the Parthian danger to Rome was over for the time being.

In 40 BC Quintus Labienus, the ally of Brutus and Cassius, joined the Parthians and persuaded them, under Pacorus, to cross the Euphrates and invade Syria. Apamea and Antioch surrendered to the Parthian army.[5] Labienus seized large parts of Asia Minor for Parthia and Pacorus took all the Phoenician coast towns (apart from Tyre) and Palestine, deposed the high priest Hyrcanus, and set up in his place his rival Aristobulus. This Parthian empire now included Syria and extended deep into Asia Minor. Labienus took the title of 'imperator Parthicus' (cf. p. 62).[6]

In 39 BC Publius Ventidius Bassus, acting for Marcus Antonius, made war on Labienus and the Parthians were driven out of Asia Minor. They also evacuated Syria, retiring across the Euphrates.[7] In 38 BC Pacorus gathered an army and invaded Syria again. But Ventidius met him at Cyrrhestica in Syria and defeated him; Pacorus was killed.[8] Orodes now resigned his throne, shortly before his death in 37 BC, to his son, Phraates IV.[9]

A very large number of silver and bronze coins with Orodes' portrait on their obverses have survived (*Ills. 321–2*).[10] His diademed bust faces left.

A few drachms and bronze pieces have been attributed to Pacorus I. The drachms show on their obverses a youthful, beardless, diademed bust facing to the left; the king wears ear-rings and a necklace. The nose and chin are not unlike those of Orodes (*Ill. 323*).[11]

1　Plutarch, *Crassus* 23–33.
2　DC, xl, 16.
3　Ibid., 28.
4　Ibid., 29, 30.
5　DC, xlviii, 24, 25; Appian, *Bell. Civ.*, v, 65; Livy, *Epit.*, 127. Cf. Horace, *Odes* iii, 6, 9.
6　DC, xlviii, 26; Josephus, *Ant. Iud.*, xiv, 365–6; Strabo xiv, 2, 24.
7　DC, xlviii, 39, 40.
8　Ibid., xlix, 19–23.
9　Ibid., 23.
10　*BMCGC Parthia*, 1903, pp. 68–96, nos. 1–247, pl. 14, nos. 1–12, pl. 15, nos. 1–17, pl. 16, nos. 1–16, pl. 17, nos. 1–14, pl. 18, nos. 1–11 – here probably wrongly named Orodes I; Newell 1937, pl. 13, no. 17; Richter 1965, fig. 1960.
11　*BMCGC Parthia*, 1903, pp. 97–8, nos. 1–8, pl. 18, nos. 12–14.

PHRAATES IV (37–*c.* 2 BC) and
TIRIDATES II(?) (26 BC)
Ills. 324, 325
Phraates IV, the son of Orodes II, began his reign by killing all those of his relatives that he feared as rivals to himself. As a protest against his cruelty, many of the Parthian nobles, including Monaeses, fled to Marcus Antonius in 37 BC. At Monaeses'

321–3　Orodes II (left and centre) and Pacorus I (right) : silver coin obverse portraits of father and son who after a period of rivalry came to terms with each other.

He has the same hair-style, short beard, and dress as Mithradates III, but his nose is slightly more hooked and sharply pointed, and his chin is rather more jutting. Some portraits show him with a very high and narrow diadem encircling the crown of his head. He is often depicted wearing a heavy spiral necklace.

instigation, Antonius marched to make war on Parthia, although Monaeses was persuaded by Phraates to return to him. Antonius' expedition against Parthia was a complete failure.[1] In 30 BC another rebellion broke out in Parthia against Phraates and a certain Tiridates (II?) was proclaimed king. Phraates was, however, soon restored and Tiridates took refuge in Syria, but returned to Parthia and rebelled against Phraates again. Octavian entered into friendly negotiations with Phraates' envoys, taking one of his sons as a hostage

his chin in a square-trimmed 'tab'. He wears a spiral necklace. He occasionally has a wart on his brow, reminding us of the most veristic of Roman republican portraits.

324, 325   Phraates IV and Tiridates II (?): silver coin portraits of the Parthian king and the usurper of his throne; Phraates is shown with a wart on his brow (a feature which recurs on several other royal portraits).

to Rome; and Tiridates was once more turned out of Parthia.[2] In 23 BC, when Tiridates came to Rome in person, as did envoys from Phraates demanding the surrender of Tiridates and the return of Phraates' son, Augustus did not surrender Tiridates to Phraates, but sent back to him his son on the condition that he restored the captives and standards taken by the Parthians from Crassus and Marcus Antonius.[3] In 20 BC the standards were restored amid universal jubilation in Rome;[4] and Augustus made Phraates the present of a young Italian slave-girl, Thesmusa or Musa, who bore him an illegitimate son, later Phraates V (q.v.), and whom he eventually made his wife.[5] In this year Rome and Phraates possibly came to some general friendly agreement (Propertius iv, 6, 79, calls it a *foedus*); but it was not until 10/9 BC that a real pact of peace and friendship was made between Rome and Parthia and Phraates, at Thesmusa's persuasion, sent his legitimate children to Rome to seal the pact and also to get them out of the way.[6] Phraates was afterwards murdered by Phraataces (Phraates V) and Thesmusa.[7]

Phraates IV's coin portraits on his silver tetradrachms and drachms and on his bronze are very numerous (*Ill. 324*).[8] Facing to the left, he is diademed and his hair-style and dress are very close to those of his father Orodes; and some of his likenesses display a similar beard. On other portraits, however, Phraates' beard hangs down from

Some tetradrachms have been attributed to the brief usurpations of Tiridates II (?) (*Ill. 325*).[9] The diademed personage portrayed on the obverses has the usual oriental hair-style and the usual costume. He has a thick, pointed beard.

1 DC, xlix, 23–31; Plutarch, *Antonius* 37–52; Livy, *Epit.*, 130. Cf. Horace, *Odes* iii, 6, 9.
2 DC, li, 18.
3 Ibid., liii, 33. Cf. *Res Gestae* 32: 'ad me supplices confugerunt reges Parthorum Tiridates . . .'; cf. p. 162, note 4.
4 *Res Gestae* 29: 'Parthos trium exercitum Romanorum spolia et signa redere mihi supplicesque amicitiam populi Romani petere'; Livy, *Epit.*, 141; Suetonius, *Augustus* 21; *Tiberius* 9; DC, liv, 8; Velleius Paterculus ii, 91; Horace, *Epistles* i, 12, 27/8.
5 Josephus, *Ant. Iud.*, xviii, 39–42.
6 Ibid.; Tacitus, *Ann.*, ii, 1; Velleius Paterculus ii, 94; *Res Gestae* 32: 'ad me rex Parthorum Phrates Orodis filius filios suos nepotesque omnes misit in Italiam, non bello superatus sed amicitiam nostram per liberorum suorum pignora petens'. See *Klio*, lv, 1973, pp. 247–8. *CIL*, vi, 1799, is the funerary inscription of two of Phraates IV's sons who died in Rome: 'Seraspadanes Phraatis Arsacis regum regis f[ilius] Parthus Rhodaspes Phraatis Arsacis regum regis f[ilius] Parthus'.
7 See note 5.
8 *BMCG Parthia*, 1903, pp. 99–134, nos. 1–279, pl. 18, nos. 15–17, pl. 19, nos. 1–9, pl. 20, nos. 1–11, pl. 21, nos. 1–27, pl. 22, nos. 1–21, pl. 23, nos. 1–7; Newell 1937, pl. 13, nos. 18, 19; Ghirshman 1962, p. 114, fig. 141; Richter 1965, fig. 1961.
9 *BMCG Parthia*, 1903, p. 135, nos. 1, 2, pl. 23, nos. 8, 9.

PHRAATES V (PHRAATACES; 3/2 BC–AD 4)
Ill. 326

Phraates V, the illegitimate son of Phraates IV
(q.v.) by Thesmusa and murderer of his father,
reported his accession to Augustus and demanded
the return of his brothers from Rome to Parthia on
the condition of his accepting peace. The emperor
replied in a letter addressing Phraates without the
title of 'King' and told him to withdraw from
Armenia, where his forces had joined a revolt
against Rome.[1] Phraates in his turn replied styling
himself as 'King of Kings' and addressing Augustus
simply as 'Caesar',[2] But when in AD 1 Gaius Caesar
appeared in Syria, Phraates came to terms with the
Roman power on condition that he renounced
Armenia and that his brothers remained in Italy. It
was then that there took place the famous meeting
of Romans and Parthians on an island in the
Euphrates.[3] Phraates made his mother Thesmusa
his queen and co-regent. He was so much hated by
his subjects that he was banished, fled to Roman
territory, and died there.[4]

Phraates V's silver and bronze coin portraits
show his diademed bust facing to the left, with the
same hair-style and costume as those worn by
Phraates IV. He has a low brow with a wart (cf. p.
161), a large nose, a pointed beard that is sometimes turned up at the tip, and a moustache turned
up at the corners. He wears a necklace and ear-
rings (*Ill. 326*). Tetradrachms, drachms and
bronze pieces have on the reverses Thesmusa's bust
facing either to the left or to the right. She wears a
high, conical, tiered tiara with diadem, ear-rings
and necklace and her hair is bunched up in a great
roll at the nape of the neck. She has a straight nose,
large eyes, a disagreeable mouth and chin, and
plump cheeks. Her titles are 'Thea Ourania Mousa
Basilissa'.[5]

1 Velleius Paterculus ii, 100: 'Parthus desciscens a
   societate Romana adiecit Armeniae manum'.
2 DC, lv, 10 (18, 20).
3 Ibid., 10a (4); Velleius Paterculus ii, 101.
4 Josephus, *Ant. Iud.*, xviii, 42–4; *Res Gestae* 32: 'ad me
   supplices confugerunt reges Parthorum Tiridates et
   postea Phrates regis Phratis filius', (cf. p. 161, note 3).
5 *BMCGC Parthia*, 1903, pp. 136–41, nos. 1–38, pl. 23,
   nos. 10–17, pl. 24, nos. 3–4; Newell 1937, pl. 13, nos.
   20, 21, p. 80, fig. 22; Ghirshman 1962, p. 114, fig.
   142.

ORODES III(?) (AD 4–6)
Ill. 327

Orodes III(?) who was offered the throne of
Parthia by the nobles (see above), was at any rate a
member of the royal family, if unpopular on
account of his viciousness and cruelty. He was, in

fact, very speedily made away with.[1] His tetradrachms show his diademed bust facing to the left,
with the same coiffure and costume as his predecessors. He has a particularly heavy spiral necklace.
His nose is somewhat hooked and his moustache is
turned down at the corners, and on some portraits
he has a long silky, pointed, beard (*Ill. 327*).[2] On
other likenesses his beard is short and curly and
covers the throat; he also has a wart on his brow (cf.
p. 161).[3]

1 Josephus, *Ant. Iud.*, xviii, 44, 45.
2 *BMCGC Parthia*, 1903, p. 142, pl. 24, no. 5.
3 Ghirshman 1962, p. 114, fig. 144; probably wrongly
   numbered as II.

326 Phraates V: obverse of silver coin showing the king
with a wart on his brow (as seen in his father's likeness; *Ill.
324*).

327 Orodes III(?): obverse of silver tetradrachm
showing the king with long beard.

VONONES I (AD 8/9–11/12; died 19)
Ill. 328

Vonones was one of the sons of Phraates IV who had been kept as hostages in Rome. After the death of Orodes III(?) a Parthian embassy to Rome asked for him to be made king (*Res Gestae* 33), but Vonones had become too much romanized to please his Parthian subjects: he had no interest in hunting or riding or in any other of the traditional Parthian pursuits, and always travelled in a litter.[1] There was therefore a revolt against him and Artabanus (said by Josephus to be the king of Media, by Tacitus to be an Arsacid) was offered the throne of Parthia. Vonones first defeated Artabanus, but was then himself defeated by him and fled first to Armenia, where he was briefly accepted as king, and then to Syria, where the governor, Creticus Silanus, kept him in safety and in the enjoyment of his royal title and Roman way of life.[2] He was then interned in Cilicia and killed in an attempt to escape.[3]

Vonones' silver and bronze coins display his likeness on their obverses. His bust is diademed and his hair, instead of hanging in stiff, wig-like ringlets, forms two tiers of thick locks on the nape of the neck. He has a long, pointed nose, a spreading moustache and a long beard squared at the tip. On his drachms, which are less plastically worked than are his tetradrachms, the strings of his diadem are tied in a great bow that projects horizontally behind his head (*Ill. 328*). Some of his reverses bear the legend 'Basileus Onones neikesas Artabanon' – recording his initial victory over Artabanus.[4]

1 Josephus, *Ant. Iud.*, xviii, 47, 48; Tacitus, *Ann.*, ii, 2; *Res Gestae* 33: 'acceperunt Parthi Vononem regis Phratis filium, regis Orodis nepotem'.
2 Josephus, *Ant. Iud.*, xviii, 48–52; Tacitus, *Ann.*, ii, 3, 4.
3 Tacitus, *Ann.*, ii, 58, 68; Suetonius, *Tiberius* 49, 2.
4 *BMCGC Parthia*, 1903, pp. 143–5, nos. 1–23, pl. 24, nos. 6–10; Newell 1937, p. 80, figs. 23, 24; Ghirshman 1962, p. 114, fig. 145.

ARTABANUS III (AD 10/11–c. 38)
Ills. 329, 330

Artabanus III, having successfully ousted Vonones I (q.v.), in AD 18 sent ambassadors to Germanicus, now in the East, to confirm the pact of friendship between Rome and Parthia, with the promise of allowing Germanicus to approach the bank of the Euphrates.[1] In 35 an embassy of Parthian noblemen came to Rome without Artabanus' knowledge, complained of the latter's brutality, and asked for Phraates – the son of Phraates IV – as their king. To this Tiberius agreed, but Phraates, who did his best to exchange his Roman way of life for that of Parthia, died in Syria. In the same year the Armenian king Artaxias died without an heir. Artabanus promptly invaded Armenia and crowned his eldest son, Arsaces, king of the country. Tiberius then set up another prince of the Arsacid family, Tiridates, as a rival to Artabanus. Arsaces was murdered in Armenia and Artabanus was forced to evacuate that kingdom. He was now deserted by his own countrymen and fled to Scythia.[2] Tiridates, encouraged by Lucius Vitellius, the governor of Syria, advanced to the Euphrates, where the *suovetaurilia* was performed, crossed the river by a bridge of boats, and was crowned king at Ctesiphon. But some of the Parthian nobility went over to Artabanus, who collected some troops and forced Tiridates to retreat. The latter took refuge in Syria.[3]

In 37, soon after Gaius became emperor, Artabanus and Vitellius met in the middle of a bridge over the Euphrates, for the purpose of renewing friendship between the two empires.[4] Later in 37 Artabanus was plotted against again by the nobility but was restored to his throne, dying not long afterwards in 38.[5]

Artabanus' portraits on his silver and bronze coins are of three types (*Ills. 329, 330*). Some of his tetradrachms portray him facing to the left, with a diadem and the wig-like rows of ringlets hanging

328 Vonones I: obverse of silver drachm showing the more stylized type of coin portrait.

329 Artabanus III: obverse of silver drachm with stylized profile portrait (cf. full-face portrait, *Ill. 330*).

down the back and sides of his neck. He has a thick, pointed beard, a moustache that is down-turned at the corners, and a slightly aquiline nose. On other tetradrachms he is shown full-face, with the strings of his diadem forming a bow that projects on either side of his face, which is framed by two great masses of flowing locks. There his beard is trimmed square. Drachms and bronze pieces present him facing left, with flowing hair rendered by rippling, wavy lines and a very sharply pointed beard, while the big bow of his diadem strings projects horizontally behind.[6]

1 Tacitus, *Ann.*, ii, 58: 'ad ea Germanicus de societate Romanorum Parthorumque magnifice, de adventu regis et cultu sui cum decore et modestia respondit'. For Artabanus' public mourning for Germanicus, see Suetonius, *Gaius* 5.
2 Tacitus, *Ann.*, vi, 31–6; DC, lviii, 26.
3 Tacitus, *Ann.*, vi, 37, 42–4; DC, lviii, 26.
4 Josephus, *Ant. Iud.*, xviii, 101 (Josephus places this incident in the reign of Tiberius); Suetonius, *Gaius* 14; *Vitellius* 2, 4; DC, lix, 27, 3 (where it is stated that some of Artabanus' sons were secured as hostages by Rome).
5 Josephus, *Ant. Iud.*, xx, 54–69.
6 *BMCGC Parthia*, 1903, pp. 146–52, nos. 1–57, pl. 25, nos. 1–12; Newell 1937, p. 80, fig. 25; Ghirshman 1962, p. 114, fig. 138 (wrongly attributed to Artabanus II).

therefore called in Vardanes, who had been safely abroad and now made a forced march on Parthia, drove out Gotarzes, besieged Seleucia and succeeded to the Parthian throne. Meanwhile the exiled Gotarzes collected forces and continued to make war on Vardanes.[1] Vardanes and Gotarzes then came to terms, the latter retiring in favour of the former, and Seleucia surrendered to Vardanes.[2] But Gotarzes renewed hostilities against his brother, who again defeated him. However, when Vardanes was murdered at a hunt in AD 45, Gotarzes finally secured the Parthian throne.[3]

In 47 the Parthian nobility rose against Gotarzes and sent envoys to Rome requesting as king Meherdates, the son of Vonones I and the grandson of Phraates IV, who in 49 was conducted to the Euphrates by Caius Cassius, legate of Syria.[4] But Gotarzes defeated him and his ears were cut off, which made him ineligible for Parthian kingship. In 51 Gotarzes died and was succeeded by Vonones II, a brother of Artabanus III and king of Atropatene, of whom no coin portraits are known to us.[5]

Vardanes' coin portraits on his silver and bronze all show him facing left, but are of two types. On his tetradrachms his diademed head has the wigcoiffure, a necklace, and an ornamented cuirass (or

330	Artabanus III: obverse of silver tetradrachm with plastically treated full-face portrait.

331	Vardanes I: obverse of silver coin with portrait including a wart on the brow.

VARDANES I (*c.* AD 40–45) and
GOTARZES II (*c.* AD 45–51)
Ills. 331, 332

Vardanes I was the youngest son of Artabanus III. His older brother was Gotarzes II (see below), who, probably soon after Artabanus' death, killed off various members of his family with a view to enjoying undisputed rule. The Parthian nobles

embroidered robe?). He has a very straight nose, large eyes, a horizontally spreading moustache, and a flowing, pointed beard (*Ill. 331*). But on drachms and bronze pieces his hair flows down in rippling, wavy locks, and the locks of his beard are straight and stiff. The bow of his diadem strings sticks out behind. He has a wart on his brow in some portraits (cf. pp. 161, 162).

Gotarzes has the same two types of coiffure on his leftward-facing diademed portraits and the same costume as his brother. But on his tetradrachms, with the wig-coiffure, his beard is longer and more stiffly curled than in Vardanes' case (*Ill. 332*); and on the drachms, where he has the rippling, wavy hair, with the diadem strings forming a projecting bow behind, his beard is trimmed square at the base.[7] The reverse type of some of his bronze coins is a bust of his queen, facing to the right and wearing a tall, conical head-dress with a diadem.[8]

1 Tacitus, *Ann.*, xi, 8.
2 Ibid., 9.
3 Ibid., 10; Josephus, *Ant. Iud.*, xx, 73.
4 Tacitus, *Ann.*, xi, 10; xii, 10, 11.
5 Ibid., xii, 12–14.
6 *BMCGC Parthia*, 1903, pp. 153–60, nos. 1–61, pl. 26, nos. 1–11.
7 Ibid., pp. 161–77, nos. 1–177, pl. 26, nos. 12–14, pl. 27, nos. 1–24, pl. 28, nos. 1–11.
8 Ibid., pl. 27, no. 18.

VOLOGESES I (AD 51–79/80)
Ill. 333

Vologeses I was the eldest son of Vonones II[1] and succeeded to the throne by permission of his brothers Mithradates, Pharasmanes and Pacorus,

vain to return.[6] In 62, however, Vologeses restored Tiridates to Armenia and crowned him king.[7] After an attempt by Vologeses to make a truce with Corbulo, open war between Rome and Parthia ensued. Tiridates finally agreed to go to Rome to do homage to Nero and in 63 he visited Corbulo's camp, near Rhandaea, for a solemn ceremony of submission to Rome; Vologeses also met Corbulo and peace between Rome and Parthia was concluded.[8] In 66 there was enacted the famous scene of Tiridates' crowning by Nero in Rome – a Parthian prince with Rome's blessing occupying the throne of Armenia.[9] The two empires were now reconciled; and Tiridates brought back with him on his return to the East an invitation to the Great King to visit Rome. Vologeses, however, refused it.

After Nero's death – probably under Otho – Vologeses sent envoys to Rome to renew the alliance and ask that honour be paid to Nero's memory.[10] In 69 he offered to supply Vespasian with forty thousand archers; and in 70 he sent a deputation to Titus at Zeugma with the gift of a golden crown.[11] Between 72 and 74 came the great invasion of the Parthian Empire by barbarians from inner Asia.[12] In 75 Vologeses appealed in vain to his ally Vespasian for help;[13] it was this refusal that caused a cooling off of the king's enthusiasm for

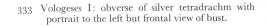

332 Gotarzes II: obverse of silver tetradrachm showing similarity of treatment to that of Vardanes I (*Ill. 331*).

333 Vologeses I: obverse of silver tetradrachm with portrait to the left but frontal view of bust.

who ruled over Armenia, Iberia and Media respectively. After the murder of Mithradates, he tried to establish his brother Tiridates as king of Armenia.[2] In AD 54 Vologeses sent hostages to Rome.[3] In 58 we find him defending Tiridates' claim to the Armenian throne,[4] but the Roman general Cnaeus Domitius Corbulo attacked Tiridates and drove him out.[5] In 60 Tiridates tried in

Rome. He died late in 79 or early in 80. The story goes that Vespasian on his deathbed maintained that the comet then visible in the sky was an omen, not for himself, but for the long-haired Parthian king.[14]

Some of Vologeses' tetradrachms show him in the usual dress, looking to the left, while his bust is frontal, diademed, and with the wig-like ringlets;

other tetradrachms present him with both face and bust turned to the left. The bow of his diadem strings projects behind his head. He has a formal row of curls above his brow, a short, formal beard, a large nose, a moustache that is down-turned at the corners, and sometimes a wart on his temple (cf. pp. 161, 162, 164). His beard is generally pointed, occasionally trimmed square at the tip. He always wears a heavy necklace. On his drachms his hair is dressed in the flowing, rippling style. An irregular cluster of curls or a large ornament crowns his head on some tetradrachms (*Ill. 333*).[15]

334 Vardanes II(?): obverse of silver coin probably depicting the son of Vologeses I who claimed power for a brief period in AD 55.

1 Tacitus, *Ann.*, xii, 14.
2 Ibid., 44, 51; xv, 2; Josephus, *Ant. Iud.*, xx, 74.
3 Tacitus, *Ann.*, xiii, 9.
4 Ibid., 34.
5 Ibid., 37–41.
6 Ibid., xiv, 26.
7 Ibid., xv, 1, 2.
8 Ibid., 3–17, 24, 25–31; DC, lxii, 19–23.
9 Tacitus, *Ann.*, xvi, 23, 24; Suetonius, *Nero* 13; DC, lxiii, 1–7.
10 Suetonius, *Nero* 57: 'de instauranda societate'.
11 *Vespasianus* 6, 4; Tacitus, *Hist.*, v, 51; Josephus, *Bell. Iud.*, vii, 105.
12 Ibid., 244–5.
13 Suetonius, *Domitianus* 2; DC, lxvi, 15.
14 Ibid., 17; Suetonius, *Vespasianus* 23.
15 *BMCGC Parthia*, 1903, pp. 178–89, nos. 1–97, pl. 28, nos. 12–16, pl. 29, nos. 1–14; Ghirshman 1962, p. 115, fig. 147.

VARDANES II(?) (AD 55)
Ill. 334

According to Tacitus, Vologeses had a son, Vardanes II, who revolted against him in AD 55;[1] and to this brief period of his claim to kingship some drachms and bronze pieces have been attributed. These depict a full-face bust wearing a conical, diademed helmet, with the bows and strings of the diadem fluttering out on either side. The personage has a moustache, but is beardless, and wears the usual spiral necklace (*Ill. 334*).[2]

335 Pacorus II: obverse of silver coin with the youthful, beardless portrait occurring on his earlier coins.

1 *Ann.*, xiii, 7.
2 *BMCGC Parthia*, 1903, pp. 190–2, nos. 1–24, pl. 29, nos. 15–18.

PACORUS II (AD 78–109/10?)
Ill. 335

Pacorus II seems to have been the eldest son of Vologeses I and it is probable that the latter chose him as his successor shortly before his death. Pacorus' attitude to Rome was unfriendly. In AD 80 the Dacian king, Decebalus (q.v.) sought Pacorus' help against Rome and sent him a Greek slave ship captured from the Romans.[1] Pacorus appears to

336 Artabanus IV: obverse of silver tetradrachm probably representing a brother of Pacorus II who held power briefly in 80 and 81.

have died *c.* 109, when the coinage of Osroes (q.v.) begins.

The earliest of Pacorus II's silver and bronze coin-portraits depict him beardless and youthful, with his diademed bust facing to the left, the wig-like coiffure and the usual dress. He has a very large nose and rounded cheeks (*Ill. 335*). Later coins show him with his head to the left, but his bust frontal, and he has a very slight beard and side-burns. On his latest coins he has a close, sheath-like beard and side-burns and a 'tea-cosy'-shaped tiara or helmet, with the strings of his diadem streaming out behind.[2]

1 Pliny, *Epistolae* x, 74.
2 *BMCGC Parthia*, 1903, pp. 193–202, nos. 1–52, pl. 30, nos. 1–13; pl. 31, nos. 1–4.

ARTABANUS IV (AD 80–81)
Ill. 336

On coins of AD 80 and 81 there appears a Parthian king named Artabanus, probably another son of Vologeses I, who gave sanctuary to the false Nero, Terentius Maximus.[1] Artabanus was swiftly overthrown by Pacorus II (q.v.) but he issued some tetradrachms, on the obverse of which is seen his portrait bust, diademed, facing to the left, and wearing the usual necklace and costume. He has the rippling hair-style, a very straight nose, and a pointed beard composed of straight locks (*Ill. 336*). On some portraits he wears a conical tiara or helmet, wound round with a diadem, whose strings project in a bow or loop behind his head and hang like streamers down the back of his neck.[2]

1 DC, lxvi, 19, 3c; Suetonius, *Nero* 57; Tacitus, *Hist.*, i, 2.
2 *BMCGC Parthia*, 1903, p. 203, nos. 1–4, pl. 31, no. 5; Ghirshman 1962, p. 115, fig. 148.

OSROES or CHOSROES (AD 109–130)
Ill. 337

Osroes or Chosroes, who appears to have been yet another son of Vologeses I, in *c.* AD 109 set himself up as Parthian king in opposition to his brother Pacorus II (q.v.) and ruled Parthia after that brother's death.[1] Between 110 and 113 he was alleged to have crowned Exedares as king of Armenia without the consent of Rome. But in 113, when Trajan was on his way to the Parthian war, an embassy from Osroes met him at Athens, asking for peace and offering gifts and also requesting that, since he had deposed Exedares for unsatisfactory conduct, Armenia should be given to Pacorus II's son Parthamasiris. Trajan, however, rejected the gifts and made no answer to Osroes' requests.[2] In

114 Parthamasiris was received by Trajan in his camp and made to stand before him like a captive. Trajan then declared Armenia a Roman province and Parthamasiris was dismissed, but put to death at the emperor's order.[3]

In 116 Seleucia was taken by Trajan's lieutenants and Ctesiphon fell to the emperor, Osroes' daughter and his golden throne being captured by him. Parthamaspes, the son of Osroes, was placed on the Parthian throne by Trajan;[4] but he was not recognized by the majority of the Parthians, whose opposition gathered round Osroes. Hadrian made peace with Parthia and seems to have taken Osroes' side.[5] In 129 the emperor invited him to a private conference (*ad amicitiam*), and he sent back the king's daughter, with the promise – actually implemented by Antonius Pius (SHA, *Pius* 9) – of also returning the golden throne.[6] It is most unlikely that Osroes accepted the invitation.

Osroes' drachms and bronze pieces present his bust facing left. He has a high diadem topped by a circular bunch of tight curls (*korymbos*; cf. p. 169), while a slightly larger circular bunch of similar curls conceals each ear: The hair in these bunches is probably not the king's own. His diadem has two sets of strings, one wavy and fluttering horizontally behind his head, the other straight, dangling down the back of his neck. His beard is pointed and composed of straight, rigid locks. His eyes are peculiarly large and his nose is aquiline and sharply pointed. Sometimes there is a conical tiara or helmet replacing or concealing the circular bunch of curls at the top of his head (*Ill. 337*).[7]

1 DC, lxviii, 19.
2 Ibid., 17.
3 Ibid., 20; Fronto (Loeb ed) ii, pp. 212–14.
4 DC, lxviii, 30; cf. the REX PARTHIS DATVS sestertius of Trajan: *RIC*, ii, 1926, pl. 11, no. 194.
5 DC, lxviii, 33; SHA, *Hadrianus* 5, 12: 'bellum Parthorum . . . Hadriani conloquio repressum est'.
6 Ibid., 12, 13.
7 *BMCGC Parthia*, 1903, pp. 204–8, nos. 1–28, pl. 31, nos. 6–15, pl. 32, nos. 1–5; Ghirshman 1962, p. 115, fig. 150.

337 Osroes (Chosroes) : obverse of silver coin showing side curls and *korymbos*.

VOLOGESES II (*c.*AD 130–47)
Ill. 338

Vologeses II was the son of Osroes and seems to have been set up as a rival to his father and to Pacorus II in AD 109. In *c.*130 Osroes appears to have died; and from that year until his death in 147 Vologeses was the undisputed ruler of the whole Parthian Empire. In about 134 he sent envoys to Hadrian; and in that year he stopped an invasion of Alani by bribing them with gifts.[1]

On his silver and bronze coins Vologeses' bust faces to the left, wearing the usual dress. He has a conical helmet adorned with hook-like features along the crown and encircled by a wide diadem, whose broad strings hang down behind his neck and shoulders. His hair is arranged in two tiers of loose curls at the base of the neck. He has a short, curly, pointed beard and wears ear-rings (*Ill. 338*).[2]

338 Vologeses II: obverse of silver coin showing the king wearing ear-rings and a conical helmet with hook-like features along the crown.

1 DC, lxix, 15, 1.
2 *BMCGC Parthia*, 1903, pp. 209–14, nos. 1–45, pl. 32, nos. 6–14, pl. 33, nos. 1–4.

MITHRADATES IV (*c.*AD 130)
Ill. 339

Mithradates IV would seem to have been set up as Parthian king for a very brief period about the time of the death of Osroes (q.v.) in AD 130. His portrait, on drachms and bronze pieces, shows his head facing left. A broad diadem with a horizontally projecting bow or loop and vertically dangling strings, binds his hair which ripples down the sides and back of his neck. He has a low brow, a prominent nose, and a sharply pointed beard of rigid locks (*Ill. 339*).[1]

339 Mithradates IV: obverse of silver drachm with portrait displaying individual treatment of hair and beard.

1 *BMCGC Parthia*, 1903, pp. 217–23, nos. 1–64, pl. 33, nos. 6–23.

VOLOGESES III (AD 147/8–193)
Ills. 340, 341

Vologeses III, the son of Vologeses II, enjoyed undisputed rule for more than forty years. This made initially for the strengthening of the Parthian Empire and for its bolder attitude to Rome. Vologeses seems, in fact, to have planned a campaign against Armenia,[1] which Antoninus Pius persuaded him by letter to forgo.[2]

In AD 161, however, Vologeses' general Chosroes attacked Armenia and besieged the legate of Cappadocia, Caius Sedatius Severianus, in the Armenian stronghold of Elegeia, which the Parthians took.[3] In 162 Lucius Verus and his generals,

Avidius Cassius and others, took over the Parthian war; and in 163 Rome occupied Armenia. In 164 and 165 Avidius Cassius invaded Parthia, capturing Dura-Europos and pursuing Vologeses to Seleucia, which he destroyed by fire, and to Ctesiphon, where he razed the Great King's palace to the ground.[4] In 166 came the outbreak of the great plague;[5] and in the same year, after a second Roman expedition into Mesopotamia, Marcus Aurelius and Lucius Verus held their joint Parthian triumph.[6] Of Vologeses' subsequent history we have little record, but he must have concluded peace with Rome,[7] losing north-west Mesopotamia.

Vologeses' coin portraits on tetradrachms, drachms and bronze coins display his bust facing left. He wears the ornamented cuirass (or embroidered robe?) and a 'tea-cosy'-shaped tiara or helmet, with hook-like features along the crown,

340, 341 Vologeses III: obverse of silver coin and (*below*)
stone relief with frontal portrait showing square-cut beard
and a conical helmet or tiara.

342 Vologeses IV: obverse of silver coin showing the more
common type of full-face portrait, featuring the side-curls
and *korymbos* seen in *Ill. 337*.

entwined by a broad diadem, and equipped with
ear-flaps. He has large eyes, a sharply pointed nose,
and a long beard that is composed of rows of stiff
curls and is blunted at the tip (*Ill. 340*).[8] A stone
relief with rounded top in a private collection shows
Vologeses' bust facing the spectator and wearing a
diademed and conical tiara or helmet: he has a
spreading moustache and a long beard trimmed
square at the base, but composed of locks that are
more flowing than on his coin portraits (*Ill. 341*).[9]
Cf. Waël (p. 138).

1 SHA, *Marcus Antoninus* 8, 6.
2 Ibid., *Antoninus Pius* 9, 6.
3 DC, lxxi, 2; SHA, *Marcus Antoninus* 8, 6.
4 DC, lxxi, 2.
5 Ibid.; SHA, *Verus* 8.
6 SHA, *Marcus Antoninus* 9.
7 According to SHA, *Marcus Antoninus* 26, when Marcus
   was at Antioch in 76 he 'pacem confirmavit occurren-
   tibus . . . legatis Persarum [sc. Parthorum?]'.
8 *BMCGC Parthia*, 1903, pp. 224–36, nos. 1–99, pl. 34,
   nos. 1–16, pl. 35, nos. 1–6; Ghirshman 1962, p. 115,
   fig. 151.
9 Ghirshman 1962, p. 69, fig. 82.

VOLOGESES IV (AD 191–207/8)
Ill. 342

Vologeses IV would appear to have begun his reign
as co-ruler with Vologeses III. In AD 193, the first
year of his sole reign, Pescennius Niger sent a letter
to the Great King requesting an alliance against
Septimius Severus, and Vologeses promised to
order his satraps to muster their troops.[1] In 194,
after defeating Niger, Septimius crossed the Euphrates and advanced to Nisibis;[2] but he had to return
to the West to cope with Clodius Albinus. Meanwhile the king had an interval of peace from
Roman attack in which to try to build up his power
in Mesopotamia.[3] But in 198 came the new Roman
onslaught. The Parthian army retreated beyond the
Euphrates and Septimius occupied Seleucia and
Babylon and seized Ctesiphon,[4] but failed to take
Hatra.[5] In 199 Rome must have concluded peace
with the humiliated Great King (although no
record of it has come down to us), since Vologeses'
coins continue till 207/8. North-western Mesopotamia was firmly in Roman hands.

Vologeses IV's portraits on his tetradrachms,
drachms and bronze coins are of two types. One
type shows him facing to the left, diademed and
with a circular bunch of tight curls on the top of his
head (*korymbos*; cf. pp. 167, 173) and another one
concealing each ear. He has very large eyes, a
very hooked nose, a moustache turned up at the
corners, and a long, pointed beard. But the majority
of his likenesses present him facing the spectator,

with the same coiffure and features as on the profile portrait, but more arrestingly displayed (*Ill. 342*).[6]

1 Herodian iii, 1, 2.
2 DC, lxxv, 2.
3 Ibid., 9.
4 Ibid.; SHA, *Severus* 16.
5 Herodian iii, 9; DC, lxxv, 10–12.
6 *BMCGC Parthia*, 1903, pp. 237–40, nos. 1–31, pl. 35, nos. 7–13; Ghirshman 1962, p. 115, fig. 153.

VOLOGESES V (AD 207/8–221/2)
Ill. 343

In AD 213 Vologeses V's brother, Artabanus V (q.v.), revolted against him.[1] In 215 Vologeses refused to surrender to Caracalla Tiridates, king of Armenia, and the pseudo-Cynic, Antiochus of Cilicia. But when the emperor threatened war, the Parthian king surrendered both those personages and Caracalla called off his Parthian expedition.[2]

Vologeses' portrait, seen on his tetradrachms, drachms and bronze pieces, depicts him always in profile to the left. He wears the diademed tiara or helmet, 'tea-cosy'-shaped and equipped with 'hooks' along the crown and ear-flaps. He has enormous eyes, a huge nose, a spreading moustache, and a long, pointed beard. On some coins the loop or bow and the strings of his diadem are visible behind his head (*Ill. 343*).[3]

1 DC, lxxvii, 12, 2a, 3.
2 Ibid., 19, 21, 1.
3 *BMCGC Parthia*, 1903, pp. 241–6, nos. 1–49, pl. 35, nos. 14, 15, pl. 36, nos. 1–7; Ghirshman 1962, p. 115, fig. 154.

343   Vologeses V: obverse of silver coin with stylized portrait typical of the later Parthian kings.

ARTABANUS V (AD 213–27)
Ill. 344

In AD 213 Artabanus V disputed the claim of his brother, Vologeses V (q.v.), to the Parthian throne. In 216 Caracalla made war on Parthia on the

pretext that Artabanus had refused to give him his daughter in marriage, since Artabanus realized that in this the emperor's aim was to annex the Parthian to the Roman Empire. Caracalla invaded Adiabene and Media and violated the Parthian royal tombs. But in 217 Artabanus raised a large army and broke into Roman Mesopotamia. Caracalla was murdered somewhere between Edessa and Carrhae.[1] Artabanus defeated Macrinus in 218 and made peace with him, receiving a bribe of two hundred million sesterces.[2]

344   Artabanus V: obverse of silver drachm with characteristic stylized features as seen in *Ill. 343*.

Artabanus' drachms and bronze pieces present him facing to the left, with the same headgear and facial features as those of Vologeses V (*Ill. 344*).[3]

1 DC, lxxviii, 1–6; Herodian iv, 10–13; SHA, *Antoninus Caracalla* 6.
2 Herodian iv, 5, 6–9; v, 1; DC, lxxviii, 26, 27.
3 *BMCGC Parthia*, 1903, pp. 247–50, nos. 1–34, pl. 36, nos. 8–13.

345   Artavasdes: obverse of silver drachm showing the last king of the Arsacid dynasty in Persia.

ARTAVASDES (AD 227–8)
Ill. 345

In AD 220 the Sassanid Ardashir gained the Persian throne. In 222/3 he began war against Parthia and in 227 overcame and killed Artabanus V (q.v.).

The latter's son, Artavasdes, managed to hold the Parthian kingship for one year, but was captured by the Persians and put to death. So ended the Arsacid line and the empire of Parthia – an empire which had never failed to maintain its status as a sovereign power on equal terms with Rome.[1]

Artavasdes issued a few drachms with his portrait – which is almost identical with that of his father – on the obverses (*Ill. 345*).[2] The royal portrait had, indeed, now ceased to claim to be a likeness and had become a mere convention, devoid of artistic interest.

1 Strabo xi, 9, 2; Pliny, *NH*, v, 21 (88); Josephus, *Ant. Iud.*, xviii, 46; Tacitus, *Ann.*, ii, 56; Herodian iv, 10, 2.
2 *BMCGC Parthia*, 1903, p. 251, nos. 1–3, pl. 36, nos. 14, 15; Ghirshman 1962, p. 115, fig. 155.

Persia: the Sassanian Kings[1]

ARDASHIR (ARTAXERXES) I (AD 224–41), Shahpur I as crown prince and Denak
Ills. 346–53

Ardashir I, known to the Romans as Artaxerxes, was the real founder of the new Persian Empire. In AD 224 or 227 he brought the Parthian Empire to an end by his victory over Artabanus V (q.v.) and in 230 he attacked Roman Mesopotamia, maintaining to Alexander Severus that, as the rightful heir of the Achaemenid Persian kings, he had a claim to all the territories that had once belonged to them.[2] Alexander in person conducted a campaign against Persia and then, according to the *Augustan History*, recognized Ardashir as 'potentissimus rex tam iure quam nomine'.[3] In 237 and 241 the Persians attacked Mesopotamia again and Nisibis and Carrhae fell to them.

At Firuzabad, south-west of Persepolis, Ardashir founded a new city, circular in plan; and on the rock-face of a gorge leading to it he had carved the scene of his decisive victory over Artabanus V (*Ill. 346*).[4] Ardashir is shown unseating Artabanus, whose horse is turning a somersault, while the crown prince, afterwards Shahpur I (q.v.), wearing a 'Phrygian' helmet, is doing likewise to the Parthian grand vizier (*Ill. 347*). On the top of the Persian king's head, shown in profile to the right, is a great mass of closely packed curls, roughly oval in shape, namely the *korymbos* (cf. pp. 167, 169), which on his coins and rock-cut reliefs appears as circular and generally bunched up inside a veil, probably of silk. Similar curls cover like a skull-cap the crown of his head, while at the side a great wave again of similar curls spreads across his shoulders. He has an enormous nose and a neat pointed beard tied by a ribbon. He has a heavy necklace and the ties of his diadem stream out behind him. Shahpur, too, is diademed, has a long beard blunted at the tip and a broad necklace.

Three rock-carvings depict Ardashir's investiture by the god Ahuramazda, who hands him a diadem. One, a little further up the gorge at Firuzabad, shows the god on the left and the king on the right standing confronted.[5] The king's head is badly weathered so that his features have disappeared. All that can be discerned are his *korymbos* inside a veil, his long, pointed beard, and the ribbon of his diadem behind his neck. Immediately behind Ardashir is his fan-bearer and behind him a figure, wearing a tall hat encircled by a diadem, who might be the crown prince; he has a long beard. A second investiture scene, at Naqsh-i Rajab, three miles north of Persepolis, in which the god and king again stand, but in reversed directions, is better preserved and displays Ardashir's skull-cap-shaped head-dress topped by the *korymbos* in a veil, with the diadem ribbons fluttering behind. He has a long, pointed beard, but no lateral curls or braids of hair and wears a heavy necklace.[6] The man on the extreme left (beyond the king's fan-bearer), who wears a conical cap with a diadem and has a large, hooked nose, a long beard blunted at the tip, and a heavy bunch of curls falling onto his shoulder, is probably again the future Shahpur I. The best rendering of the theme is at Naqsh-i Rustam, a few miles north-east of Persepolis, where the god facing left and the king facing right are both on horseback (*Ill. 348*).[7] The king's head-dress is the same, with the addition of ear-flaps and a neck-guard to his skull-cap, but his long, pointed beard is pulled through a ring and he has two waves of braided hair falling onto his shoulder, while the very long and broad ribbon of his diadem reaches to his horse's back. Beside the hooves of Ardashir's horse is the

346, 347   Ardashir I and his son Shahpur (later Shahpur I; cf. pp. 176ff.): details of rock-reliefs at Firuzabad showing the king and crown prince unseating respectively Artabanus V and the Parthian grand vizier in the course of the battle which brought the Parthian empire to an end (AD 224 or 227).

head, with pointed beard, of his fallen foe, Artabanus V, wearing the 'tea-cosy'-shaped, diademed Parthian tiara or helmet edged along the top with 'teeth' or hooks and furnished with ear-flaps and a neck-guard. On all of these reliefs the Persian king wears a long-sleeved, belted tunic and trousers.[8]

A now very badly worn rock-cut relief at the ancient Salmas, modern Shahpur, a short distance to the west of Lake Urmia, in the north-western extremity of modern Iran, shows Ardashir I and his son Shahpur I both on horseback and moving slowly to the left, while a groom holds each horse's head.[9] The details of the picture can today be best studied in the somewhat embellished and not com-

extend the right hand forward. Hinz suggests that the two standing figures are, on the left, Chosroes I of Armenia (c.225–50), a vassal of Ardashir, and, on the right, his grand vizier.

Hinz convincingly dates the Salmas relief to the last years of Ardashir's reign, when Shahpur I was co-regent with his father. It is to be noted that Shahpur wears his father's head-dress, not the mural crown that characterizes his portraits during his sole rule (cf. p. 176). It was, moreover, in 237–8 that the Persians overran Mesopotamia and annexed Armenia, without devastating that country (see above). G. Herrmann, on the other hand, would place the relief early in Ardashir's reign on stylistic grounds and connect it with the king's early

348 Ardashir I: rock-carving at Naqsh-i Rustam depicting the investiture of the king by the god Ahuramazda (*right*); the standing figure behind the king (*far left*) may represent his son Shahpur.

pletely accurate drawings made of it by Charles Texier in 1839 and Eugène Flandin in 1841. The left-hand horseman is somewhat taller than his companion on the right and must be Ardashir himself. Both riders have a moustache, a pointed beard drawn through a ring, and a veiled *korymbos* balanced on a diademed skull-cap. Shahpur, on the right, has a great bunch of curls on either side of his face. An examination of the original relief shows that Texier was wrong in giving these bunches to Ardashir as well. Both figures have two pairs of ribbons fluttering behind them from neck and back respectively. Both wear tunic and trousers, grasp with the left hand the hilt of a long sword, and

campaigns up the Tigris into Armenia.[10] As she rightly points out, the rigid frontality of all the human figures and the flat method of carving link it more closely with Parthian work than with the developed Ardashiran style of rock carving as seen at Naqsh-i Rajab and Naqsh-i Rustam. But it must be remembered that Salmas is far distant from those sites, as well as from Firuzabad (see above) and Darabgird (see below), and close to northern Parthia, from which, indeed, carvers could well have been brought to cut the Ardashir–Shahpur relief.

The most striking and complex of all Ardashir's rock-carved reliefs is that at Darabgird, south-east of Persepolis, the centre of which is occupied by the equestrian figure of the king facing to the right (*Ill. 349*).[11] He wears his usual diademed head-dress – the skull-cap surmounted by the *korymbos*, while his hair forms two great bunches of curls on either side of his face. The broad ribbons of his diadem stream out behind. His face is badly worn, so that the details of his features and beard cannot now be determined. But his heavy necklace, long-sleeved tunic, fluttering cloak and trousers are clear enough. Approaching the king from the right are three male figures – an old man on whose bowed head Ardashir lays his hand, a young man striding rapidly towards the king, and a man, perhaps an attendant, leading a donkey-cart. On the left of this central group is massed a great crowd of Persians, mostly long-bearded, facing right, and wearing tall hats or 'Phrygian' helmets: the heads of the background figures are raised in tiers above those in the foreground. On the right of the central group is a similar throng of tiered, bare-headed personages, thought to be Romans,[12] facing left and wearing short beards that sheathe the chin. Just to the right of the horse's forelegs can be seen the diademed and slightly bearded head of a corpse on the ground.

Both the old man and the young man are diademed, and the latter's legs are swathed in oriental leggings. The old man's face, with its huge hooked nose, curving mouth and fat cheeks, is definitely portrait-like. He may be beardless (but this is by no means certain) and he wears a dejected look. He does not resemble any known Roman emperor. The young man has a slight beard.

G. Herrmann's arguments for ascribing the relief to Ardashir I rather than to Shahpur I are wholly convincing. The problem is to identify the occasion that the whole scene depicts. If, as she plausibly suggests, the old and young man and the corpse represent minor oriental kings subdued by or allied to or slain by Ardashir, what would be the role of the Romans (if indeed they are Romans, as she assumes) massed in their tiers behind and above those two easteners? If they stand for a Roman defeat, where is their defeated Roman leader? Could they not be a crowd of non-Persian orientals, supporting the old and young man, both of whom are orientals, just as the Persians on the other side, of whom those in the bottom row may be royal princes, support their king? Their features – great hooked noses, moustaches turned down at the corners, and large, rather staring eyes – resemble those of the old man who submits himself to Ardashir and they could as well be those of easterners as of 'caricatured Romans', to cite G. Herrmann's interpretation of these personages. Their short beards are paralleled by that of the young striding oriental in the centre of the picture. The occasion of the whole carving would then be the celebration of a general triumph by Ardashir over Persia's neighbours to the north and west of her.

Ardashir's earliest coin portraits show him on the obverses facing the spectator and wearing the Parthian 'tea-cosy' helmet or tiara edged round the top with pearls(?) and fitted with ear-flaps and neck-guard. He has a moustache and a long, tapering beard slightly blunted at the tip, while a great bunch of tight curls hangs down on either side of his face (*Ill. 350*). On the reverses of some is the bust of Ardashir's father, Papak, facing to the left and wearing the same headgear.[13] Other early coin portraits depict him facing to the right, with the same beard and wearing the same Parthian headgear. He has a very large, hooked nose, a moustache that is down-turned at the corners, and the same type of beard, but he lacks the lateral bunches of hair; he wears a heavy necklace or chain of office.[14]

There are a few coins that present Ardashir facing to the right and wearing a diademed mural crown, within which, on the top of the head, can be seen a circular mass of tight curls representing the *korymbos*. His long beard is plaited and his hair hangs in broad plaits over his shoulder and behind

349   Ardashir I: detail of rock-relief at Darabgird showing the king, mounted, on the left.

350–2 Ardashir I: examples of coin obverses showing (*above*) early type of full-face portrait, and (*below*) profiles with mural crown, and with diadem alone, both with veiled *korymbos* (actual size).

Right
353 Denak: amethyst seal with bust of Ardashir I's queen.

emperor in combat; both are on horseback, with the former grasping the latter by the wrist, as though taking him prisoner.[19] It is difficult to hold that it represents, as it is so often said to do, the victory of Shahpur I over Valerian, since the king does not wear Shahpur's characteristic mural crown (cf. p. 173). Here the king has Ardashir's skull-cap head-dress surmounted by the veiled *korymbos* and not combined with either braided side-locks or lateral bunches of tight curls, features which are also lacking on some of that monarch's rock-cut and coin portraits (cf. pp. 173, 174). The king's beard on the cameo is pulled through a ring or tied with a ribbon. All these details fit Ardashir, although he is never shown elsewhere wearing cheek-pieces, as on the cameo; furthermore, Ardashir never took a Roman emperor captive. No

his neck (*Ill. 351*).[15] But on the great majority of the king's later coins, where his bust faces to the right, very occasionally to the left, the same plaited beard and braided hair is combined with the skull-cap head-dress topped by the ball-like veiled *korymbos*, as on some of his portraits on his rock-cut reliefs referred to above (*Ill. 352*).[16] On one coin type the curls of the *korymbos* are exposed.[17] On coins dating from the years of Shahpur I's co-regency the bust of Ardashir, with the veiled *korymbos* and braided hair, faces to the right and confronts the leftward-facing bust of his son, who wears the 'tea-cosy' Parthian headgear.[18]

On a cameo in the Bibliothèque Nationale, Paris, are depicted a Sassanian king and a Roman

later king wore the head-dress of the king on the cameo, whose interpretation must remain an enigma.

An inscribed amethyst seal carries a bust of Denak, the queen of Ardashir I, facing right. She has a long, straight nose, large eyes, a small mouth, a heavy chin and a full neck. Her hair is wound round her head in a series of neat plaits, the ends of which hang down beside her neck; while the rest is gathered up into a great top-knot of tight, round curls (*Ill. 353*).[20]

1 For a general account of the relations between Rome and the Sassanids from the fall of Parthia in AD 227 to the end of the fourth century, see K.-H. Ziegler, *Die Beziehungen zwischen Rom und dem Partherreich*, 1964, pp.

141–53, where it is argued that Rome regarded the Sassanid empire as the direct successor of the Parthian and as a 'brother' empire on an equal footing with her own (cf. p. 171 and note 1). For an account and catalogue of Sassanian coins from the third to the early seventh century, see F. D. J. Paruck, *Sassanian Coins*, 1924, and R. Göbl, *Sasanian Numismatics*, 1971. For a full discussion with illustration of the successive headgears worn by the Sassanian kings, see E. Herzfeld, *Archäologische Mitteilungen aus Iran*, ix, 1938, pp. 91–158, pls. 1–12 and fig. on p. 102.

2 DC, lxxx, 3, 4; Herodian vi, 2–6; 4, 5.
3 SHA, *Alexander Severus* 56, 7.
4 Ghirshman 1962, figs. 163–6; *Iran*, vii, 1969, pl. i and pp. 71–3, figs. 5, 6.
5 Ghirshman 1962, fig. 167; *Iran*, vii, 1969, p. 66–7, pl. 2.
6 E. Herzfeld and F. Sarre, *Iranische Felsreliefs*, 1910, pl. 12; *Iran*, vii, 1969, pp. 67–9, fig. 3 and pl. 3. Here the two children between the king and the god are identified as Ardashir's son and grandson and the diademed woman on the right as his queen; the woman with her could be the crown prince's wife.
7 Ibid., pp. 69–71, fig. 4 and pl. 4; Herzfeld and Sarre, op. cit., pl. 5; Herzfeld, op. cit., pl. 2, a.
8 On the Firuzabad battle relief the king's *korymbos* could be either his own hair or a wig composed of someone else's and fastened on. Where it is covered with a veil, the hair would, if it were his own, have had to be pulled through a hole in the top of the skull-cap and then puffed out into a kind of football. But it would seem to be more likely that the contents of the veil, if it were hair, did not grow from the king's head.
9 H. Hinz, 'Das sassanidische Felsrelief von Salmas', in *Iranica antiqua*, v, 1965, pp. 148–60, pls. 44–51.
10 *Iran*, vii, 1969, pp. 73–4.
11 Ibid., pp. 83–8, fig. 10 and pls. 12–16; Ghirshman 1962, fig. 206 (wrongly ascribed to Shahpur I).
12 Cf. *JRS*, xliv, 1954, p. 76.
13 Paruck, op. cit., pl. 1, nos. 4–12; Göbl, op. cit., pl. 1, nos. 1–3.
14 Paruck, op. cit., pl. 1, nos. 13–23, pl. 2, nos. 24–8; Göbl, op. cit., pl. 1, nos, 7, 8, 10; Ghirshman 1962, p. 245, fig. 304.
15 Paruck, op. cit., pl. 2, nos. 29–33; *CAH*, vol. v of plates, 1939, p. 235, g; Göbl, op. cit., pl. 1, nos. 14, 15. It has bee suggested (*CAH*, xii, 1939, p. 130) that the mural crown records Ardashir's capture of the cities of Nisibis and Carrhae (cf. p. 171).
16 Paruck, op. cit., pl. 2, nos. 34–44, pl. 3, nos. 45–56; *CAH*, vol. v of plates, 1939, p. 235, a; Göbl, op. cit., pl. 1 nos. 9–13; cf. Herzfeld, op. cit., p. 102, fig. 1.
17 Paruck, op. cit., pl. 3, no. 57; Göbl, op. cit., pl. 1, nos. 16, 17; L. Vanden Berghe, *La signification iconographique du relief rupestre sassanide de Sarab-i Qandil (Iran)*, 1973, fig. 20.
18 Paruck, op. cit., pl. 3, nos. 58–63; Göbl, op. cit., pl. 2, nos. 19, 20.
19 Ghirshman 1962, p. 152, fig. 195.
20 Vanden Berghe, op. cit., fig. 21.

SHAHPUR (SAPOR) I (AD 241–72)
Ills. 354–362

In AD 241 Shahpur I took Hatra and other Roman outposts in Mesopotamia. The Roman counter-offensive in 243, under Gordian III's praetorian prefect Timesitheus, secured Antioch against Shahpur and recovered Nisibis and Carrhae for Rome. But after the deaths of Gordian and Timesitheus in 243–4, Philip the Arabian made peace with Persia. In 252, however, Shahpur seized Armenia, expelling the last Arsacid king of that country. He now styled himself 'King of Kings of Iran and non-Iran'.[1] In 259 Nisibis again passed to Persia. In 257 and 259 Valerian had withstood renewed Persian invasions. But in 260 Shahpur besieged Edessa; and the emperor, in view of the depressed state of his army, sought to negotiate with the king and offered him a large money-payment as the price of peace. He agreed to a personal interview with Shahpur, who immediately took him prisoner. Shahpur then took Antioch and invaded Asia Minor, but was defeated there and forced to withdraw his troops beyond the Euphrates into Persia. On his way he was attacked by Odenathus of Palmyra (cf. p. 148), who inflicted crippling losses on him.

Shahpur I's portraits as crown prince on the rock-cut reliefs and coins of his father Ardashir I have already been described (pp. 171, 172).

Of Shahpur I's own rock-carved reliefs probably the earliest is that which shows his investiture by the god at Naqsh-i Rajab. Both god and king are on horseback, the king facing to the left, but his head and the upper part of his body are almost completely worn away, leaving no discernible details of his crown or hair-style. Only the figure of the god is well preserved.[2] In his second equestrian investiture relief, that at Bishapur, south-west of Persepolis, the king's figure, facing left, is again destroyed and that of the god is much less well-preserved than on the Naqsh-i Rajab relief.[3] But close in front of the forelegs of the king's horse is the kneeling figure of a Roman supplicating Shahpur I, which must represent Philip the Arabian suing for peace in 244; while under the hooves of the king's horse is a prostrate figure, who must be the dead Gordian III. The relief can therefore be dated to 244 or 245.[4]

Next in date would seem to be Shahpur I's triumph scene carved at Naqsh-i Rustam, where the king appears on horseback, facing to the left and grasping the hand of a man who stands facing him, while a wreathed Roman facing right kneels in supplication towards him (*Ill. 354*).[5] The king's head is reasonably well preserved. He wears a mural crown encircling a large veiled *korymbos* (for which a niche has been cut in the rock; cf. p. 177) and two great masses of curls frame his face. His beard is pulled through a ring and he has a heavy necklace. The kneeling wreathed Roman is clearly Philip the Arabian, since his features closely resemble those of that emperor on his coin portraits. The racial identity of the standing figure whose hand the king grasps, whether Roman or oriental, is difficult to determine. But he must be a prisoner of

354 Shahpur I: rock relief at Naqsh-i Rustam showing the king's triumph over Philip the Arabian (kneeling at left); the carving dates from soon after 244 or 245.

some importance. The carving of this rock-relief can be dated to soon after Philip's supplication for peace in 244 or 245.

On a relief at Naqsh-i Rajab, Shahpur I on horseback, facing right, occupies the right-hand portion of the scene, while behind him, also looking to the right, stand nine men who all wear tall hats which are, apparently with one exception, diademed. They have been convincingly equated by G. Herrmann with Shahpur's sons, the tallest one, immediately behind the horse's rump, with a huge bunch of curls at the right-hand side of his neck, being the heir to the throne, later Hormizd I: she dates the relief on stylistic grounds to the first decade of Shahpur's reign (*Ill. 355*).[6]

In two more reliefs at Bishapur, nos. IV and VI, the central scene containing the figure of Shahpur I is framed by subsidiary panels or friezes containing figures of riders and men on foot – the king's noblemen and troops – arranged in four or two superimposed registers.[7] These two reliefs are carved on either side of the gorge; and while the supporting panels or friezes differ, the central picture is almost precisely the same in both. It shows the king on horseback to the right, grasping

the wrist of a man in Roman dress who stands just behind him, while another Roman kneels in supplication to the left before him, and a dead Roman lies prostrate beneath the horse's hooves. As G. Herrmann points out,[8] the style and technique of the two reliefs differ markedly, no. IV (*Ill. 356*),[9] although much damaged, being considerably more lively, naturalistic and plastic than no. VI (*Ill. 357*);[10] and she suggests that no. IV was the work of Roman carvers taken prisoner at the time of Valerian's defeat, and whose production the Sassanian carvers of no. VI copied. This view is supported by the fact that both scenes contain a wholly Graeco-Roman motif – a Cupid flying towards the king with the gift of a diadem. In both Shahpur wears the mural crown with veiled *korymbos*, for which again a special niche is cut in each case in the rock-face (cf. p. 176) and he has great bunches of curls framing his face. Behind the kneeling Roman are two Persians wearing tall hats, who may be princes or nobles: the pairs in IV and VI are not identical. On no. VI, where the heads of all three Romans are well preserved, they wear thick rolls round their brows, no doubt Sassanian versions of laurel-wreaths.

There would seem to be little doubt that the three Romans are emperors and that B. C. MacDermot is right in identifying them as Gordian III lying dead beneath the hooves of the king's horse, Philip the Arabian suing for peace, and Valerian held firmly captive – all three, as he points out, being mentioned in Shahpur's great bilingual inscription at Kaaba-i-Zardusht.[11] To the present writer's mind there can be no difficulty in believing that Shahpur combined in a single picture symbolic scenes of his victories over no less than three Roman emperors – Gordian III in 243–4, Philip the Arabian in 244–5, and Valerian in 260 – a signal achievement, truly worthy of commemoration in the presence of the king's people.

The case against identifying the Persian king and Roman emperor on the Bibliothèque Nationale cameo as Shahpur I and Valerian has already been argued (cf. p. 175), although R. Göbl (op. cit. [note 11], pl. 1, fig. 5) illustrates a rock-relief at Darab

showing Shahpur wearing a crown without crenellations, and suggests that the head-dress could be a special 'Kriegskrone' – hence the cheek-pieces. However, Shahpur is certainly depicted on the interior of a silver bowl in the British Museum. He is shown hunting deer and is striding towards the right; he is here characterized by his mural crown with veiled *korymbos* and by bunches of curled hair framing his face (*Ill. 358*).[12] Most striking of all the king's portraits is the colossal statue of him carved in a pillar of stone that connected the roof and floor of a cave in the mountains near Bishapur (*Ill. 359*).[13] The king's *korymbos*, encircled by his mural crown, was actually carved in the roof and was left there when an earthquake, perhaps, caused the statue itself to snap at the ankles, hurling the figure to the ground. Shahpur is shown diademed and has a great bunch of curls on either side of his face, huge staring eyes, a long, horizontal moustache that curves away on either side of his mouth, and a close

355–7 Shahpur I: rock-reliefs depicting (*below*) the king accompanied by his sons, at Naqsh-i Rajab; and (*opposite*) two scenes at Bishapur (nos. IV and VI) showing marked differences in style.

358–62 Shahpur I: (*above*) interior of silver bowl with hunting scene; (*below*) colossal statue from a cave near Bishapur; (*right*) two coin portraits showing mural crown with veiled *korymbos* (actual size), and one a conical helmet.

beard that is pulled through a ring. He wears earrings and a heavy necklace and the texture of his long-sleeved tunic is rendered by a series of curious wavy, vertical wisps. The king may have been buried in the cave, in which case the statue would be his funerary portrait.

Shahpur I's coin portraits present his bust facing to the right. He wears the mural crown, sometimes equipped with ear-flaps and always topped by the veiled *korymbos*. An enormous bunch of tight curls projects behind his neck and his neat beard is passed through a ring (*Ills. 360–61*).[14] On one silver coin he has the same hair-style and beard, but wears a conical hat or helmet surmounted by an eagle's head (*Ill. 362*).[15] Some coin portraits show a very hooked nose.

1   *Orientis Graeci Inscriptiones Selectae*, i, 1903, no. 434.
2   Herzfeld and Sarre, op. cit., pl. 13; *Iran*, vii, 1969, pp. 75–6, fig. 8 and pl. 5.
3   Herzfeld and Sarre, op. cit., pl. 44: *Iran*, vii, 1969, pp. 76–7, pl. 6; Ghirshman 1962, figs. 202, 203.
4   *Iran*, vii, 1969, p. 77.
5   Ibid., pp. 77–8, pl. 7; Herzfeld and Sarre, op. cit., pl. 7; *CAH*, vol. v of plates, 1939, p. 149; *JRS*, xliv, 1954, pl. 4, fig. 2; Ghirshman 1962, fig. 205; Herzfeld, op. cit., pl. 2, b.
6   Herzfeld and Sarre, op. cit., pl. 11; *Iran*, vii, 1969, pp. 78–80, fig. 9 and pl. 8; Herzfeld, op. cit., pl. 1.
7   Ghirshman 1962, fig. 196 (= Bishapur VI); *Iran*, vii, 1969, pl. 9 (= Bishapur IV).
8   Ibid., pp. 80–3.
9   Ibid., pls. 9, 10; Herzfeld and Sarre, op. cit., pl. 43; Ghirshman 1962, fig. 200.
10   *Iran*, vii, 1969, pl. 11; Herzfeld and Sarre, op. cit., pl. 45; Ghirshman 1962, figs. 197–9.
11   *JRS*, xliv, 1954, pp. 78–80, pl. 4, fig. 1, Cf. R. Göbl, *Der Triumph des Sasaniden Sahpur über die Kaiser Gordianus, Philippus und Valerianus*, 1974.
12   *CAH*, vol. v of plates, 1939, p. 147, a.
13   Ghirshman 1962, pp. 162–5, figs. 207–9.
14   Ibid., p. 245, fig. 305; Paruck, op. cit., pl. 4, nos. 64–89, pl. 5, nos. 90–6; R. Göbl, *Sasanian Numismatics*, pl. 2, nos. 21–33; *CAH*, vol. v of plates, 1939, p. 235, b; Herzfeld, op. cit., pl. 4, fig. 4.
15   Paruck, op. cit., pl. 5, no. 97; Göbl, op. cit., pl. 2, no. 34; *CAH*, vol. v of plates, 1939, p. 235, h.

363   Hormizd I: obverse of silver drachm showing the characteristic veiled *korymbos*.

HORMIZD I (272–3)
Ill. 363

The brief reign of Hormizd I, the son of Shahpur I, witnessed no important contacts with Rome. His coin portraits show his bust facing to the right. He wears a large, veiled *korymbos* and the skull-cap of his crown is adorned above the diadem that binds his brow with a series of close-set spirals. A huge bunch of curls projects behind his neck. He has large eyes, an aquiline nose, a small mouth, and a beard composed of neat curls and drawn through a ring. He wears a heavy necklace and ear-rings (*Ill. 363*).[1]

1   Paruck, op. cit., pl. 5, nos. 99–104; Göbl, op. cit., pl. 3, nos. 35–9; Ghirshman 1962, p. 245, fig. 306.

BAHRAM, or VARHRAN, I (AD 273–6)
Ill. 364

The reign of Bahram, or Varhran, I, the brother of Hormizd I, was an equally uneventful period, so far as relations with Rome were concerned. On his coins his bust faces either to the right or to the left, his veiled *korymbos* rests on a skull-cap that is encircled by rays projecting upwards from just

above the band of his diadem, and his crown is equipped with ear-flaps. His hair and beard are dressed in straight, tight braids. Three braids of hair joined to form a long, bean-shaped feature hang down diagonally behind his head. Four braids depend beside his neck behind and below the ear-flap and are completely straight and vertical, as are also the four braids of his beard as seen in profile. These braids and those of the beard are all of equal length and together form an almost straight, horizontal line at their terminations. The king's nose is long, pointed and somewhat aquiline. He has his brother's small mouth (*Ill. 364*).[1]

In view of his rayed crown, which is not worn by any other Sassanian monarch, we should almost certainly identify as Bahram I the king on horseback, facing to the left and being invested with a diadem by a rightward-facing god, also on horseback, depicted on a rock-cut relief at Bishapur.[2] He has here the veiled *korymbos*, but his hair and beard are worn in a style quite different from that which his coin likenesses affect. There are no tight, straight braids, but his hair spreads out behind his head in a great triangular mass of curls and his pointed beard is drawn through a ring. On the

364   Bahram I: obverse of silver drachm showing a rayed crown not seen in any other portraits of Sassanian kings.

other hand, the nose and mouth are those of
Bahram's coin portraits.

1 Paruck, op. cit., pl. 5, nos. 105–10; pl. 6, nos. 111–14;
  Göbl, op. cit., pl. 3, nos. 40–7; *CAH*, vol. v of plates,
  1939, p. 235, c; Ghirshman 1962, p. 246, fig. 307.
2 Herzfeld and Sarre, op. cit., pl. 41; Ghirshman 1962,
  p. 167, fig. 211.

BAHRAM, or VAHRHAN, II (AD 276–93) with son
and queen
Ills. 365–9

With Bahram, or Varhran, II we return to confrontations between Rome and Persia. Probus (AD
276–83) is said to have rejected with contempt the
gifts sent to him by the Persian king, who must be
Bahram II.[1] In 283 the latter was at war with the
Emperor Carus, who took Seleucia and Ctesiphon,
but died there.[2] Rome and Persia came to terms
and Mesopotamia remained in Roman hands. In
288 Diocletian induced Bahram to resign formally
all claim to Mesopotamia and in the same year he
set on the throne of Armenia his own nominee,
Tiridates III.

365, 366 Bahram II: silver coin portraits showing (*above*)
the king confronted by his son (actual size), and jugate with
his queen and confronted by their son.

Bahram II's coin portraits depict his bust facing
right. He has the veiled *korymbos*, and wings, one on
each side, sprout from the skull-cap just above the
diadem. The wings are generally straight along
their upper edge, but occasionally slightly up-
turned at the tips. A vast bunch of curls projects
behind his neck. He wears ear-rings and a necklace.
He has a large nose and a small mouth and his neat,
curly beard is drawn through a ring. Some coins
show him facing the full-size bust of his son, who is
beardless and wears the 'tea-cosy'-shaped type of
'Parthian' head-dress with ear-flaps (*Ill. 365*; cf. p.
174); on others he confronts a miniature bust of his
son, who wears a 'Phrygian' cap terminating at the
top in a boar's head. On other coins again are the
rightward-facing jugate busts of Bahram and his
queen, either by themselves or confronted by the
miniature 'Phrygian'-capped bust of their son, who
extends a diadem towards his parents. The queen's
head-dress terminates at the top in a wolf's head
(*Ill. 366*). A silver cup found at Sargvechi in
Georgia and now in the Tbilisi Museum is adorned
on the exterior with medallions containing coin-
like portraits of Bahram II with up-turned head-
wings and of his wife and son.[4]

A rock-cut relief at Naqsh-i Rustam presents
Bahram II standing in the centre and flanked on
either side by members of his family and court. The
king's body faces the spectator, but his face is
turned towards the personages on his right; he rests
both hands on the hilt of a mighty sword. The top of
his head is in deep shadow, but one can see traces of
a veiled *korymbos* and of a skull-cap with wings,
while a great mass of curls is visible behind his neck.
His beard is passed through a ring and he wears a
necklace (*Ill. 367*).[5] On a rock-relief at Naqsh-i
Bahram the king sits enthroned, facing the spectator and flanked by four dignitaries, two on either
side. His facial features are worn away, but his
veiled *korymbos*, two wings sprouting from his skull-
cap, and two great bunches of curls on either side of
his neck are well preserved.[6] A rock-relief at Sar
Meshed portrays the king at a lion-hunt, accompanied by his queen. The king's head is seen in
profile to the left, with a veiled *korymbos*, a winged
skull-cap, a mass of curls on either side of his face, a
beard drawn through a ring, ear-rings and necklace (*Ill. 368*). The queen has a domed, 'tea-cosy'-
shaped and diademed head-dress, long, straight
ringlets of hair hanging down beside her neck, and
a necklace. Her facial features have been badly
damaged, but her full cheeks and rounded chin are
relatively intact (*Ill. 369*).[7]

Of the other rock-cut reliefs that have been
ascribed by Vanden Berghe to Bahram II,[8] the one
at Sarab-i Qandil shows three figures of which the
central and tallest one must be the king.[9] The
latter's head and face are badly worn, the veiled

367   Bahram II: rock-relief at Naqsh-i Rustam showing the king surrounded by members of his family and court; the king's
hands are resting on the hilt of his sword.

korymbos is just identifiable, there are no clear traces of wings sprouting from the skull-cap, and since the beard is broken off we cannot know whether or not it was passed through a ring. However, Bahram's characteristic huge bunches of curls framing the face are well preserved; and Vanden Berghe's general arguments for identifying him as the king

here depicted are acceptable. The king's body faces the spectator while his face is turned to his right towards the figure, on the left of the group, of a woman who offers him a flower.[10] The reasons for equating her with Bahram's queen are convincing, although her head-dress does not correspond either with that of her coin portraits described above or with that worn by her in the lion-hunt scene at Sar Meshed. Here her hair-style recalls, rather, that of Denak, queen of Ardashir I (cf. p. 175). The third figure in the group, on the spectator's right, is male and looks towards the king to whom he extends a diadem. His head, too, is weathered, but his head-dress could be a 'Phrygian' cap, as worn by Bahram's son on his coins (cf. p. 182). He could well be the crown prince, Bahram III, who has left no independent coin portraits of himself, since he reigned only for a few months in 293.[11] On the relief at Barm-i Dilak the woman on the left who receives a flower from a king on the right has the domed head-dress of Bahram II's queen on the lion-hunt relief (cf. p. 182). But the king, so far as the poor condition of the carving enables us to judge, has

none of the characteristic features of crown, hair and beard that we find on Bahram II's coin likenesses.[12] On the other hand, a relief at Bishapur shows a group of horsemen on the right confronting the equestrian figure of a king who has Bahram II's veiled *korymbos*, winged skull-cap, and a great bunch of curls beside the neck.[13]

1 Not Narses, as stated in SHA, *Probus* 17, 5.
2 SHA, *Carus* 8 and 9.
3 Paruck, op. cit., pls. 6–8, nos. 115–60; Göbl, op. cit., pl. 3, nos. 48–53, pl. 4, nos. 54–70, pl. 5, nos. 71, 72; *CAH*, vol. v of plates, 1939, p. 235, d; Ghirshman 1962, p. 246, fig. 308; Vanden Berghe, op. cit., p. 23, fig. 14; cf. the Bishapur rock-relief – Herzfeld, op. cit., pl. 3, a, pl. 4, figs. 1, 3.
4 Vanden Berghe, op. cit., p. 22, fig. 13.
5 Ghirshman 1962, pp. 169–71, figs. 212, 213.

368, 369   Bahram II and his queen: details of rock-relief at Sar Meshed depicting a lion-hunt; the coiffure and head-dress can be clearly seen in both portraits.

6 Ibid., p. 172, fig. 214.
7 Ibid., pp. 173–5, figs. 215–17.
8 Vanden Berghe, op. cit., pp. 13–16 and notes 6–14.
9 Ibid., figs. 2–8.
10 Ibid., figs. 2, 3, 15, 16.
11 The coin portraits ascribed to Bahram III by Ghirshman 1962 (p. 240, fig. 309) and Paruck (op. cit., pl. 8, nos. 161–4) are those of Narseh.
12 Vanden Berghe, op. cit., p. 15, fig. 10; Herzfeld and Sarre, op. cit., pl. 32 (above).
13 Ibid., pl. 42.

NARSEH (NARSES) (AD 293–302)

Ills. 370, 371

Bahram III was displaced from the Persian throne (cf. p. 184) by his great-uncle Narseh, a son of Shahpur I. Narseh made war on Rome and drove from the throne of Armenia the Roman nominee, Tiridates III (cf. p. 182). In 296 he invaded Syria and defeated Galerius at Callinicus. Galerius then brought up reinforcements from the Danubian provinces and routed the Persian king in Armenia Maior, capturing Narseh's wives and children. The king retired and Galerius took Ctesiphon, whereupon Narseh renounced his aggressive policy and concentrated on negotiating for his wives' and children's return. Peace was concluded between the imperial secretary, Secorius Probus, and the Persians on the river Asprudas. Mesopotamia was ceded to Rome and Armenia acknowledged as a Roman protectorate; Narseh recovered the captives, and under Constantine I the Persian king and the Roman emperor were to be declared 'brothers' (Eusebius, *Vita Constantini* iv, 11). The arch of Galerius at Thessalonica was erected to commemorate Rome's victory over Narseh.

Narseh's coin portraits present him facing to the right. His crown is topped by a veiled *korymbos* and

370 Narseh: obverse of silver drachm showing one type of portrait with bunch of curls behind (cf. *Ill. 371*).

is always adorned with a series of vertical flutes along the lower edge of the skull-cap. He has a neat, curly beard passed through a ring, and a long, slightly hooked nose, and he wears ear-rings and a necklace. Some likenesses display a great bunch of curls at the neck; on others his hair falls to his shoulders in long, straight, rigid ringlets; and with this coiffure are combined three leafy sprays springing upwards from the skull-cap (*Ills. 370–1*).

371 Narseh: obverse of gold dinar with portrait featuring straight, rigid hair-style and leafy sprays above the crown.

A rock-cut relief at Naqsh-i Rustam depicts Narseh's investiture by the goddess Anahita. The king's body is shown frontally, but his head is turned to the right towards the goddess. A special niche has been cut in the surface of the rock in which the scene is recessed to hold his great *korymbos* and below that the fluting of his skull-cap is very prominent. His hair is heaped in a large bunch of curls on either shoulder and his beard is passed through a ring.[2] Cf. p. 176.

1 Paruck, op. cit., pl. 8, nos. 161–4 (not Bahram III), 165–72; Göbl, op. cit., pl. 5, nos. 73–9; *CAH*, vol. v of plates, p. 235, e; Ghirshman 1962, p. 246, fig. 309 (not Bahram III), p. 247, fig. 310.
2 Ghirshman 1962, p. 176, fig. 218; Herzfeld and Sarre, op. cit., pl. 9; Herzfeld, op. cit., pl. 3, b.

HORMIZD II (AD 302–9)

Ill. 372

The reign of Hormizd II, son of Narseh, was uneventful, so far as relations with Rome were concerned. His coin portraits face mainly to the right, occasionally to the left. A great *korymbos* tops his skull-cap, from which spread backwards wings with up-turned and markedly curled tips, while an eagle's beak projects in front. A row of large pearls(?) outlines the skull-cap's lower edge, just above the diadem. The hair flows behind the neck in a great mass of curls. The king has a large, pointed nose and wears ear-rings and a necklace (*Ill. 372*).[1]

372   Hormizd II: obverse of silver drachm (actual size) showing distinctive head-dress with eagle's head and wings.

A rock-cut relief at Naqsh-i Rustam may well portray Hormizd II on horseback, charging towards the right against a foe, whom he is unseating. The king's *korymbos* is lost, but there is a circular depression in the rock-face where it may once have been. There are also what look like scars – the remains of the now destroyed masses of side curls. The wings on the skull-cap spread backwards and are up-turned and curled over at the tips, but there is no trace of a projecting eagle's head in front or of a row of pearls(?). The beard, drawn through a ring, is visible.[2] Another rock-relief from Naqsh-i Rustam shows a king who is likely to be Hormizd II, since he has wings on his skull-cap with up-turned and noticeably curled-over tips. He is on horseback on the left and is charging another horseman who confronts him from the right. He has a big *korymbos* in a specially cut arched niche and a mass of curls on either side of the neck (cf. pp. 176, 185). The face of the king and the front of his crown are lost.[3] On the other hand, it could be argued that both of these reliefs belong to Bahram II (q.v.), since he, too, sometimes has up-turned wings, if not as curly at the tips as those of Hormizd II.

1   Paruck, op. cit., pl. 8, nos. 173–5, pl. 9, nos. 176–89; Göbl, op. cit., pl. 5, nos. 80–7; *CAH*, vol. v of plates, 1939, p. 235, f; Ghirshman 1962, p. 247, fig. 311; Paruck, op. cit., pl. 8, nos, 191–3, gives a portrait in which two horns flank the *korymbos* and there is no eagle's head.
2   Ghirshman 1962, p. 179, fig. 220.
3   Herzfeld and Sarre, op. cit., pl. 8.

SHAHPUR (SAPOR) II (AD 309–79)
Ills. 373–7

Shahpur II was an infant when his father Hormizd II died and during his minority his mother and the great nobles jointly ruled the Persian Empire. On coming of age he displayed remarkable independence and strength of character. But it was not until his later twenties that he began, in AD 338, his movements against Rome.

First Shahpur besieged Nisibis and occupied a number of the Mesopotamian fortresses. Later he forced Chosroes, Tiridates III's successor on the Armenian throne, to pay him tribute and cede to him Atropatene. Clashes between Persian and Roman forces, the latter commanded on two occasions by the Emperor Constantius himself, soon ensued. In 348 Shahpur defeated Constantius at Singara; but his son was captured, tortured and executed by the Romans. After many unsuccessful attempts to take Nisibis, Shahpur was obliged to raise the siege. Between 356 and 358 Rome opened negotiations with Persia, but could not accept the king's terms, namely the cession to him of all Mesopotamia and Armenia. In 359 Shahpur invaded Mesopotamia and besieged and took Amida, incurring very heavy losses thereby. Ammianus Marcellinus (xix, 1, 3) vividly describes his appearance on that occasion: 'insidens autem equo ante alios celsior ipse praeibat agminibus cunctis, aureum capitis arietini figmentum instinctum lapillis pro diademate gestans' ('the king rode on horseback in front of the lines, towering above the rest and wearing, in place of a diadem, a ram's head worked in gold and set with precious stones'). Shahpur then reduced Singara and Bezabde and captured five Roman legions.

In 362 the Emperor Julian made a resolve to conquer Persia finally. He rejected all Shahpur's overtures for negotiations and marched from Constantinople through Asia Minor to Antioch. In the spring of 363 he advanced to the Euphrates and then to Carrhae. Thence he returned to the Euphrates at Callinicus and followed the course of the river, now crowded with Roman shipping, to Circesium, where his army entered Persian territory, divided into three columns, and met with some successes. Assyria was devastated by Roman troops and two fortresses, Perisator and Maogamalcha, were reduced. The Roman fleet was transferred by artificial channels to the Tigris, which the army successfully crossed and forced the Persians, waiting on the further bank, to retreat. Julian now realized that he would never be able to take Ctesiphon, but again refused Shahpur's offer to negotiate for peace. Partly on the advice of a deserter from the Persian side and partly, no doubt, realizing that his river fleet on the Tigris would be incapable of returning upstream, he had his ships destroyed to prevent them from falling into Persian hands. The Roman army now started to retreat and was surrounded and continually harassed by Persian forces. Julian himself was mortally wounded in a brilliant attempt to relieve his rearguard and Jovian was saluted emperor by the troops. Shahpur now attacked the Roman rearguard and the position of the imperial army on the Tigris became desperate. Shahpur, fearing that Rome might produce a new army to avenge Julian, sent envoys to the Roman camp to arrange a thirty years' peace. The terms were the return to the Persian Empire of the five regions beyond the Tigris that Narseh (q.v.) had ceded to Rome. Included were Nisibis and Singara; and Rome was to abandon Armenia for ever. The Roman army crossed the Tigris with enormous losses and retired across the plains of Mesopotamia to the neighbourhood of Nisibis, which was evacuated of its inhabitants and, as stipulated, passed out of Roman hands, despite the protests of the citizens.

In 365 Shahpur entered Armenia. The king, Tiranus, was put to death and the country declared a Persian province. The Persian king was now faced with internal troubles; and although the Emperor Valens respected the treaty made with him by Jovian, he ventured to support the romanizing parties in Iberia and Armenia. In 379 Shahpur died and the two Empires mutually consented to Iberian and Armenian neutrality.

Shahpur II's portrait busts on his coins face right. He has a large, veiled *korymbos*, from the base of which ribbons sometimes flutter behind, emerging from a mural crown (cf. Shahpur I, p. 176). Below the three crenellations of the mural crown is a horizontal row of pearls(?) and below that again is the diadem with streamers flying out behind the neck. The king has a large, aquiline nose, a small mouth and a close beard drawn through a ring. At the back of the neck is a bunch of thick curls (*Ills. 373–4*).[1]

An almost life-size silver-gilt portrait head of a Sassanian monarch in the Metropolitan Museum of Art, New York, with a vertically ribbed (veiled?) *korymbos* (cf. the Paris cameo: Ghirshman 1962, p. 152, fig. 195, and above, p. 175) rising from a mural crown, is more likely to portray Shahpur II than Shahpur I, since it has the row of pearls(?) above the brow, which Shahpur I's crown lacks. There is a crescent on the central crenellation of the mural crown. As on most of his coin likenesses the king is moustached, the moustache here being particularly fine and curly, and the lower part of his beard is gathered into a narrow braid that reaches

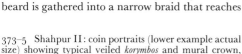

373–5 Shahpur II: coin portraits (lower example actual size) showing typical veiled *korymbos* and mural crown, and (*below*) silver-gilt head, almost life-size.

to the base of the neck. Curls are massed on either side of the face. The nose is pronouncedly aquiline (*Ill. 375*).[2]

A rock-cut relief at Bishapur, carved with two superimposed tiers of figures, shows a king seated frontally, and on a larger scale than the rest, at the centre of the upper tier. The king has been identified as Shahpur II in triumph, surrounded by courtiers and soldiers, some of whom present captives and the severed heads of foes. The monarch holds a sceptre in his raised right hand and rests his left hand on the hilt of an enormous sword. A great bolster-like feature behind his head may represent

lateral bunches of curls, incompletely worked. His *korymbos* is partially preserved, but below it the crown reveals no trace of crenellations or of a row of pearls(?) and is flat and triangular in shape. The identification is far from certain.[3] A rock relief at Taq-i-Bustan presents two kings standing side by side and identified by inscriptions as Shahpur II and Shahpur III. Both heads are badly worn, but a crescent is clearly visible on the crown of Shahpur III on the left, recalling the crescent on the central crenellation of the New York head of Shahpur II (see above).[4]

Three silver plates almost certainly portray Shahpur II hunting. One, in the Freer Gallery of Art, Washington, D.C., shows him on horseback to the right. His skull-cap with its mural crown is topped by a ribbed *korymbos*, as on the New York head, but lacks a row of pearls(?), while both *korymbos* and diadem have broad, fluttering streamers. He has the side bunches of curls, but his close-fitting beard is not pulled through a ring (*Ill. 376*).[5] A second plate, in the Hermitage, Leningrad, depicts the king on horseback to the left, but looking back towards the right, with lions as his quarry. His head-dress consists of a plain *korymbos*, a mural crown, a row of pearls(?) and a bunch of curls behind. His beard is ringed (*Ill. 377*).[6] On yet a third plate, in a private collection, the king is on foot towards the left, kneeling on the back of a deer which he is killing. He has the plain *korymbos*, the mural crown, the bunch of curls at the neck, and the ringed beard, but no row of pearls on his head-dress.[7] On the second and third of these plates the diadem has flying streamers.

1   Paruck, op. cit., pl. 9, nos. 194–202, pl. 10, nos. 203–30, pl. 11, nos. 231–57; Göbl, op. cit., pl. 6, nos. 88–106, pl. 7, nos. 107–20; Herzfeld, op. cit., pl. 4, figs. 5, 6; Ghirshman 1962, p. 247, fig. 312.
2   P. O. Harper in *Metropolitan Museum of Art Bulletin*, n.s., xxv, 1966–7, pp. 137–44, figs. 1, 6, 18.
3   Ghirshman 1962, p. 184, figs. 225–6.
4   Harper, op. cit., p. 138, figs. 4, 5.
5   Ibid., p. 140, fig. 8.
6   Ghirshman 1962, p. 212, fig. 253.
7   Ibid., p. 213, fig. 254.

376, 377 Shahpur II: silver-gilt plates with scenes of boar-and lion-hunting (Freer Gallery, Washington, D.C.; Hermitage, Leningrad).

ARDASHIR (ARTAXERXES) II (AD 379–83)
Ills. 378, 379

Ardashir II was a relative, but not the brother, of Shahpur II. His coin portraits show him wearing a crown topped by a veiled *korymbos*, to which a fluttering ribbon is attached, a skull-cap ornamented with rosettes, and a row of large pearls(?) or small plaques(?) above the diadem, the tassel-ended ties of which emerge either above or from behind a mass of curls at the neck. The king has

large eyes and a prominent nose and his curly beard is passed through a ring (*Ill. 378*).[1]

A rock-cut relief at Taq-i-Bustan shows the investiture of Ardashir II, standing in the centre, by Ahuramazda, on the right, who presents the king with a diadem, while Mithras, wearing a rayed head-dress, supports him on the left. The king's small *korymbos* has large ties and the very broad and heavy ribbon of his diadem passes across the top of his lateral bunch of curls and hangs down behind his back. There are no traces of decoration on the skull-cap. The beard is ringed. Beneath the feet of Ardashir and Ahuramazda lies a dead enemy, wearing a decorated cap. The fringe of straight hair on the brow and the long beard suggest that he may be meant to represent Julian – an allusion to the victories over Rome of Ardashir's predecessor, Shahpur II (*Ill. 379*).[2]

1 Paruck, op. cit., pl. 12, nos. 258–61; Göbl, op. cit., pl. 7, nos. 121–4; Ghirshman 1962, p. 247, fig. 313.
2 Ghirshman 1962, pp. 190, 191, figs. 233, 234; Harper, op. cit., p. 143, fig. 15.

SHAHPUR (SAPOR) III (AD 383–88)
Ills. 380, 381

Shahpur III was the son of Shahpur II. His first act was to place Chosroes III on the throne of Armenia, whereupon Theodosius sent an army against Persia. No battle took place; and in AD 384 Shahpur sent an embassy to Constantinople asking for a renewal of peace with Rome.[1]

Coin likenesses of Shahpur III as crown prince on four pieces, three of gold and one of bronze, display his bust facing to the right, with his hair forming a

378, 379 Ardashir II: coin portrait and detail of rock-relief at Taq-i Bustan showing the investiture of the king by the god Ahuramazda (right); at the left can be seen part of the rayed head-dress of Mithras.

380, 381 Shahpur III: coin portraits depicting Shahpur as crown prince (*left*), and as king.

dome-shaped mass of round curls all over his head, curiously outlined along its upper edge and bound by a diadem, whose tasselled ribbons fly out above a bunch of curls behind the neck (*Ill. 380*).[2] On his coin portraits as king his *korymbos* with its two short strings surmounts a flat cap, wider at the top than at the bottom, and decorated either with three arched panels, each of which contains an attempt at a classical palmette, or with vertical striations. The close beard is held in a ring. The king has a large nose and a rather wide mouth (*Ill. 381*).[3]

1 Pacatus, *Panegyricus Theodosio*, 22, 4, 5.
2 Paruck, op. cit., pl. 12, nos. 275–8, 280, 283; Herzfeld, op cit., pl. 4, fig. 2; Göbl, op. cit., classes (tables vi and viii; pl. 7, no. 113, pl. 8, no. 143) the coins with this coiffure as special issues of Shahpur II and Bahram IV.
3 Paruck, op. cit., pl. 12, nos. 262–74; Göbl, op. cit., pl. 8, nos. 125–35; Ghirshman 1962, p. 250, fig. 315.

BAHRAM, or VARHRAN, IV (AD 388–99)
Ill. 382

Bahram IV was the brother of Shahpur III. In AD 388 he made peace and a pact of friendship with Theodosius, by which the Persians received the lion's share of Armenia – a division that lasted until the Arab conquest.

On his rightward-facing coin portraits Bahram's veiled and beribboned *korymbos* tops a cap that is adorned with a crenellation in front of two wings, one seen behind the other, with curled-back tips and with a row of pearls(?) at the base. The broad streamers of his diadem fly out behind the usual bunch of curls at the neck.[1] One coin type shows him full-face, with the crenellation, both wings, and both lateral bunches of hair completely visible (*Ill. 382*).[2] The king has a pointed nose and a small, curving mouth. His beard is ringed.

1 Paruck, op. cit., pl. 12, nos. 279–82, pl. 13, nos. 284–95; Göbl, op. cit., pl. 8, nos. 136–142; Herzfeld, op. cit., pl. 5, fig. 1. Paruck no. 296 gives another type of crown for Bahram IV, with three crenellations or palmettes, no wings, and a fluttering tie on either side of the *korymbos*.
2 Göbl, op. cit., pl. 8, no. 144.

382 Bahram IV: full-face coin portrait showing elaborate winged head-dress, *korymbos* and lateral bunches of hair (actual size).

YAZDGARD I (AD 399–420)
Ill. 383

Yazdgard I was the son either of Bahram IV or of Shahpur II. He was noted for his good relations with Rome, with whom he made a treaty in AD 408, and his friendly attitude, initially, towards the Christians.

On Yazdgard's coin portraits a small beribboned *korymbos* surmounts a skull-cap which carries in front a crescent and on the side a crenellation. The bunch of curls at the neck is somewhat conventionalized and behind it and above it float the broad streamers of the diadem. The king has large eyes, a large and prominent nose and a small mouth. His beard is pulled through a ring (*Ill. 383*).[1]

1 Paruck, op. cit., pl. 13, nos. 298–305, pl. 14, nos. 306–12; Göbl, op. cit., pl. 9, nos, 145–52; Ghirshman 1962, p. 250, fig. 316. Paruck, op. cit., pl. 13, nos. 297, 304, and Göbl, op. cit., pl. 9, no. 152, show Yazdgard I wearing a 'cap' of all-over curls (cf. Shahpur III) with a crescent in front.

383 Yazdgard I: coin portrait with small *korymbos* and crescent in front of the skull-cap (actual size).

BAHRAM, or VARHRAN, V (AD 420–38)
Ill. 384

Bahram V, the son of Yazdgard I, made war on Rome. The imperial army attacked Nisibis, but the city was relieved; and in AD 422 the Persian king concluded a hundred years' peace with Rome, both sides promising religious freedom.

Bahram's coin portraits present his rightward-facing bust. His crown consists of two crenellations, one on either side of a small globe, on which rests a large crescent – a feature that appears here for the first time in Sassanid iconography – cupping the *korymbos*. The diadem has wide, flying ties, as in the coin likenesses of most of Bahram's successors. The bunch of curls at the neck is rosette-like and unnaturalistic. The king has large eyes, a very large, jutting nose and a narrow beard sheathing his chin and passed through a ring below. Some dies show a row of pearls(?) at the base of the skull-cap, probably part of the diadem (*Ill. 384*).[1]

1 Paruck, op. cit., pl. 14, nos. 313–24, pl. 15, nos. 325–30; Göbl, op. cit., pl. 9, nos. 153–8; Herzfeld, op. cit., pl. 5, fig. 2; Ghirshman 1962, p. 250, fig. 317. Paruck, pl. 15, nos. 331–2, gives a portrait of Bahram V wearing a pair of curly ram's horns, one on either side of the *korymbos*.

384 Bahram V: coin portrait showing crescent below the *korymbos*, a novel feature in Sassanid iconography (actual size).
385 Yazdgard II: coin portrait with mural crown and crescent below the *korymbos*.

YAZDGARD II (AD 438–57)
Ill. 385

Yazdgard II was the son of Bahram V. He maintained his father's treaty of peace with Rome, but was antagonistic to the Christians.

Yazdgard's coin likenesses, facing to the right, show a mural crown with three crenellations and a row of pearls(?) on the diadem below them. The large crescent cupping the *korymbos* surmounts the central crenellation and sometimes has fluttering ties. The king has a large lateral bunch of curls and his short beard appears to be ringed (*Ill. 385*).[1]

1 Paruck, op. cit., pl. 15, nos. 333–40; Göbl, op. cit., pl. 10, nos. 159–66.

PEROZ (AD 457–84)
Ills. 386–9

In AD 464 and again in 466–7 Peroz tried to enter into negotiations with the Emperor Leo I, with a view to enlisting Rome's help against his eastern foes. But Leo rejected both these requests; and he declined yet a third approach. The Persian king died in battle fighting against the Huns.

Peroz's rightward-facing coin portraits depict two types of head-dress. On one type there are two crenellations, one behind and one at the centre, and on the latter is poised the large crescent, furnished with ribbons, that cups the veiled *korymbos*; in front, above the brow, is a smaller crescent. The diadem is adorned with a row of pearls(?). A variant of this type shows a dome-shaped skull-cap with only the central crenellation and the small crescent above the brow. The second main type has on the cap the two crenellations and the small crescent in front, but two wings with curled-back tips spread outwards and upwards from below the crescent cup of the *korymbos*. In both types the king's beard is short and not passed through a ring, and the lateral bunch of hair is stylized. In both types again the diadem has wide flying ribbons (*Ills. 386–7*).[1]

386, 387 Peroz: coin portraits showing the two main types – (*above*; actual size) with large and small crescents, and (*below*) with wings below the crescent supporting the *korymbos*.

388 Peroz: detail of silver plate with hunting scene showing nimbus behind the king's head (Metropolitan Museum of Art, New York).

king's right hand. Behind the head there is a nimbus (*Ill. 388*).[3] On the second plate, in a private collection, Peroz's diadem has a double row of pearls(?), a central jewel, and ties behind; the bunch of neck curls is extremely small. The beard closely resembles that on the New York plate (*Ill. 389*).[4] Despite the minor discrepancies, there can be little doubt that the same king, Peroz, is depicted on both plates.

1 Paruck, op. cit., pl. 15, nos. 341–6, pl. 16, nos. 347–57; Göbl, op. cit., pl. 10, nos. 167–77; Herzfeld, op. cit., pl. 4, figs. 7–9; Ghirshman 1962, p. 250, fig. 318.
2 Ghirshman 1962, p. 192, fig. 235.
3 Herzfeld, op. cit., pl. 8.
4 Ghirshman 1962, p. 207, fig. 247; p. 249, fig. 314.

BALASH, or VALKAS (AD 484–88)
Ill. 390

Balash was the son of Yazdgard II and the brother of Peroz, after whose death he was made king. He was friendly to Rome and sent the Bishop of Nisibis to Constantinople to announce his accession to the Emperor Zeno. In AD 488 he was dethroned in favour of his nephew Kavad I, after a reign of only four years.

The coin portraits of Balash, facing to the right, carry a crown sometimes with a domed skull-cap and always adorned with two crenellations, one at the back, the other at the front, and between them a pyramidal feature supporting the *korymbos* in its beribboned crescent cup. The diadem, which has wide-ended streamers, consists of a double row of pearls(?). The narrow beard fits closely round the chin and is not ringed. The bunch of neck curls, although conventionalized, is recognizable as hair (*Ill. 390*).[1]

1 Paruck, op. cit., pl. 16, nos. 358–69, pl. 17, nos. 370–2; Göbl, op. cit., pl. 11, nos. 178, 179; Ghirshman 1962, p. 250, fig. 320 (wrongly dated).

JAMASP, or ZAMASP (AD 497–9)
Ill. 391

Jamasp is said to have been the brother of Kavad I (cf. p. 194), whom he dethroned and compelled to fly to the Huns. But with their assistance Kavad recovered his throne from Jamasp after two years of exile.

Jamasp's coin portraits, facing right, depict a crown that is composed of a back and a front crenellation (or palmette?) with a small projection between them on which rests a small crescent

A rock-cut relief at Taq-i-Bustan portrays in the upper tier of carving Peroz's investiture. The king's features are badly defaced. But the head-dress of the winged type is well preserved and there seem to be remnants of his neck curls.[2]

The most striking portraits of Peroz are on two silver plates, both of which show him hunting on horseback to the right and, as on the Shahpur II plate in Leningrad (cf. p. 188), aiming an arrow at his quarry. Both likenesses show a domed skull-cap adorned with two crenellations and the small crescent in front above the brow: neither has head wings. On the plate in the Metropolitan Museum of Art, New York, there is a single row of pearls(?) on the diadem, the thick beard is rounded at the base, and a large bunch of curls is visible behind the

Opposite
389 Peroz: detail of silver plate with hunting scene (private collection).

embracing a tiny ball. On this ball is balanced a
larger crescent cupping the *korymbos*. The diadem
has one row of pearls(?). The king has a tight beard
cut square at the base, a long, pointed nose, and a
triple ear-ring. Facing him from the right is a small
male bust offering him a diadem. The king's neck
curls are much conventionalized (*Ill. 391*).[1]

1 Paruck, op. cit., pl. 17, nos. 382–6; Göbl, op. cit., pl.
   11, nos. 180, 181, 181a.

390 Balash: coin portrait (actual size) showing crown
with two crenellations.

391 Jamasp: coin portrait featuring a small crescent with
ball supporting the larger one above.

KAVAD, or KOBAD, I (AD 488–97; 499–531)
Ills. 392, 393

Kavad I was the son of Peroz and the brother of
Jamasp (q.v.), who dethroned him between AD 497
and 499. In 502 Kavad declared war on Rome on
the pretext that the Emperor Anastatius refused to
pay the annual sum of money to Persia that had
been agreed in the hundred years' treaty made by
Bahram V (q.v.). The king was at first successful,
defeating the Roman generals and capturing a
number of fortified cities in Mesopotamia. But the

Huns turned against him and in 505 he made peace
with Anastatius, who paid him an indemnity, while
Kavad restored Mesopotamia, which he could no
longer hold, to Rome. In 521 war was renewed
between Persia and the emperor, now Justin I, and
Kavad was successful again, until he was deserted
by his best generals.

Kavad's rightward-facing coin portraits issued
during his first period of rule show a crown consisting of a crenellation (or palmette?) behind, a
pyramidal feature at the centre, on which rests a
large beribboned crescent enclosing the *korymbos*,
and a small crescent above the brow. This type of
head-dress appears again on the earlier coins of his
second reign, but was then replaced by another
type, where there is a dome-shaped skull-cap with
a crenellation (or palmette?) at the back and a
small crescent in front above the brow. The
korymbos-bearing large crescent surmounts the
'dome' and from just below it two wide-ended
streamers fly upwards on either side of the *korymbos*.
The king has a square jaw, large eyes and nose, a
close beard, and a bunch of curls at the neck that is
reduced to a small ball (*Ill. 392*).[1]

The cameo portrait of a Persian king in the
Cabinet des Médailles, Paris, has a head-dress
whose elements correspond most closely with those
of Kavad I's portraits. Here the king faces to the left
and his crown consists of a dome-shaped skull-cap
adorned with a small crescent in front, a crenellation supporting a large *korymbos*-enclosing crescent at the centre, and another crenellation at the
back. There is a jewelled diadem just above the
brow. The neck curls are more like real hair than
are those on the coins. The face has Kavad's large
eyes and nose, close beard and square jaw (*Ill.
393*).[2]

1 Paruck, op. cit., pl. 17, nos. 373–81, 387–91, pl. 18,
   nos. 392–413; Göbl, op. cit., pl. 11, nos. 182–93;
   Herzfeld, op. cit., pl. 5, figs. 3, 4; Ghirshman 1962, p.
   250, fig. 319.
2 Ghirshman 1962, p. 240, fig. 293.

392 Kavad I: coin portrait of the later type with dome-
shaped skull-cap (actual size).

393 Kavad I: cameo portrait with detailed features closely resembling this king's coin portraits.

XUSRO, or KHUSRAU (CHOSROES), I (AD 531–79)
Ills. 394–6

Chosroes I, one of the greatest of all the Persian kings, inherited war against Rome from his father, Kavad I, who is said to have wanted the Emperor Justinian I to adopt him and who bequeathed his empire to him. In AD 532 Justinian purchased peace from him at the price of a large annual subsidy. But in 540 war between the two Empires broke out again and Chosroes invaded Syria and took Antioch. But the presence of Justinian's great general Belisarius induced Chosroes to recross the Euphrates. War, however, continued between truces made in 546, 553 and finally in 562, when Persia was again promised an annual sum by Constantinople. Ten years later war was once more renewed. The imperial army, sent to do battle with the Persians, was suddenly disbanded and the Persian king ravaged Syria. But Chosroes died before his war with Rome was concluded.

Most of Chosroes' coin portraits present him facing to the right. His skull-cap is domed and decorated with a back and central crenellation and a small crescent above the brow. Supported on the top of the 'dome' is the large crescent that cups the veiled *korymbos*. The king has a large, aquiline nose, a small mouth and a short beard. The bunch of curls at the neck is distinguishable as such (*Ill. 394*). A few coins show Chosroes full-face, with a crenellation at either side and a small crescent at the centre. His beard is thick and trimmed square and he has a large mass of curls on either side of his neck. In both types the broad ties of his diadem fly upwards on either side of his bust.[1]

394, 395 Chosroes I: obverse of coin with profile portrait, and detail of gold plate with central medallion of rock-crystal showing the type of full-face portrait also seen on some coins.

Almost certainly a portrait of Chosroes I is the full-face, enthroned figure of a king carved on a rock-crystal cameo medallion which is set at the centre of a gold plate or shallow bowl, now in the Cabinet des Médailles, Paris. The medallion is surrounded by an elaborate pattern of polychrome rosettes of inlaid glass. The king's crown is precisely

396 Chosroes I(?): silver plate from Strelka showing a
nimbed king; the general features are consistent with
Chosroes' other known portraits, but the beard is absent
here.

the same as that on Chosroes' full-face coin portraits and he has the same bunch of curls on either
side of the neck. But the beard here is more pointed.
Here again the broad ribbons of the diadem fly
upwards on either side of the head (*Ill. 395*).[2] Less
certainly depicting Chosroes is the nimbed king
seated frontally on a silver plate from Strelka, in
the Hermitage, Leningrad. Here we have Chosroes' head-dress, lateral bunches of curls and the
upward-flying streamers of his diadem. But this
king is beardless (*Ill. 396*).[3]

1 Paruck, op. cit., pl. 19, nos. 414–30, pl. 20, nos. 431–3;
   Göbl, op. cit., pl. 12, nos. 194–9; Herzfeld, op. cit., pl.
   7, fig. 3; Ghirshman 1962, p. 250, fig. 321.
2 Ibid., p. 205, fig. 244; p. 304, fig. 401.
3 Ibid., p. 206, fig. 245.

HORMIZD IV (AD 579–90)
Ill. 397
Hormizd IV was the son of Chosroes I (q.v.) and
carried on his father's war with Rome. In this he
was successful until AD 586, when he was severely
defeated by the Emperor Mauricius at Solacon.
Again, in 588, he suffered a crushing reverse at
Sisarbene. In 590 he was murdered by the Persian
nobility.

    Hormizd's coin likenesses depict him wearing a
high, domed skull-cap adorned with a back and a
central crenellation and a small crescent at the
brow. The large crescent cupping the *korymbos* rests
on the apex of the 'dome'. The diadem consists of

two rows of pearls(?). The nose is long and pointed.
The neck curls are mere rosettes (*Ill. 397*).[1]

1 Paruck, op. cit., pl. 20, nos. 434–40; Göbl, op. cit., pl.
   12, nos. 200–2; Herzfeld, op. cit., pl. 5, fig. 5;
   Ghirshman 1962, p. 250, fig. 323.

BAHRAM, or VARHRAN, VI (AD 590–1)
Ill. 398
After the death of Hormizd IV, Bahram, a prince
of the royal house, who had served his predecessor
gallantly in war, got himself crowned at Ctesiphon.
But the Emperor Mauricius supported the claim of
Chosroes II (q.v.) to the Persian throne; and in the
ensuing battle Bahram fled.

    In Bahram VI's scant coin portraits he wears a
crown composed of much the same elements as that
of Hormizd IV. But the *korymbos* cupped in the
large crescent is smaller and more ball-like. The
neck curls are again mere rosettes. A double row of
pearls(?) adorns the diadem (*Ill. 398*).[1]

1 Paruck, op. cit., pl. 20, nos. 441–3; Göbl, op. cit., pl.
   12, nos. 203, 204.

397 Hormizd IV: coin portrait (actual size) showing
dome-shaped skull-cap with crescent and *korymbos* above.

398 Bahram VI: coin portrait (actual size) showing a
reduction in the size of the *korymbos*.

BISTAN, or VISTAHM (AD 591/2–597?)
Ill. 399

Bistan, one of Chosroes II's more distant provincial
governors, made himself king in Media. Defeated
by Chosroes, he took refuge with the Turks, by
whom he was put to death.

Bistan's coin portrait depicts him with a high,
domed crown that is adorned with two crenellations and a small crescent and surmounted by a
very attenuated *korymbos* in a large crescent. Two
rows of pearls(?) form the diadem. The king is
moustached and bearded. He has large, round
eyes, a pronouncedly aquiline nose and a square
jaw. A few, wispish locks of hair take the place of
neck curls (*Ill. 399*).[1]

399 Bistan: coin portrait (actual size) featuring a very
attenuated *korymbos* within a large crescent.

---

1 Paruck, op. cit., pl. 20, no. 444; Göbl, op. cit., pl. 13,
   nos. 205–7.

XUSRO, or KHUSRAU (CHOSROES), II
(AD 591–628)
Ills. 400–3

Chosroes II rivals in fame his grandfather and
namesake Chosroes I (q.v.). He owed his throne to
the Emperor Mauricius (cf. p. 196), whose murder
by Phocas he was determined to avenge. At first he
met with great success, occupying Mesopotamia,
Syria and Palestine, while in Asia Minor he advanced to Chalcedon, opposite Constantinople. But in
AD 622 the Emperor Heraclitus struck a counter-
blow, forced Chosroes to retreat, and pursued him
right into the heart of the Persian Empire. In 628
the king was murdered by his son.

Chosroes' coins display three types of portrait.
On a few pieces he has a domed skull-cap, surmounted by the *korymbos* in its crescent, and a
diadem composed of two rows of pearls(?). The
great majority of coins present him with a pair of
wings springing from the base of the slender stem
on which the surmounting crescent is supported;
and in that crescent, in place of a *korymbos*, there is a
star. The wings spread outwards and upwards and
are curled back at the tips. The skull-cap is
decorated with a crenellation at the back and at the
centre and a tiny crescent at the brow (*Ill. 400*). A
third type portrays the king full-face, with three
crenellations on the skull-cap and the wings flank-
ing the star-in-crescent (*Ill. 401*). There is always a
double-stranded pearl(?) diadem and the bunches
of curls at the neck are generally large and naturalistic. The king has a large hooked nose, a very
square jaw, and a thick beard trimmed square at
the base.[1]

Two bronze portrait busts, one in the Louvre
(*Ill. 402*), the other in the E. Borowski Collection at
Basle (*Ill. 403*), represent a Sassanian king.[2] They

are obviously by the same hand and obviously
depict the same personage, whom we may, ten-
tatively at any rate, identify as Chosroes II. Both
have square faces, large, almond-shaped eyes, a fine
moustache, a small mouth, and a sheath-like beard
caught in a ring below the chin. Both have a large
crescent above the brow and a larger one, cupping a
ribbed *korymbos*, on the crown of the head. On both
there are luxuriant curls at the sides of the neck and
both wear a heavy necklace. The head-dress of the
Louvre bust is the better preserved and has two
wings curving outwards and upwards and curled
inwards at the tips – just like the wings on the coin

400, 401 Chosroes II: profile and full-face coin portraits
(actual size) featuring a head-dress with prominent wings.

402, 403   Chosroes II(?): bronze portrait busts depicting a Sassanian king and featuring an elaborate head-dress with
wings as seen in the coins of Chosroes (Louvre, Paris; E. Borowski Collection, Basle).

404 Kavad II: coin portrait (actual size) featuring a
head-dress with a ribbed *korymbos* within the prominent
supporting crescent.

405 Ardashir III: coin portrait (actual size) of the type
including wings below the crescent supporting the
korymbos.

portraits of Chosroes II. On the Basle bust both wings are fragmentary. The main deviation from the coin portraits lies in the ringing of the end of the beard.

It is possible that we have yet another likeness of Chosroes II on a silver-gilt plate in the Cabinet des Médailles, Paris, which shows a Sassanian king on horseback on the right, hunting a large assortment of animals. His crown has all the features of that of Chosroes – back and central crenellations, small crescent at the brow, large crescent on a slender stem, rising from the top of the skull-cap and flanked by two wings that spread outwards and upwards and curl back at the tips. There is also the double-stranded diadem of pearls(?). The main difference is that here the large crescent encloses a *korymbos*, not a star; nor are any neck curls visible.[3]

1 Paruck, op. cit., pl. 20, nos. 445–8, pl. 21, nos. 449–64; Göbl, op. cit., pl. 13, nos. 208–15, pl. 14, nos. 216–22; Herzfeld, op. cit., pl. 5, fig. 6, pl. 6, figs. 1, 2, 3, 5, pl. 7, figs. 3, 5; Ghirshman 1962, p. 250, fig. 324.
2 Ghirshman 1962, p. 224, fig. 267 (Louvre), p. 225, fig. 269 (Basle).
3 Ibid., p. 212, fig. 253.

KAVAD, or KOBAD, II (AD 628)
Ill. 404

Kavad II murdered his father, Chosroes II (q.v.). On coming to the throne, he put to death many of his numerous brothers and made peace with Rome. He ruled for only six months.

On his coins Kavad is portrayed as wearing a flattish, rounded skull-cap decorated with two crenellations and a small crescent above the brow. Surmounting the cap is a ribbed *korymbos* cupped in a large crescent, to the stem of which two ties are fastened. The diadem has the two rows of pearls(?).

406 Buran: coin portrait (actual size) showing a domed crown with wings above, and a rather small *korymbos* within the crescent.

The king has very large eyes and nose and a square jaw with close-fitting beard. There is a large mass of curls at the neck (*Ill. 404*).[1]

1 Paruck, op. cit., pl. 22, nos. 465–7; Göbl, op. cit., pl. 14, nos. 223, 224.

ARDASHIR (ARTAXERXES) III (AD 628–30)
Ill. 405

Ardashir III was the son of Kavad II by a Roman woman. He was placed on the Persian throne as a child and seems to have been recognized throughout the Empire. He was put to death by the most powerful of his generals, Ferruchan Schahrveraz.

Ardashir's coin portraits are of two types. One shows the skull-cap ornamented with three crenellations and topped by the veiled *korymbos* in its crescent, from the stem of which flutter two short ties. In the second type there is a pair of wings spreading outwards and upwards, and curled back at the tips, from the stem that upholds the crescent. The bunch of curls at the neck is well in evidence in both types, as is also the double row of pearls(?) of the diadem. The king is beardless (*Ill. 405*).[1]

1 Paruck, op. cit., pl. 22, nos. 468–74; Göbl, op. cit., pl. 14, nos. 225–7; Herzfeld, op. cit., pl. 5, fig. 8; Ghirshman 1962, p. 250, fig. 326.

BURAN (AD 630–1)
Ill. 406

Buran was the daughter of Chosroes II and reigned for sixteen or seventeen months as queen of Persia. Her relations with Rome are uncertain.

Buran's coin portrait presents her with a domed crown decorated with rosettes and carrying on top the crescent that cups the *korymbos*. On either side of the crescent's stem is a wing springing outwards and upwards and curled inwards at the tip. She has two rows of pearls(?) on her diadem and her hair hangs down in long tresses beside her neck (*Ill. 406*).[1]

1 Paruck, op. cit., pl. 22, nos. 474–7; Göbl, op. cit., pl. 15, nos. 228, 229; Ghirshman 1962, p. 251, fig. 327.

HORMIZD V (AD 631–2)
Ill. 407

Hormizd V was the grandson of Chosroes II and was put forward as king by the army at Nisibis, where he reigned for a brief period.

In his coin likenesses Hormizd wears a skull-cap adorned with two crenellations and the small

crescent on the brow. Two wings, curled inwards at
the tips, spread outwards and upwards on either
side of a small crescent enclosing a star. The king
has a double row of pearls(?) on his diadem, a
bunch of curls at his neck, a square, thickly
bearded jaw and a hooked nose (*Ill. 407*).[1]

1 Paruck, op. cit., pl. 22, nos. 478, 479, pl. 23, no. 480;
   Göbl, op. cit., pl. 15, nos. 230, 231; Ghirshman 1962,
   p. 251, fig. 328.

407 Hormizd V: coin portraits (actual size) showing
     head-dress with wings and star within crescent.

XUSRO, or KHUSRAU (CHOSROES), V (AD
631–633?)
Ill. 408

Chosroes V was held to be the son of Chosroes II
and seems to have reigned at Ctesiphon for a few
years as a child. He was murdered.

This king's head-dress is virtually the same as
that of Hormizd V (q.v.) and he has the same
bunch of neck curls. Some of his coin portraits show
him beardless, others with a close, square-cut beard
(*Ill. 408*).[1]

1 Paruck, op. cit., pl. 23, nos. 481, 482; Göbl, op. cit., pl.
   15, nos. 232, 233.

408 Chosroes V: coin portrait (actual size) with details
     closely resembling those of Hormizd V.

409 Yazdgard III: coin portrait showing the beardless
     likeness of the last Sassanian king of Persia.

YAZDGARD III (AD 632–651?)
Ill. 409

Yazdgard III was the last Sassanian king of Persia.
He was a grandson of Chosroes II and was placed
on the throne as a child by members of the Persian
nobility. In AD 636 the Arabs took Seleucia and
Ctesiphon and Yazdgard fled. Between 640 and
642 the Arabs shattered the Persian army, but
Yazdgard retained the appearance of sovereignty
until about 651. The exact date of his death is not
known.

In his coin portraits Yazdgard III has practically
the same head-dress as his two predecessors, Hormizd V and Chosroes V (qq.v.). He has the bunch
of neck curls and is shown sometimes clean-shaven,
sometimes bearded (*Ill. 409*).[1]

1 Paruck, op. cit., pl. 23, nos. 483–94; Göbl, op. cit., pl.
   15, nos. 234, 235; Ghirshman 1962, p. 251, fig. 329.

Sources of Illustrations

With the exception of those listed below the majority of coins illustrated are from specimens in the British Museum.

Index

The general index includes personal names, together with names of tribes, peoples, countries, sites and places; for museums, collections etc. *see p. 208.*

INDEX OF MUSEUMS AND OTHER COLLECTIONS